Prais

The End of the Perfect 10

"Like a backstage pass to the mysterious world of Olympic athletics."

—*Library Journal*

"Brimming with energetic intelligence, wit, and insight-a-page storytelling, *The End of the Perfect 10* is more than an instant classic of gymnastics reporting: it's an indispensable read for anyone who's ever wondered what we really mean when we speak about perfection."

—Avi Steinberg, author of *Running the Books*
and *The Lost Book of Mormon*

"An incredibly thorough yet accessible account of one of the most mystifying aspects of the sport. The publication of *The End of the Perfect 10* provides an opportunity for the casual fan to take a deep dive into gymnastics."

—*Pittsburg Post-Gazette*

"A gripping analysis not just of the gymnastics world, but of what our desire for perfection does to us as athletes and as viewers. . . . *The End of the Perfect 10* is far less about the death of a benchmark score than it is about the birth of a new era in gymnastics."

—*New Republic*

"*The End of the Perfect Ten* will help you understand and appreciate the spectacle of gymnastics before and after the next quadrennial."

—*Providence Journal*

THE END OF THE
PERFECT
10

The Making and Breaking of Gymnastics'
Top Score—from Nadia to Now

DVORA MEYERS

TOUCHSTONE
New York   London   Toronto   Sydney   New Delhi

Touchstone
An Imprint of Simon & Schuster, Inc.
1230 Avenue of the Americas
New York, NY 10020

First Touchstone trade paperback edition July 2017

TOUCHSTONE and colophon are registered trademarks of Simon & Schuster, Inc.

For information about special discounts for bulk purchases, please contact Simon & Schuster Special Sales at 1-866-506-1949 or business@simonandschuster.com.

The Simon & Schuster Speakers Bureau can bring authors to your live event. For more information or to book an event, contact the Simon & Schuster Speakers Bureau at 1-866-248-3049 or visit our website at www.simonspeakers.com.

Parts of the author's account of Simone Biles in Chapter Six were previously published in her article for *Deadspin*.

Interior design by Jill Putorti

Manufactured in the United States of America

10 9 8 7 6 5 4 3 2 1

The Library of Congress has cataloged the hardcover edition as follows:

Names: Meyers, Dvora.
Title: The end of the perfect ten : the making and breaking of gymnastics' top score—from Nadia to now / by Dvora Meyers.
Description: New York : Touchstone, [2016] | Includes bibliographical references and index. | Description based on print version record and CIP data provided by publisher; resource not viewed.
Identifiers: LCCN 2016021446 (print) | LCCN 2015049288 (ebook) | ISBN 9781501101403 (e-book) | ISBN 9781501101366 (Hardcover : alk. paper)
Subjects: LCSH: Gymnastics—History. | Gymnasts—Rating of.
Classification: LCC GV461 (print) | LCC GV461 .M46 2016 (ebook) | DDC 796.4409—dc23
LC record available at https://lccn.loc.gov/2016021446

ISBN 978-1-5011-0136-6
ISBN 978-1-5011-0159-5 (pbk)
ISBN 978-1-5011-0140-3 (ebook)

To my mother

If you look for perfection, you'll never be content.

—Leo Tolstoy, *Anna Karenina*

CONTENTS

CONTENTS

INTRODUCTION

In the team finals of the women's gymnastics competition in 2012, sixteen-year-old U.S. gymnast McKayla Maroney performed what is arguably the best vault of all-time. She hurdled toward the table, did a round-off, and then a back flip off. Hitting the table with a perfectly hollowed body shape and straight arms, she pinged up and off, higher than all of the gymnasts—male and female—at the Olympics. She even launched higher into the air than Japanese demigod, Kohei Uchimura, did on the same vault. Maroney flipped one and a half times and wrapped two and half twists in before opening up for a perfect landing. As she saluted the judges, the Swarovski crystals on her red leotard catching the light of a thousand camera flashes, an astute viewer caught the image of American judge Cheryl Hamilton staring, openmouthed, in shock. Maroney jumped up and down excitedly and leapt into the arms of her coach and her teammates. It was, without a doubt, the best piece of gymnastics performed in London.

"That's a 16.5," Alexandra Raisman, the American team captain, said on the sidelines as she congratulated her teammate. This would have been the highest possible score that this vault could've been awarded under the 2009–2012 *Code of Points*. This would've been a "perfect" mark.

INTRODUCTION

The reward Maroney received for her efforts: 16.233. The vault, which had appeared flawless to everyone in the audience and the commentators on TV, had received nearly three tenths in deductions.

"Where were these taken from?" demanded commentators and fans alike. Maroney was known, not just for the explosiveness and complexity of her vaults, but also for the tightness of her form and body shape. When she vaults, Maroney glues her legs together and keeps them straight. Her toes are pointed throughout. Typically, her only fault on the two-and-a-half twister was a failure to stick the landing. She usually bounded forward, unable to control her power. But in the air, she was faultless. And this time, she stuck the landing. So where was Maroney's Perfect 10?

Perfect scores, however, are a thing of the past in elite gymnastics. No matter how flawless seeming a performance is, judges behave like undergraduates in a creative writing workshop. They can always find something wrong with your routine. Close scrutiny of Maroney's vault showed that her legs came apart just slightly on her preflight, as she flipped backward toward the apparatus.

In the past, however, that sort of infraction might've escaped notice. Perfect marks were handed out for a lot less. A generation earlier, the 1988 Olympic competition was rife with 10s. The judges were having a fire sale on the mark. Soviet Yelena Shushunova won the gold with a vault that contained similar faults to Maroney's—and yet Shushunova was still awarded a 10, which allowed her to edge Romania's Daniela Silivas for the all-around title. Silivas also received her share of perfect scores over the course of her career for routines with minor breaks and shuffles on landings.

And let us not forget the first perfect mark in Olympic competition—that of Nadia Comaneci—was also awarded to a routine slightly less than faultless. In 1976, the fourteen-year-old from Onesti, Romania, in the foothills of the Carpathian Mountains, entered the record books for her performance on a compulsory bars routine. She did the same routine as everyone else in the meet, but better—her form was tighter, her technique was more precise, her positions were perfect. Well, almost. She had a tiny shuffle forward on her dismount landing. It was nearly a stick.

Even Comaneci admits as much. In her memoir, *Letters to a Young Gymnast*, she writes, "I felt an almost invisible hop on the landing but knew that my routine was good enough. It wasn't perfect, though."

Comaneci understood that a 10 does not necessarily mean perfection. Sports scores can't be tasked with evaluating the intrinsic value of a performance. Rather, they are supposed to rank the athletes. And it was undeniable that Comaneci was better than the rest of her competitors in 1976.

The Summer Games in Rio de Janeiro will mark the fortieth anniversary of Comaneci's feat in Montreal. Her routines changed the nature of the game for women's gymnastics seemingly overnight. The teams of athletes, which had once been comprised of reformed dancers and women, were suddenly made up of young girls in their early and mid-teens. And this new crop of gymnasts in the late 1970s and early 1980s were small—both in height and width—for their age. The Olympic mantra, as it pertained to gymnastics, was tweaked to *"Younger, smaller, stronger."* Every four years, Olympic fans were introduced to a new superstar gymnast, cuter and smaller than the last.

The anniversary of Comaneci's accomplishments in Montreal coincide with a different anniversary—2016 also marks ten years since international elite level gymnastics rid itself of the Perfect 10 in favor of open-ended scoring. Now, a gymnast receives two scores—

one that measures the difficulty of her exercise and the other that determines how well she performs it. Both are added together. That's how you end up with something like Maroney's vault score, an inelegant 16.233. It doesn't quite roll off the tongue in the same way that 9.9 did. Or a Perfect 10.

The new *Code of Points* did more than change the way the scores looked—it also changed the way the gymnasts looked. Since Nadia, elite gymnastics had been the domain of wispy, prepubescent girls. But in the last decade, the rules have favored a different breed of gymnast—older, powerfully built, more athlete than artist.

And in this brave new world of gymnastics, where the sky is the limit in terms of difficulty, the United States has emerged triumphant, winning the lion's share of international medals in the past decade. The United States is what the Soviet Union once was—the most dominant force in women's gymnastics. When American gymnasts enter competitions, they are expected to win. And they usually do.

The key to American success is the semicentralized training camp system established by Bela Karolyi in 1999 and administered by his more knowledgeable half, Martha, since 2001. Every month, American gymnasts and their coaches travel to the Karolyi ranch in New Waverly, Texas, where they are assessed for physical fitness and skill level. It is also at these camps where all international teams—including those for the World Championships and Olympics—are decided. Forty years since Nadia has also meant forty years of the Karolyis.

Though Bela and Martha may have helped create the Perfect 10 world, they have been willing to deconstruct it. They have been nimble when it comes to adapting to the new *Code* and demands of the postmodern gymnastics era in which age minimums have been raised and difficulty caps have been removed. Martha Karolyi has demonstrated that she is willing to be above all pragmatic. She doesn't favor a single body type or race when it comes to team selection. The only thing she cares about is whether the gymnast can hit when it matters most.

The difficulty levels have also escalated since open-ended scoring was introduced to gymnastics. Now, the gymnasts must cram as many hard moves into a ninety-second exercise—the better to rack up the highest start score in the open-ended system—and as a result injuries have been on the rise, especially tears to the ACL and Achilles' tendon. Nearly every top-shelf female gymnast has been felled by one or the other at this point. It's not a matter of "if" but "when" an elite gymnast will face a potential career-ending injury.

You'd think that with rising levels of difficulty and injuries, older gymnasts would be pushed out of the medals—and you'd be wrong. At the same time the sport has gotten riskier, the medalists have seemingly matured, too. In London, twenty-four-year-old Romanian gymnast Catalina Ponor won the silver on the floor exercise with a routine of surpassing difficulty and beguiling dance. This medal came a full *eight years* after she won a gold medal on the same event at the Olympics in Athens. Oksana Chusovitina is aiming for Rio, which will be her seventh Olympic Games. She'll be 41 in 2016—and has a child that will be age-eligible for the Games. British gymnast Beth Tweddle won a bronze on the uneven bars at age twenty-seven in 2012. These are not the only athletes extending their careers and reversing the Comaneci legacy; there are several others who seem to be defying the odds, which no longer look so steep.

Nearly forty years after Comaneci ushered in the era of youthful perfection, gymnastics has changed course. It's now more sport than art. It's hard and, at times, messy.

It's not perfect. But then again, neither was Nadia.

PART I

NEW WAYS TO SCORE

PART 1

NEW WAYS
TO SCORE

1

SINEW AND SPANDEX:
THE FIRST—AND LAST—PERFECT 10S

The 1976 Olympics hadn't gotten off to a particularly auspicious start. On the eve of the Games, twenty-two African nations had withdrawn their athletes from Montreal in protest of New Zealand's inclusion in the competition. It was at the height of apartheid in South Africa, and the Kiwi rugby team was touring the pariah nation, in defiance of a worldwide sporting boycott.

Once a symbol of global unity, the Olympic Games were feeling a bit tarnished and tired in 1976. It was, after all, just four years after the camaraderie was marred by the massacre of eleven Israeli athletes by Palestinian terrorists at the 1972 Munich Olympics. Which came four years after Tommie Smith and John Carlos, two American track and field stars, had raised their fists in a black power salute to protest racism in the United States and human rights abuses abroad in Mexico City, 1968. Smith and Carlos were thrown out of the Games for this act of defiance by Avery Brundage, the president of the International Olympic Committee (IOC). Brundage harbored well-documented anti-Semitic and racist sentiments; in addition to tossing Smith and Carlos out of the Mexico City Games, he had made the controversial decision four years later not to cancel the Munich Games after the massacre, declaring, "The Games must go on." In fact, he had decried the politicization of sports at the memorial service for the slain Israelis. So Brundage had overseen two consecutive Olympic Games where protest, politics, and terrorism dominated the headlines—and in 1976, with the South Africa/New Zealand controversy, it looked like a third was heading down the same path.

Then on the first night of competition in Montreal, Nadia Comaneci, a fourteen-year-old gymnast from Romania, stepped onto the podium. Comaneci stood at just four feet eleven and weighed little more than 80 pounds. Her hair was pulled back into a ponytail and tied with ribbons. She wore a white leotard with a V-neck that exposed her sharp clavicle and drew the eye to a medallion in the middle of her chest. There was piping on the sides of her leotard, one stripe for each of the colors of the Romanian flag—red, yellow, and blue. Her look was all about lines—from stripes on her leotard to the shape of her legs, to her perfect handstands. No curves disrupted the lines. With her body, she could create perfect geometric shapes, different angles depending on the skill.

Standing at a distance from the uneven bars, Comaneci saluted the judges and ran toward the apparatus. She jumped on the springboard to vault herself over the low bar and grab the high rail. Martha Karolyi, the Romanian national team coach, pulled the board out of the way and jumped down from the podium.

Comaneci casted up to a handstand, stretching all the way to vertical, a straight line from her wrists to her toes. Then she swung down and beat her hips against the low bar, the force of which propelled her body back up until she was almost in a handstand once again. Comaneci then switched her grip and moved to the low and back to the high, before casting up for the final handstand of the routine. When she hit the peak again, the crowd audibly gasped.

"It was not such a big deal," the Olympic gold medalist recalled in a Sky Sports documentary about her life. "It was the A, B, C, D of gymnastics." These were the compulsory exercises, so the routine Comaneci was performing was identical to the five teammates who preceded her and to the rest of the female gymnastics competitors in Montreal. The skills were all basic; the point was to show how well you could perform the ABCs of mid-'70s women's gymnastics. If you had sat through the entire competition in 1976, you would've watched this routine eighty-six times. Depending on the spectator, this sort of repetition might have been boring or it could have been challenging, like a sommelier trying to discern the variations between a range of cabernet sauvignons produced in different regions and in different years and then ranking them.

From the last handstand, Comaneci swung down, wrapping her hips around the low bar and circling underneath, hands free, before landing on the mat several feet in front of the apparatus, almost exactly where the springboard had been less than a minute earlier. Comaneci threw her arms up overhead, arching her back, the side piping on her leotard clearly visible, creating an arc of sinew and spandex. The crowd cheered wildly, but the gymnast didn't bask in it—she jogged off the podium and rejoined her team.

"Then I heard a huge amount of noise," Comaneci recalled. The digital scoreboard had flashed "1.00" below her bib number, 073. Bela Karolyi, the other Romanian coach, and Comaneci were confused. A score of only 1 out of 10? How could this be? She had performed to her usual standard. The coach started to wander over to the officials' table to find out if some bizarre penalty had been levied against his gymnast. Suddenly, the announcer's voice came on the loudspeaker, to explain the confusion over Comaneci's score. The announcer said, "Ladies and gentlemen, for the first time in Olympic history, Nadia Comaneci has received the score of a Perfect 10." As with the early computer programmers who left only two spaces to denote the year, prompting the Y2K panic, the gymnastics organizers failed to anticipate the possibility of a Perfect 10 when they ordered the scoreboard for the event. The audience, the gymnastics community, and the scoreboard—none were quite prepared for Nadia Comaneci.

The gymnast came out for a curtain call, remounting the podium and waving to the crowd, not once, but twice. Then she marched to her next event. This scene would repeat itself six more times in Montreal. By the time the gymnastics competition was over in 1976, Comaneci would have earned seven perfect scores, three gold medals, one silver, and a bronze. Comaneci had become the new face of women's gymnastics.

Nearly forty years later in late 2014, Comaneci was attending the LA premiere of *Unbroken*, an Angelina Jolie–directed film, with her husband, 1984 Olympic gold medalist Bart Conner, when she approached the actress Kirsten Dunst. The legendary Olympic champion was a fan of Dunst and wanted to introduce herself. Standing alongside the actress at the soiree was a young woman, presumably Dunst's friend. Ever polite, Comaneci introduced herself to her too.

"Hi, I'm Nadia Comaneci," she said to the woman.

"I'm Nellie Kim," Dunst's friend responded, invoking the name of the former Soviet champion who had been Comaneci's fiercest rival throughout much of her career in the '70s. The Romanian expat thought this young woman was being sarcastic, that she didn't believe that Comaneci was who she claimed to be and was responding to the Olympian with a rhetorical eye roll. "I thought she knew the story," Comaneci told me outside her office in Norman, Oklahoma. We were sitting at the conference table at Paul Ziert & Associates, an unassuming but neat building nestled off Bart Conner Drive, right across from the gym that shares its name with the street and the 1984 Olympic gold medalist. Though Conner hails from Illinois, he won the majority of his titles, including his Olympic gold, as a Sooner with Ziert as his coach. Now that Ziert and Conner have retired from coaching and competing, respectively, the two produce gymnastics shows and other forms of gymtertainment. Ziert, along with Conner, is also the publisher of *International Gymnast* magazine. Its production is housed inside the complex, as are its archives dating all the way back to the 1950s, just as the modern sport of gymnastics was taking shape.

Comaneci first met Conner back in 1976, when they both won their respective divisions at the inaugural American Cup in Madison Square Garden. He was a high school senior and she was fourteen— her grade in school was indeterminate. They shared a childish peck on the cheek on the winner's podium. This kiss had been Comaneci's first. Nearly thirty years later in 1994, the pair married in Romania in a celebrated state affair. Despite her defection to the United States in 1989, Comaneci remains a beloved figure in her native country.

Their courtship and romance is the sort of implausible plot line that Hollywood routinely packages into romantic comedies starring Katherine Heigl or whichever actress is the rom-com queen of the moment. It feels as scripted as an episode of reality TV. The princess of modern gymnastics grows up to marry the crown price of the sport—really!? But Comaneci's life often feels like it is being masterminded by something other than fate—from her meeting and marrying Conner all those years later, to her harrowing defection from Communist-controlled Romania, to her bib number, 073 in 1976 (its digits added up to 10), to her seven Perfect 10s at age fourteen at the Olympics.

To the story that Comaneci was telling me about the movie premiere and meeting a woman named Nellie Kim. I asked Comaneci how many times this gymnastics "Who's on first?" routine—"I'm Nadia" and "I'm Nellie"—went back and forth. "A couple of times," she said. Eventually, the younger Kim proved her earnestness. Her name actually was Nellie Kim. And she knew all about her namesake.

"She said, 'I got a 10, too,'" Comaneci recalled. "And I said, 'Yeah I know.'"

Kim, an explosive athlete who competed with more difficulty than just about anyone on floor and vault, received her first 10 (of two) a couple of days after Comaneci earned hers in that iconic performance on the uneven bars. Kim would also go on to earn another "perfect" mark on the floor exercise whereas all of Comaneci's subsequent 10s were on bars or beam. Kim put her reaction to her own milestones succinctly. "I was just happy," she told me after the women's competition at the 2015 World Gymnastics Championships had finished. Kim is the current president of the Women's Technical Committee, which oversees the rules and judging on the women's side of the sport. Kim, with her chin-length, straight dark hair, was still wearing her official judging blazer and sipping from a glass of wine. After ten days of competition, it was job done for her at these championships. And after a relatively smoothly run meet with few glitches, she was happy yet again. Though perhaps not as happy as she was on the day she received her 10s as a gymnast. "I was rewarded for my work and innovation," she added. That was all she had to say about her 10s.

Perhaps this is because the Perfect 10 didn't change Kim's life the way it had changed Comaneci's. Most casual Olympic fans don't even remember her. It was Comaneci, not Kim, who became the star of the 1976 Olympics, whose life was turned into a melodramatic made-for-TV movie in 1984, and who graced a Jockey for Her billboard in Times Square in the early '90s wearing only her bra, underwear, and thigh highs. "10 Years of Perfect Fit on a Perfect 10" was the tagline, nearly ten feet high.

The Comaneci sitting in front of me more closely resembled her billboard in Times Square than she did the fourteen-year-old who had become the star of the Montreal Olympics. Her brown hair was set in cascading waves, the same style she wore to the movie premiere. She had posted photos of herself and Conner with various celebrities, including Brad Pitt, to her Facebook fan page. She cut a slim figure in a white pantsuit over a black off-the-shoulder top. As a young teen, Comaneci's large brown eyes, framed by brown bangs seemingly combed forward from the middle of her head, were her most salient feature. Forty years later, her cheekbones are the most prominent. They jut out as though the cheek flesh underneath had been scooped out by a small spoon. The Comaneci of 2014 would have a difficult time passing as her fourteen-year-old self.

When asked why she had come to symbolize the 10 in a way that her nearest rival never had, Comaneci was pragmatic. She got there first.

"That's how society works, I think. Who was the second person who went to the moon?" she asked. "It could've been anybody else.

It had to do with [being] the first. What if the orders were different, if they [the Soviets] had competed [first]? If things had been different, Kim would've scored a 10 because she did," Comaneci added.

But was it simply a matter of timing? Would Kim even have scored a 10 had she not competed after Comaneci? Did Comaneci's mark create an appetite for perfect scores that the judges and officials sought to satisfy? Or did the Soviets, who exerted tremendous influence over the judging panels, pressure the judges to reward one of their gymnasts a 10, too?

"Do you think it's possible that you created momentum for her 10?" I asked Comaneci.

"I don't think I created momentum for the 10," she responded flatly, refusing to take credit for another gymnast's scores. Kim earned her 10s just as Comaneci had earned her own.

Even if that is true, it is undeniable that the 10 transformed Comaneci's life in a way that it didn't for Kim. Comaneci became the physical embodiment of perfection. She and the 10 have become interchangeable. It's unlikely you even remember Nellie Kim's 10s.

Unless, of course, you're also named Nellie Kim.

———

For most, the history of the Perfect 10 begins with Comaneci, since she was the first Olympic gymnast to earn it at the Games. But just because no one had been awarded a perfect score in modern Olympic competition before Comaneci doesn't mean that no one else merited this mark. Going through archival gymnastics footage, you can find many examples of "perfect" routines—if "perfect" is defined as "without flaw"—that predated the Romanian in Montreal.

Comaneci's milestone could have belonged to the graceful Ludmilla Tourischeva or Vera Caslavska, the Czechoslovakian superstar who won the all-around at the 1964 and 1968 Olympics. Each had done routines that appeared to be flawless several times during the Olympics, yet they weren't anointed the way Comaneci was. Perfection in gymnastics existed before Comaneci. This begs the question: Why was *she* singled out the way she was for her performance in Montreal?

Olga Korbut, the darling of the 1972 Olympics, has frequently asserted that she deserved to be awarded a perfect mark for her work in Munich. In her autobiography, she wrote about her routine on the uneven bars in the event finals, "The judges gave me a 9.85. . . . [B]ut my routine had been perfect and the crowd wanted more. They shouted and cheered and stamped their feet until the Games had to be stopped . . . I had made no mistake, so I think my routine really deserved a 10, but they never gave out 10s in those days. Clearly, the crowd thought it was time to break that unwritten rule."

At that time, the *Code of Points* was quite short—just a handful of pages—and there were probably more unwritten rules than the ones that had been jotted down. Korbut was the breakout star of the 1972 Olympics, yes, but she was not favored by the Soviet gymnastics establishment. It is likely that they didn't throw their full weight and influence behind her to sway the judging panels. In her memoir, Korbut posited that her silver on the bars in that final was the result of behind-the-scenes deal making and that all of the individual winners were predetermined.

This, like most allegations of cheating in gymnastics judging, is both highly plausible but also impossible to prove. And few would argue against Tourischeva's all-around win in 1972, except perhaps Korbut, who was often compared to the older gymnast and found lacking. Tourischeva was everything that a purist would want in a gymnast—athletic, powerful yet elegant. Shapely too—she cut a womanly figure in a leotard with a noticeable widening below her waist as compared to her upper body. Tourischeva was also famously stoic. At the World Cup Finals in 1975, the uneven bars completely collapsed as she was dismounting. Tourischeva stuck her dismount, saluted the judges, and never glanced behind her at the wreckage of the apparatus as meet officials scrambled to see what went wrong. She was just like the action hero who blows up a building and doesn't even deign to look behind him.

Korbut, by contrast, was too short to be truly elegant. Her body was androgynous instead of curvy. And her brand of gymnastics favored complex acrobatics at the expense of the balletic style that the Russians had brought to the sport. As Roslyn Kerr pointed out in her history of women's gymnastics, Korbut's coach, Renald Knysh, was something of a renegade. He believed that any skill that you could do on the floor—such as a back flip—could be done up on the apparatus. So Korbut famously stood on the high rail of the uneven bars and did a back flip over it to catch the bar. She became the first woman to do a back tuck somersault on the four-inch wide balance beam. Korbut won gold medals in Munich but not the overall title, owing to her major error in the all-around finals. And she didn't get any of the 10s she believed she deserved.

As recently as 2012, Korbut was asserting her claims about the injustice of her bar score in Munich. In an interview with a gymnastics fan site, she said, "Not to brag, but in 1972, in Munich my bar routine wasn't judged properly and the sixteen thousand fans knew it was the first 'unofficial Perfect 10.' . . . There was nothing wrong with my routine. It should have been the first Perfect 10," Korbut said.

But it was Kim, not Korbut, who became the first Soviet to earn perfect scores in Olympic competition. She received 10s in

1976—two to Nadia's seven—and picked up the gold medals that the Romanian had missed. (The two divvied up all of the individual titles at the 1976 Olympics among themselves, leaving only silver and bronzes for everyone else.) They were clearly the most dominant gymnasts of the Games.

Kim's first perfect mark came during the all-around competition on the vault. After running and jumping onto the springboard, she did a half twist onto the horse and then blocked from her hands to propel herself backward into a full twisting tuck flip. This vault was years ahead of its time. Everyone else in the competition was doing the same approach but with just a straight flip off, no twist. Kim stuck this vault cold. Despite taking a literal giant leap forward on the vault, Kim's 10 did not leap ahead of the field on the event. "The distance between my vault and all other vaults was almost nothing. It was maybe 0.1 or 0.15," she pointed out. Even in that magical Olympic Games when those first 10s were electrifying the audience, the limits of the perfect mark were already in evidence. If everyone's vaults are worth a 10, then how do you reward a gymnast who has pushed the envelope? Of course, (almost) no one was thinking about that back then. It was only forty years later, as the president of the Women's Technical Committee who oversaw the transition to a points-based scoring system, did she note the problems with her vault score—that it didn't reflect the true distance between her and the other competitors on the apparatus—in the language of open-ended scoring.

Back then, the best the judges could do was give Kim a 10. Unlike Comaneci's first 10, which was awarded for performing elementary moves flawlessly, the Soviet's score was given for striking the right balance between difficulty and execution. It wasn't about the purity of her technique or the lines of her body. It was a very hard vault done extremely well. For Kim, the 10 was more score than symbol. It didn't necessarily signify anything about her as a gymnast. For some reason, Kim's 10 somehow didn't express perfection as much as a lack of missteps; but in the eyes of viewers, Comaneci's wasn't the errorless 10, it was the *perfect* 10—but, why?

With the exception of Korbut, most of the champions who came before Comaneci were women in both age and appearance. They were esteemed as paragons of beauty and grace. They were feminine according to the standards of their times, curves and all. Their athleticism was almost secondary. At the time of many of her triumphs, Tourischeva was in her late teens and early twenties. Larisa Latynina—whose Olympic medal record of eighteen medals (fourteen individual, four team) was surpassed only recently, by Michael Phelps in 2012—was actually pregnant at the 1958 World Championships. But by 1976, Comaneci modeled a new look for an Olympic champion. She wasn't a woman yet in age or appearance. She was a child. Is it a coincidence that this new type of pre-woman champion was also the first to achieve "perfection"?

And it wasn't just about body type. The "perfect" champion must also be free of compromised (adult) associations like politics. Consider Caslavska, often considered gymnastics' last "feminine" star. She famously protested the Soviet domination of her homeland by turning her head down and to the side while the USSR anthem played during the medal ceremony. Before the 1968 Olympics, Caslavska had openly supported the Prague Spring, putting her name on a petition. When the Soviet tanks rolled into Czechoslovakia, she was forced into hiding and actually had to train on makeshift apparatuses in the woods. It's hard to imagine Comaneci or any other young teenage girls voicing strong political opinions or bringing more to the table than just her acrobatics and performance. Politics are messy and often violent. They are, by definition, imperfect, and to be involved in the process is to sully oneself. In politics, there is very little consensus. But in Comaneci, the world finally had someone who was free of sex and politics: in other words, the perfect female champion.

Awarding a Perfect 10, however, is an exercise in near-complete consensus. After the high and low scores are tossed out, the average of the remaining marks is what determines the final score. And for that mark to be a 10, the remaining judges need to be in agreement that they all saw the same thing and that the thing was without flaw. Or to award a Perfect 10 to an imperfect routine, the judges need to mutually agree that they're going to ignore the same obvious mistake. It's either collusion or collective human error.

Latynina, who was the Soviet head coach in 1976, commented at the time, "Nobody is perfect. Comaneci has her faults, too."

Korbut chalked up Comaneci's 10s to politics. "Politics made it a Perfect 10. The routine had mistakes, but that's how the cookie crumbles," she said. Cookies in gymnastics, of course, are for crumbling, not eating.

———

Cathy Rigby, who won the first World Championship medal for the American women—a silver on the balance beam—in 1970, was in Montreal in 1976 as an analyst for ABC. She, like Korbut and Latynina, also questioned the validity of some of these high scores to *Newsweek*. "The judges are in a box," Rigby said. "They started out giving high scores, and Nadia is so superior to every girl here that they have no choice but to give her 10s."

When asked if that meant that Comaneci was undeserving of those marks, she backtracked a little. "If Nadia were doing what she's been doing, all alone in an empty room, I'd still have to say that she would get the 10s," she said.

But Korbut and Latynina were correct. Comaneci was not absolutely perfect. There was a slight flaw in Comaneci's first routine—a small slide forward on the landing of her dismount that she herself acknowledged in her own memoir. Yet she still might have deserved the 10 anyway. The score, not the designation of "perfect." The Romanian gymnast who went before her on the apparatus received a 9.90 and Comaneci was demonstrably better than her teammate. That 10 was the judges' way of ranking her correctly. It wasn't perfect; it was better than.

Abie Grossfeld, an American gymnast from the '50s and '60s, who watched Comaneci perform in Montreal, also noted the imperfection on the dismount but acknowledged that she was superior to her competitors. "She was an eleven compared to those girls," he told me. Grossfeld wished that "perfect" had not been used as a modifier for the ten. "You know what's the proper term? Maximum score," he observed.

Following the 1976 Olympics, one annoyed fan sent a letter to *International Gymnast* that expressed this idea. "After watching in person and on TV the competition in Montreal, I think that the International Federation should consider some changes in the judging of World level competition. Videotape replay of Nadia's first, imperfect 10.0 compulsory uneven bars routine illustrated the dangers inherent to a flurry of perfect scores. Perhaps the scoring of all routines over 9.9 could be done in 1/100ths or 3/100ths of points to allow for better ranking of performances," he wrote. Perhaps if the judges had been able to award 9.975s, Comaneci wouldn't have been awarded that first 10. This would reduce Comaneci's first 10—and all of the fame that came with it—to what is essentially a rounding error.

Sports Illustrated's Frank Deford said as much at the time. "It is quite obvious that perfect scores are a great hype. Comaneci could have won 9.95s across the board, earned just as many gold medals, been every bit as good, and attracted about one half the publicity for herself and women's gymnastics." He also noted that a small, yet noticeable contingent of fans in the audience had started chanting "No more 10s!" as Comaneci continued racking up more perfect scores.

Comaneci had scored 10s before the Olympics, but those don't really count either. "They care about the Super Bowl, the Olympics," Comaneci said when I brought up her previous perfect marks to her.

Her legend status may have been cemented in Montreal, but the hype around the young teen had been growing steadily for at least a year before the Olympics when the Romanian turned thirteen and was old enough to compete internationally at the senior level. In 1975, Comaneci won the European all-around title in Skien, Norway, defeating Tourischeva. The European Championships ranked just behind the World Championships and Olympics in terms of prestige, especially back in the '70s, '80s, and '90s, when the strongest gymnastics powers still hailed from Europe. A win at the Europeans was usually considered a harbinger of future Olympic success. Many a European champion has gone on to win the all-around at the subsequent Games.

But it was more than simply winning the European title that got everyone talking about this talented teen. It was the way that she performed her skills. Comaneci demonstrated a technical perfection that had heretofore not been seen in the sport. And to that, she added an ease of performance. Comaneci gave the impression that not only could she do the extremely difficult skill perfectly but also that she could do it repeatedly without error. Her perfection was not spectacular—it was mundane.

This ability to perform flawlessly repeatedly was likely borne out of the intense conditioning that Bela Karolyi subjected his gymnasts to. Karolyi had known little of gymnastics until he met his future wife, Martha, who had been a gymnast, but he had been an accomplished track and field athlete as well as a boxer during his youth. He brought this expertise to gymnastics.

Comaneci wrote about the conditioning regimen. "Bela had a vision of bringing all of his experience in boxing, rugby, handball, and general athletics to gymnastics ... We spent a few hours a day working with weights and ropes and did lots of jumping, running, and other training."

She reiterated this idea when I asked her about the impact her coaches had on the sport. "I think conditioning was something that people didn't know how important it is to do conditioning in gymnastics. You can't do tricks unless you're really prepared and fit."

Rod Hill, the U.S. Olympic team manager in 1976, recalled being on tour with the young Romanian squad and wrote about it. "She could throw ten, twenty, or thirty routines and score a 9.8 or better in each of them. I have seen her throw six consecutive bar routines and hit every one of them and not be breathing hard."

But it's more than the fact that Comaneci was incredibly consistent in her routines. "When she hits a position, she does not ease into it, she HITS it. It is crisp and to the point," Hill marveled in his magazine account. This description speaks of more than not missing but of taking skills, even the seemingly easy ones, to the limit. At the Olympics, the crowd gasped, not just at the spectacular release moves—she had been the first woman to release, flip, and regrasp the same bar—but at a simple handstand in Comaneci's compulsory bar routine. Their collective awe was not in error. The way in which Comaneci performed the most basic of elements such as that handstand was to take it to absolute vertical. It was so close to the edge it was reasonable to fear that she might tip over and fall off the other side. But she always managed to stay in control, right on top of the sweet spot. Comaneci made no errors while leaving no margin for errors.

"Not every gymnast can do everything technically correct," Ziert asserted. "There are limitations to some with their bodies, but that's why Nadia was so good. She had done so many repetitions that her body had the aptitude to do it correctly and it taught itself that." Ziert didn't seem to put much stock into Karolyi's ability as a technical teacher. "It wasn't a coach that taught her that. The coach made her do so much, her body taught herself that."

Ziert's theory imbues Comaneci with almost magical qualities— she had so much talent that she learned proper technique almost without instruction. It's gymnastics' equivalent of little Abe Lincoln teaching himself how to read all alone in a log cabin.

Ioan Chirila, a Romanian writer who had been chronicling Comaneci, the Karolyis, and the Romanian gymnastics effort since the early '70s, quoted a Romanian professor, Gheorghe Brasoveanu, who also minimized the role that Karolyi played in the gymnast's success. Brasoveanu was the principal of a high school in Comaneci's hometown of Onesti, where the experimental gymnastics school that the Karolyis established was located. "For anybody, even for those who don't know a lot about gymnastics, it would have been apparent that the girl was made for sports in general, gymnastics in particular. I am convinced that if our city would have been a place for fencing and not gymnastics, the selector would have discovered in Nadia Comaneci a big champion of the foil." According to Ziert and Brasoveanu, finding Comaneci was more than half the battle.

And for Latynina, it was not finding a Russian Nadia that proved to be her undoing. She resigned from her post as the head coach of the USSR team after it lost the majority of the individual titles to the Romanians in 1976. She reportedly said at the time, "I don't know why I should be blamed that Nadia was born in Romania, not Russia."

Comaneci, for her part, didn't downplay the role of her coaches. The day after our conversation, she and Conner were headed to New York for a U.S. Olympic Committee (USOC) luncheon honoring Bela and Martha. "Bela called me two months ago and of course, we have to be there. Time goes by so fast. Bela is in his seventies. I'm in my fifties," she said, her tone wistful. We were talking about her youthful accomplishments, something she was often asked to do, and yet the fact was neither she nor Bela were young anymore.

Perhaps it was age and distance that have freed Comaneci to deconstruct some of the apocryphal stories that had been told about her, especially that of her discovery by Karolyi. He has frequently spoken of finding her and Viorica Dumitru, who went on to become one of Romania's premiere ballerinas, doing cartwheels on the playground. (It was a simpler time—a grown man could lurk around playgrounds without arousing suspicion.) They had run off before he could get their names. Then, the story goes, he went from classroom to classroom, searching for the two little girls he had seen, asking the students if they enjoyed gymnastics.

But Karolyi hadn't actually "discovered" the young girl's innate athletic talent. Comaneci had already been taking gymnastics for about a year before the famed coach spotted her and invited her to train at the experimental gymnastics school. "I had other coaches before them [the Karolyis]," she said. "Actually, Martha was coaching me before Bela got involved."

"I think I was in kindergarten when she came and visited the school and put together a ballet routine for us. I think we met her first and then Bela," she told me. This revelation doesn't diminish the impact the Karolyis had on Comaneci's career. They were her primary coaches throughout most of her time as a gymnast and contributed significantly to her greatest athletic achievements. But it does tweak the fairy tale a bit. The clarification of this timeline makes Comaneci's story seem slightly less constructed, less "perfect" if you will.

And as many of Karolyi's past gymnasts have pointed out, he was an excellent motivator and knew how to get his athletes to do more than they thought possible. Sometimes he pushed his athletes too far, but he could never quite crack Comaneci. In her memoir, she recalled, "I've heard my old coach Bela Karolyi say that I was the only young gymnast he could never break."

Later in the book, she delved into this idea in greater detail. "Throughout my years of training and competition, I always kept a reserve of energy," she wrote. "Let's say that I knew that I could do fifteen laps of the stadium. I'd tell Bela I could do ten and give myself some reserve, some padding . . . Bela pushed me hard, but the reason he could never break me is because he never truly knew my limits."

I asked Comaneci about those passages, about what it felt like to know that she could not be broken by a coach who was known for his toughness. I wanted to know if this realization came later or if she recognized it at the time.

"I don't even know how to explain it," she said. "Bela was challenging us all the time, 'I bet you can't do twelve.' And I was like, 'I bet I can do more than twelve.' I always did two more, and I realized I could do more than that, but that's okay, I'll keep it for next time . . . I didn't know how much more but I felt that I could do more . . . I don't think I've ever pushed to the point where [I thought] 'This is it, I don't think I can do more.' "

As I listened to her, I wondered if the story she told herself about her own limits was the key, if that belief was what we talk about when we talk about perfection. Maybe twelve or fourteen really was her limit. But because she *believed* she could do more, she didn't feel broken down at twelve. This begs the question, is believing you have more in the tank the same thing as actually having more in the tank? Does *not* pushing yourself too hard create a padding, as Comaneci called it, that allowed her to not determine her limits and thus to believe in her own limitlessness? Like Latynina, I tend to doubt the existence of perfection, but I do share in the belief that Comaneci seemed to cultivate in the endlessness of her abilities—maybe that's the closest approximation we have to perfection. Maybe conditioning that belief is what, under the bright lights of the Olympic Games, creates about as flawless a performance as possible.

Even if Korbut, Comaneci's petite predecessor, had indeed merited 10s in her career, she didn't communicate cool perfection like Comaneci did. Korbut, in her daring tricks, conveyed risk and danger. She paused dramatically before her hardest elements, telegraphing them for the audience. You gasped because you thought she might actually hurt herself. That she made mistakes endeared her to

22

the audience, especially when she wept openly in disappointment, which subverted the stereotype of the cold, unemotional Soviet athlete. She was seen as talented yet human and fallible. Perfection is distancing, and Korbut wasn't distant—she was eminently relatable, especially to the Western audiences who fell in love with her.

On the other hand, Comaneci, despite doing skills far more difficult than the Belarusian (and more of them), never made you feel ill at ease. She was even keeled on the apparatus and barely wobbled on the narrow beam in all of her Olympic performances in 1976. In *Everybody's Gymnastics Book*, Dr. William Sands and Mike Conklin observed, "The Romanians provided the public with real beauty, but it is a beauty of fine engineering than that of the more esoteric forms of art such as dance, ability to emote and ability to communicate a message." The Romanian style of beauty wasn't expressive. That brand is highly unpredictable, as it was with Korbut. Rather, Comaneci's was consistent. It was the sort of sameness you'd expect from assembly-line construction. Comaneci and the Romanians were more Henry Ford than runway couture.

Korbut retired after the 1976 Olympics. It was now Comaneci's turn to shoulder unfathomable pressure to continue to excel. "After those Olympics, everything I had to go to, I had to win," she told Sky Sports.

———

"Wherever I go, I am seen as a former gymnast," Comaneci observed. This statement would probably be just as true coming from Olga Korbut, Mary Lou Retton, or any other female gymnast who won gold and global fame before they were old enough to drive a car. Their predicament is similar to that of child actors. They are expected to move on from their youthful accomplishments while constantly being forced to recall and relive them for fans.

In 2014, Retton, who won the 1984 Olympic all-around at sixteen, managed to slip back into her teen self for a Super Bowl ad for the now-defunct electronics chain Radio Shack. She donned a replica of the Stars and Stripes leotard that she had worn on the cover of the Wheaties box and a wig cut in the same pixie shape her hair had been in thirty years before. And it worked. Though Retton had visibly aged since her triumph, she still mostly looked the part. She's only marginally larger than she had been at the height of her gymnastics powers, though she probably can't flip anymore because she's had hip replacement surgery in recent years. But in appearance and context—being a suburban mother of four in Texas is not a far cry from the image of the wholesome American teenager she projected during her athletic career—she's remained largely the same. Retton is the rare former child star that you could still plausibly imagine in her younger role, even years after the fact.

Comaneci, who seems to have aged gracefully, would not be able to pull off that same feat. There was far too much time and distance, physical and geographic, between her present and younger selves.

These days, to stay fit she takes Zumba classes or does the dancercise in the privacy of her own home. "It's really fun," she said. "I don't do something that I kill myself." It is hard to reconcile the image of one of the greatest Olympic athletes of all time doing a Jazzercise workout in her living room every morning.

Forty years after her Olympic triumphs, Comaneci is a suburban mom. She lives in a college town in Oklahoma and has a young son, who has a pet lizard named Rocky. Her son, Dylan, named for the rock music legend, favors a less regimented form of acrobatic play— parkour—to the disciplined gymnastics that made both of his parents famous. I'm sure he's just following his interests, but I wanted to commend him on his decision not to enter the family business. Though certainly possessed of the perfect genes to excel, no child of Nadia Comaneci and Bart Conner should do gymnastics. That is simply too much pressure and expectation for any kid to bear. More pressure, perhaps, than being a fourteen-year-old girl expected to win the gold medal at the Olympics.

Comaneci didn't seem inclined to push her progeny to relive her and her husband's past glory. If there is any pressure, it seemed to flow from the opposite direction. Dylan forces the Olympic champion to ride roller coasters with him. Comaneci, apparently, is very afraid of roller coasters. When asked why, she said, "I'm in the seat of someone else's creation." She can trust her own body and strength—just as she always believed that she had more in reserve when she was training—but she is less certain about these man-made contraptions.

So why does she go on these rides?

"I do it for the fun of Dylan," she said. "Because he laughs at me because I close my eyes, of how I scream, 'Is it over?' " She spends the entire time on the ride clenching the harness. "You don't expect that from someone who has done flips and doubles [double twisting somersaults]."

But as she said, Comaneci is done with all of that.

Just as gymnastics is done with the 10 that made her globally famous.

On August 2, 1992, at the Olympics in Barcelona, Lavinia Milosovici was awarded a perfect score on her floor routine in event finals. None of her competitors could match this mark, so she also won the gold medal. The fifteen-year-old was hoisted onto the shoulders of her coach, Octavian Bellu, to wave to the raucous, appreciative crowd. Earlier that same evening, China's Lu Li had been similarly celebrated by her coaches and the audience when she received a 10 for her performance on the uneven bars. No one in the audience that day knew it, but they were witnessing the end of the score that had dazzled Olympic gymnastics audiences for a mere sixteen years.

Milosovici was not an obvious choice for a Perfect 10, let alone the "last perfect score." She was daring but didn't do the highest degree of difficulty in the competition on floor exercise. She was clean enough in her movements, but no one would have held her out as an example of technical perfection. That distinction would have gone to someone like Soviet Svetlana Boginskaya, 1989 World Champion, nicknamed the Belarusian Swan for her elegance, style, and purity of her technique. And of course, there was her height. She was almost five feet five in a sport dominated by the under-five-foot set. Though Boginskaya performed exceptionally well in Barcelona and without error, the nineteen-year-old Olympic veteran didn't medal individually. She had been surpassed by a bevy of much shorter fifteen-year-old tricksters.

Boginskaya moved languorously, almost with the appearance of slow motion, allowing you to see just how perfectly she did every skill. Milosovici, by contrast, performed loosely but with speed, so fast that it was hard to see the small errors. It was speed as optical illusion.

Milosovici competed early in the floor lineup, the second gymnast out of the eight who qualified to the final. First, the American Shannon Miller, not known for her tumbling prowess, had performed a fine routine to insistent violins. The crowd applauded politely to Miller's final routine in Barcelona. And then Milosovici took to the mat. She opened with the same tumbling pass Miller had used, but tacked a crowd-pleasing little front-tuck flip onto the end of it. Milosovici hopped forward on the landing of this pass, just a small slide really, the same way Comaneci had landed her bars dismount in 1976. The rest of the routine was fairly standard in terms of the difficulty of the tumbling. What buoyed her to a Perfect 10 was that extra flip in her first line and the energy of her music and dance. Performing to a jazzy number and with choreography reminiscent of Comaneci's Montreal floor exercise, Milosovici scarcely paused to catch her breath. (Gymnastics is an anaerobic sport anyway.) When she finished and saluted the judges, the audience applauded loudly. But when her score was announced, that's when crowd went wild. It was as if the audience was more excited by the 10 than by the acrobatics that preceded it.

The 1992 Games were the first Olympics where the "new life" rule applied. In the previous 1988 Games, the gymnasts carried their scores with them from session to session, like bad relationship baggage. But beginning in 1989, gymnasts started from scratch in the medal rounds. The first beneficiary of this renewed lease on scoring was Boginskaya, who won the World all-around title in 1989 despite qualifying into the finals behind two of her Soviet teammates. In years past, she would have brought that point deficit with her, but with "new life," she started the all-around final with a clean slate. Nineteen-ninety-two was the first time this new rule was introduced at the Olympic Games. In the event finals in Barcelona, every gymnast started from zero and could climb as high as 10. The 10 Milosovici earned early in the floor rotation was all that mattered. And since you couldn't get higher than a 10, Milosovici was guaranteed a gold medal, her second of the Games.

If they wanted a share of that title, the remaining six competitors would have to try to match her. Next up was the 1991 co–World Champion on the floor exercise, Oksana Chusovitina of the Unified Team. She performed a full twisting double layout, which was by far the most difficult tumbling pass in the women's competition, but she landed it out of bounds, a mandatory one-tenth deduction. A 10 was now impossible, and the commentators and even the audience seemed to lose interest in her routine. *Next!* they seem to be saying through their apparent lack of enthusiasm.

The commentators also seemed to nitpick a bit more in their discussion of the gymnasts' performances. Once a 10 had been awarded—whether deserved or dubious—the subsequent routines would *really* have to be perfect. When the Hungarian Henrietta Onodi, the co–gold medalist on vault (with Milosovici), paused slightly after landing her extremely difficult and rare triple twist on floor before going into her next pass, the commentator noted it as though it were a deduction. But it wasn't. There was no rule that you had to link tumbling passes as Onodi (and American Dominique Dawes) often did. Plus, she completed four passes to Milosovici's three. She had performed an arguably more difficult exercise, but she didn't receive a 10. Perhaps the judges agreed with the commentators that the pause was indeed a deduction. The Hungarian had created an expectation of seamlessness from her previous routines and didn't do it in the final round. She had overpromised and underdelivered. Onodi placed second behind the Romanian.

The other challengers also failed to get a perfect score. Two lurched forward on their tumbling passes; another placed her hands on the mat. And Kim Zmeskal, the defending World all-around champion from the United States, didn't make any noticeable mistakes except that she came close to going out of bounds—which is not a deduction—but it probably reminded the judges that she had, in fact, taken a large step out of bounds during the all-around. Though scores were technically no longer supposed to be carried over, the judges' memories are a bit trickier.

At the end of the night, no one managed to tie Milosovici for top honors on the floor (though three gymnasts tied for the bronze, making the third medal tier quite crowded). Little did the audience at the Palau Sant Jordi and viewers at home realize that Milosovici's 10 would be the last perfect score they would ever witness in Olympic competition.

A scoring revolution that had started with a Romanian ended with one. From 1976 to 1992, judges awarded more than 100 perfect scores in internationally sanctioned competition. The era of the Perfect 10 lasted less than twenty years.

"I always said that the 10 belonged to gymnastics," Comaneci told me.

And after 1992, it belonged to history.

I DON'T CARE ABOUT YOUR ART:
HOW GYMNASTICS BECAME LESS ARTISTIC
AND MORE ATHLETIC AFTER NADIA

In 1979, *Sports Illustrated* sent Bob Ottum to Transylvania to check up on Nadia Comaneci. There was just one year to go until the 1980 Games, which meant that gymnastics was, once again, due for some attention. When he arrived at Deva, the national team training center established by the Karolyis, Ottum discovered something shocking: three years after her seven Perfect 10s in Montreal, Comaneci had grown up. Time did not stand still, not even for gymnasts. Elite gymnasts may be able to hit the snooze bar on puberty a couple of times, but eventually it will come for them. And it had come for Comaneci.

Of course, there had been reports of this in the tabloids, stories about weight gain and losses to younger challengers. Even *People* magazine ran an article about Comaneci's encroaching womanhood.

"As a result of that much publicized puberty, Nadia now has breasts," Ottum wrote. This sort of proclamation was simultaneously ridiculous and significant, and if this had been reported during the twenty-four-hour cable news era, "Nadia now has breasts" would have probably scrolled at the bottom of a CNN newscast.

Comaneci was no longer the little sprite who had performed routine after routine unflappably in front of the Olympic audience. She was a woman in a sport that trended downward in age, which was, in part, her doing. At fourteen, she had ushered in the era of the very young gymnast, or "attack of the mini-monsters," as Ottum called this new breed of female gymnast as though they were the stars of a B horror movie instead of Olympic athletes.

Though Ottum's tone appeared to be jocular, there was also an unmistakable whiff of disgust in his wording. He seemed to believe that there was something fundamentally unnatural, monstrous even, about the size and age of this new generation of gymnast. (Fittingly, "Nadia's Theme," which is the music that was played by ABC in 1976 to accompany her performances, originally came from the movie *Bless the Beasts & Children*.) As with any sort of child prodigy, adults regard young female gymnasts with a mixture of awe and revulsion. The world had fallen in love with the likes of Olga and Nadia, to be sure, but it also seemed a bit uncomfortable with all that they represented—extreme youth, extreme diminution, and extremely arduous training commenced in childhood.

This made Ottum wistful for the past. "There was a time, not too long ago, when women's gymnastics was more of an art form than a sport. It was a lyrical exercise somewhere this side of ballet, an activity pursued by serene young ladies with swanlike necks," he wrote. When men were men, Norman Rockwell painted prosaic scenes of the American family, and gymnastics was done by women who would look as natural up on the balance beam as they would in an apron in the kitchen.

Comaneci's performances in 1976 did more than just shatter the glass scoring ceiling. They also shifted the balance of power in women's gymnastics from feminine and mature to young and acrobatic. Instead of *faster, higher, stronger*, the Olympic credo, as it pertained to women's gymnastics, had morphed into *shorter, younger, lighter*.

―――――――

That women's gymnastics would come to be dominated by young acrobatic girls was by no means a given. In its very earliest incarnation, women's gymnastics was a sport created specifically for women and freighted with all of gender expectations that dominated the prewar and early postwar eras.

Back in 1948, women's gymnastics wasn't daring. It didn't demand extreme strength, or above-average coordination, or even a full-time commitment to practice. The gymnasts were grown women in their twenties and even thirties possessed of fit yet thoroughly feminine physiques, evident breasts and wide hips. This did not hinder them at all, since they didn't do much to challenge gravity. Rather, they danced with ribbons and posed statically on the beam. Their movements were graceful and slow, not fast and explosive.

A clip of the group exercises from the 1936 Olympics shows a group of women in their twenties dressed in white cotton leotards cut like your grandmother's swimsuit, moving through calisthenics exercises, slowly as though they were afraid of breaking a hip. Another segment shows a woman in boy shorts cautiously balancing on the beam with one leg raised. The only place where these women can show any sort of power is on the vault. There, at least, they can run toward the apparatus and jump. Still, nothing they attempted was any more daring than what you'd see on the average playground (at least before the era of helicopter parenting and over-litigiousness). "They were doing what are considered primitive gymnastics today," Ziert explained to *Sports Illustrated* in 2012 about those early years.

Given the low skill level, there was literally nowhere for things to go but up. And as the athletic prowess of the female gymnasts escalated through the late '60s and '70s, culminating with Nadia, the sport attracted a much younger following. In the post-Nadia (and Olga) era, elite gymnasts were no longer mature women in their twenties. Instead, they were often girls in their early to mid-teens—probably no more than a few years older than their fiercest acolytes and athletic successors.

"The *first* time I really began dreaming about the Olympics was in 1976, when Nadia won her three gold medals at Montreal," Retton wrote in her memoir. "I was eight years old that summer, and I can remember lying on the living room floor back home in Fairmont, watching the whole thing on television." Fans of Nadia and Olga didn't have to project themselves more than a few years into the future to imagine competing at the Olympics. Younger competitors meant younger—and arguably more ardent—fans.

And increasingly, these younger girls had a different mind-set and sensibility. For one thing, they were much more active and dynamic, and that came through in their routines and the kind of gymnastics they were drawn to practicing. Since Nadia, nearly every top-flight elite gymnast's story begins with some version of the parent saying, "Well, little Bailie/Madison/Alyssa/ had so much energy, so I enrolled her in gymnastics." It's safe to say that the more measured, elegant brand of 1948 gymnastics wouldn't have appealed to the sort of rough-and-tumble kid who looked up to Nadia, Mary Lou, or today, Simone Biles, as their heroine.

Many of these differences between the 1948 gold medal Olympic team and the teams that started forming in the early 1980s probably also came down to the changing times. Most sports weren't created with women in mind; instead, women were typically added to the sports after the rules had already been standardized—for men. Women who wished to participate in most sports had to conform to the preexisting masculine ideal.

Women's gymnastics, however, was originally designed to be "feminine," whatever that means at any given time. While this view, in and of itself, is problematic on many levels, it did set up an interesting dynamic: a sport where female gymnasts got to compete without being compared to the men. How could they be? They weren't even performing on the same events. Though the men's and women's apparatuses overlap with floor exercise and vault, they demanded different things from the competitors, especially during the early years when the men tumbled and the women danced. Men's and women's gymnastics are essentially different sports.

But being designed specifically for women, as opposed to moving along a track parallel to the men, meant that women's gymnastics in the 1940s and 1950s was saddled with all of that era's beliefs about the place and potential of females—and those values, like the apparatuses the women competed on, were in constant flux. Back in the early days of women's gymnastics, the gymnasts sometimes competed with hand apparatuses, such as the ribbon, ball, and clubs, as they did in 1936 for the group exercises. (These hand apparatuses would later compose a separate discipline, rhythmic gymnastics.) Occasionally, female gymnasts would train and compete on the parallel bars, which today are the sole domain of men's gymnastics. This is why when in 2012, an eighty-six-year-old German gymnast Johanna Quaas performed an exhibition routine at the Cottbus World Cup, she elected to go up on the p-bars. (Unlike the female gymnasts in the elite field of that meet—the tiny teens who could do multiple somersaults—Quaas probably competed on that apparatus during her own heyday as a gymnast.) Quaas's performance went viral online after it was posted. It was shocking to see an older woman perform in a sport that was known for uniquely young female athletes. And it was even more surprising to some to see her go up on an apparatus that is usually associated with the men.

Quaas, in addition to the parallel bars, probably also dabbled on the rings, which, in the 1930s and 1940s, was an event that included women as well as men. The International Gymnastics Federation (FIG), in its own very brief history of the sport, states, "In 1948, the women even competed in a compulsory exercise on the rings." The modern-day rings, with its static strength holds and iron crosses, is an event dominated by strong men with overdeveloped upper-body musculature. But in 1948, the event was less about strength and more about swing. They were called the "flying rings," and women could fly with the best of them, provided there were male spotters ready to catch them when they dismounted. The mats were quite thin in those days, just a thin layer of cotton or canvas. They offered about as much cushioning as a bath towel.

"You know what I competed on for the first eight years? A wooden floor," Grossfeld told me. Like a grandfather telling his grandchild he had to walk to school barefoot in the snow, he also mentioned that he twice competed on concrete. "The '56 Olympics was the first time I had [a] canvas sheet with a one-eighth-inch felt," he recalled. We were sitting in the press box at the 2015 U.S. championships. Grossfeld motioned to the floor exercise where the current crop of elites was warming up for the second day of competition. "You've got a trampoline now," he said of the spring-based floor mat.

By 1952, the events of women's gymnastics were standardized, and the competitive opportunities for females were expanded to include individual titles and gold medals. The four events for women were vault, uneven bars, balance beam, and floor exercise. The selection of these particular events for the women was not an accident. Of the four, three are what you would call "leg events," with only the uneven bars demanding any upper-body strength at all. But even that apparatus didn't challenge the upper body all that much. The rails were close together, so close that a gymnast could pause, resting her lower body on the shorter rail while grasping the upper one with her hands.

The women were also given the danciest of the apparatuses—beam and floor. Unlike the men, the women performed their floor exercises with the musical accompaniment of a live pianist. Though there may have been a cartwheel here and handstand there, the emphasis was on presenting a highly feminine style to the judges. And the balance beam was another place to showcase their ladylike grace. "We were not allowed to do certain things, those back bends or even splits," Laddie Bakanic, a member of the U.S. team in 1948, told me in 2012, adding that she had teammates who were capable of more complicated skills like handstands and cartwheels on the narrow plank.

In the post-Comaneci gymnastics era, it's hard to imagine that at one time, the female gymnasts were actively discouraged from showcasing their daring and strength. But the women of Quaas's and Bakanic's period were supposed to be, first and foremost, ladies—on the streets *and* on the balance beam.

But that had already started to change, and earlier than the pop-culture narrative would have you believe. It didn't begin with Nadia Comaneci in 1976 or even Olga Korbut in 1972. Neither the Romanian nor her Belarusian predecessor invented the idea of the teenage gymnast. The youth trend had begun in the '60s. In 1964, the Soviet National Championships were won by a fifteen-year-old, Larisa Petrik. In 1966, Natalia Kuchinskaya, then seventeen, won golds on bars, beam, and floor at the World Championships. Caslavska, considered the last of the "feminine" champions, remarked, "The first time I really thought about leaving [competitive gymnastics] was when Kuchinskaya appeared on the World Championships podium—so young, so beautiful. It seemed to me I could not compete with her." Caslavska was then all of twenty-four years old. She would continue to compete and dominated at the 1968 Olympics but retired immediately thereafter. After the World Championships in 1970, Petrik would step away for similar reasons. Comaneci's victory in 1976 was the end, not the beginning, of a multiyear process that established the supremacy of young, prepubescent females over their adult women peers. Young teens were beating up on their older sisters for ten years before Comaneci started doing it.

Comaneci's coach Bela Karolyi was a big believer in the power of youth. "It's an odd sensation," Chirila noted as critically as he could in a book that was supposed to be a propaganda tool for the Communist party in Romania, "but Karolyi is obsessed with the idea that in gymnastics you grow old too fast, as it happens in the space stories of Jules Verne." Peter Pan would have been another literary expression of a similar idea. And the role of Peter Pan on Broadway and on tour was played for decades by Rigby, the former gymnast who had been an older teen masquerading as a younger one in pigtails and a body nearly as slim as Korbut's when she won her medal in 1970. A female gymnast playing the boy who didn't want to grow up. Art imitates sport.

In a *Sports Illustrated* article from 1976, Karolyi said that a female gymnast's best training and competing years were from eight to twenty. "During those years," he told the reporter, "there is no fear, there are no problems. Women gymnasts have done so many more difficult feats in recent years because they are younger now."

Chirila also published excerpts of what was allegedly Karolyi's diary from 1972 where he wrote about his impressions of the Munich Olympics. "I have watched almost all of the gymnastics in Munich," he wrote. "If we were there with the children, we could have placed— according to my calculations—in third place." Comaneci, one of the "children" he was referring to, whom he was coaching at his experimental gymnastics school in Onesti, Romania, was only ten at the time.

His faith in the fearlessness of youth was evident in his dim appraisal of Tourischeva, who was the overall champion at those Games, and even Korbut, its breakout star, though her success arguably set the stage for Comaneci's popularity four years later.

It was around that time, in 1972, that Karolyi started sneering at the "decline" of the balletic, graceful gymnasts like Tourischeva who had previously dominated the sport. "She wants to be a gymnastics aristocrat," he wrote. "She likes ample movements. Movements that hide a certain lack of nerve inherent to her age and wear. The secret is that Tourischeva is a gymnast made only through gymnastics. She has class, undoubtedly, but her engine is not too strong for the body she has."

But Karolyi failed to give Tourischeva her due. Though "aristocratic" in her movements, the gymnast in her younger days pushed the envelope on difficulty just as his star pupil would later do. In 1968, a fifteen-year-old Tourischeva competing in her first of three Olympic Games, performed a back flip on the beam and a full twisting somersault off—two of the more daring skills competed in Mexico City. Tourischeva was hardly the lady figure she would later morph into. A year later at the European Championships, she competed a program with such ambitious difficulty that she was actually deducted for it. This was likely done to discourage widespread adoption of greater acrobatics. But in 1970, Tourischeva was rewarded for her risk taking when she won the World all-around title.

The year 1970—two years before Korbut's big splash and six before Comaneci became a household name—was also when the first age minimum was introduced to the sport. This new rule seemed to be as much about protecting very young gymnasts from harsh training methods as it was about providing protectionism by maintaining the image of the sport as feminine pursuit suitable for adult women even as gymnasts such as Tourischeva adopted more and more complex skills. Karolyi, in his endorsement of extreme youth in gymnastics—remember, according to Chirila, he seemed to indicate that he thought his ten-year-olds should have been able to compete in 1972—was something of a free-market capitalist, opposing regulations that would eliminate competition. In 1980, the minimum would be raised once again to fifteen and, in 1997, to sixteen. The justifications were the same for those changes as they were for the first in 1970: equal parts protection and protectionism.

———

In 1978, the Soviets produced a documentary about the nation's top gymnasts called *You Are in Gymnastics*. It begins with scenes set in the mountains of Armenia, where the team is on vacation, with soft piano music wafting in the background. The young girls frolic in the snow and pose for pictures. But, as the narrator interjects, these are not simply children playing as kids are wont to do. They are world-class athletes, European and World champions. And they are far, far ahead of their predecessors, in terms of skill level.

"Today," the narrator says of the girls' abilities on the precarious balance beam, "the gymnasts perform elements on it which only a few years ago they wouldn't attempt on the floor," as young gymnasts wearing cotton leotards that slouched where their curves were supposed to be, flipped and turned to the music.

This documentary, filmed just two years after Comaneci's triumphs, demonstrated the impact that the young Romanian's win had on her nearest rivals, the Soviets. The composition of the Soviet national team onscreen in 1978 was demonstrably and aesthetically different than it was in 1976. Tourischeva, the feminine stalwart champion of the team from 1968 to 1976, had retired. Not shown in this documentary is Comaneci's nearest rival, Nellie Kim, though she continued to remain a factor in competition until 1980. The gymnasts highlighted in this film are young, at least in appearance. (Their chronological age is difficult to guess.) These young gymnasts were slight and androgynous from the neck down. They resembled Korbut in her heyday more than the powerfully built Kim or ladylike Tourischeva. They were, we are told, the new breed of female gymnast.

This new type of Soviet gymnast was exemplified in Yelena Mukhina, the 1977 European silver medalist (right behind Comaneci) and the 1978 World Champion, who was featured prominently in the film. She was actually older than Comaneci in 1976 but wasn't included on the Soviet Olympic team, which skewed several years older than the Romanians. At the same time that Comaneci was trouncing the senior ranks internationally, Mukhina was topping the juniors in the Soviet domestic sphere, winning the national junior title in 1976.

Despite being more than a year older than Comaneci, Mukhina appeared in the documentary as young and innocent, if less stoic, than the Romanian. Her sandy blond hair was swept back into a ponytail, and she seemed soft-spoken in her conversations with her coach, averting her eyes, shrugging her shoulders, mumbling responses to his criticisms.

Unlike Comaneci, who had been heralded as a promising gymnast before the age of ten, Mukhina spent her early years in gymnastics in relative obscurity within the large Soviet sports machine. But with the arrival of Comaneci on the international stage in 1975, Mukhina's gymnastics fortunes changed. To adapt to the new gymnastics reality that Comaneci's success had created, the Soviets were attempting to cultivate gymnasts a bit more like the Romanian and less like the beloved Tourischeva. And Mukhina physically fit the bill.

Mikhail Klimenko, Mukhina's coach, explained this history to her in the documentary. "Nadia Comaneci had such a great performance at the European Championships in 1975. She came out and had stronger routines than our best gymnasts," he lectured her on the gym sidelines. As Klimenko told her this, Mukhina stared off into the middle distance with her head resting in her hand. Not that it mattered. This communication was clearly not meant for her. Mukhina was well aware of the history and who the enemy was. His words were clearly directed to the average Russian viewer to help him understand the urgency in their preparation—the USSR was no longer completely dominant in women's gymnastics as it had been since 1952, when it first entered the international fray. Vladimir Zaglada, one of the coaches involved with the film, spoke of the impact of Nadia's and Bela's Olympic debuts. "Like a storm of dynamite," he told me. In the late '70s, Zaglada worked as a consultant with the national team to help develop and teach extremely difficult skills to the coaches and gymnasts. "They [the Romanians] kicked the bottom of Russian gymnastics," he added with the same sort of color that the Russians showed when they performed on the mat. Zaglada said that after the 1976 Olympics, the Soviets had a meeting to discuss how to remain competitive with the surging Romanian team.

Mukhina was to be the savior of Soviet gymnastics, a role she seemed reluctant to assume. She told Klimenko repeatedly that she was tired and frustrated when he chastened her about crying during the workouts. The only time Mukhina appeared joyful was when she was among her teammates outside of the gym—eating meals, playing in the steam room, boarding the plane for a competition in a coat and fur hat. She seemed far happier out of a leotard than in one.

During these filmed sideline conversations, Klimenko subtly manipulated Mukhina, threatening her with abandonment, asking if she wished to train on her own. This would be akin to asking a child if she wished to raise herself. As one of the coaches in the film explained, the coach in women's gymnastics occupies a parental role in a young girl's life, especially since many of the gymnasts lived too far away from home to train. This was even truer in Mukhina's case because she was an orphan. When she was five, she lost her mother in an apartment fire.

Mukhina shook her head and said no. Quitting—both the sport and the coach who molded her into a champion—was not an option. She needed him. He had made her a star. And he needed her just as much. Klimenko didn't have any other Olympic contenders waiting in the wings. She was his ticket to the 1980 Olympic Games in Moscow.

I wonder if Klimenko's tactics were actually manipulative or only appeared so because of how the story ended. Less than two weeks before the Moscow Games in 1980, Mukhina would crash land on her chin while attempting a difficult new tumbling skill on the floor exercise, the Thomas salto, a move borrowed from the men's repertoire. The impact of the fall snapped her spine. Mukhina would spend the rest of her life as a quadriplegic being cared for by the grandmother who had raised her before she was taken into the Soviet gymnastics system. After her grandmother's death, Mukhina was looked after by Yelena Gurina, a former teammate, in an apartment that had been renovated by the Soviet legend Latynina.

As an adult, Mukhina became a critic of the Soviet sports machine. In 1991 she was featured in an episode of the *More Than a Game* documentary series, where she talked about the circumstances surrounding her accident in 1980. "My injury could have been expected. It was an accident that could have been anticipated. It was inevitable. I had said more than once that I would break my neck doing that element. I had hurt myself badly several times, but he [coach Mikhail Klimenko] just replied that people like me don't break their necks."

That Klimenko was coaching a gymnast like her was a demonstration of another new trend in the sport: men's gymnastics coaches teaching the girls. Klimenko had started his career as a coach in the men's training hall. As women's gymnastics increased in global popularity, Klimenko, like many other men's gymnastics coaches, transitioned to teaching the girls. (Aman Shaniyazov, also featured in the documentary, was a former men's coach who replaced Latynina as head of the women's program after 1976.) Klimenko, like many of his peers who made the switch, brought a tremendous amount of technical expertise in teaching highly risky and difficult elements that had been formerly the exclusive domain of men.

This trend was not purely an Eastern bloc or Soviet phenomenon. It was happening in the United States, too, where Korbut and Comaneci were, arguably, more popular than they were anywhere in Eastern Europe. (Korbut, in particular, was more beloved in the West than she had ever been in her homeland.) "Many young male coaches moved into the women's side of the sport and took up the slack with coaching," observed Dr. William Sands and Mike Conklin in *Everybody's Gymnastics Books*, which was published in 1984, less than a decade after Comaneci's wins. "Their approach emphasized winning and technique because the technical aspect of men's gymnastics is more dominant than the artistic aspect." Sands and Conklin, in this excerpt, offered a possible explanation for not only the increase in difficulty that was the trademark of the post-Comaneci era but also for the seeming concomitant decrease in artistic expression. Men's coaches schooled in men's training techniques didn't know how to teach it as effectively as someone like Latynina, who danced her way to multiple gold medals, did. "You with your choreography have become out of date," the Soviet champion turned coach recalled hearing from officials after the 1976 Games.

Though also expressive and balletic like her Soviet predecessors, Mukhina, under Klimenko's tutelage, greatly upped the difficulty ante. Just two years after Comaneci and Kim had become the first women to perform a double back somersault on the floor, Mukhina added a full twist to hers, just like the men in 1976 did. As for the "simple" double back flip that Kim and Comaneci did on the floor—Mukhina performed it as her dismount off the beam. She seemed to be the next link in the escalation of gymnastics complexity.

It's important to note that the change was not necessarily about cross-gender coaching arrangements. That was nothing new. Men had long been coaching women's gymnastics with great success. Tourischeva was coached by the legendary Vladislav Rastorotsky, Korbut by Knysh. Bela Karolyi had never been a men's gymnastics coach either (though during his early days as a physical education teacher in Vulcan, he probably taught boys as well as girls). These men came up through the ranks as women's gymnastics coaches. But Klimenko and the coaches Sands was referring to had first been serious men's trainers before working with the women. Or to be more accurate, young adolescent girls who were capable of acrobatics feats similar to those of the men.

When Gary Goodson, an American coaching in Canada, arrived in Moscow in 1978 to study Soviet training techniques, he saw firsthand how the next generation of Russian gymnasts was being prepared for the brave new world of women's gymnastics at the legendary Dynamo Sports Club. "When I was in there, I saw little tiny girls doing giants [swings] on bars," he said. At this juncture, this now commonplace move was not often seen in women's gymnastics. Goodson reacted in horror at seeing such young athletes being pushed to do what he considered a dangerous skill. "You're risking the lives of these little girls," he recalled saying to Zaglada. "They're doing a very advanced, dangerous element." But Zaglada disagreed. "Gary," he said to the American, "it is no problem. It is a profile element." The Soviets, as Goodson would learn, had devised a system to teach advanced elements by grouping all of them into different families of skills. Instead of teaching them in order of increasing difficulty—a linear progression—the coaches taught the specially chosen, gifted athletes the most typical, or "profile," skill first, before teaching related variations both easier and harder than the central move. This enabled the young gymnasts to learn new moves rapidly. Which was how the young gymnasts Goodson saw in Moscow were able to swing around the uneven bars with ease.

Yet despite investing heavily in acrobatic innovation, the Russians hadn't completely abandoned their artistic soul to defeat the Romanians. Emilia Sakalova, the team choreographer, presided over their practices in 1978, teaching the girls the finer points of movement. "The most difficult thing in life is to do the simplest things," she told her young charges. "Just sit beautifully, walk nicely, and just present yourself beautifully." This was hard but not spectacular. Emotion conveyed to an audience was not measurable in feet and inches like the height on somersaults.

I imagine that if Karolyi had watched the footage of Sakalova telling a young gymnast to pay attention to her hands, for she "speaks about life with them," the brash Romanian coach would have scoffed. Though Comaneci was certainly no slouch artistically, Karolyi came from a world of athleticism. In his writing, at least, he seemed to have little patience or respect for the artistic tradition that formed the foundations of women's gymnastics. "Gymnastics through gymnastics will remain, I am sure, only a memory, somewhere in a chest drawer, like grandmother's lace dress," Karolyi wrote in his diary. And the gymnasts he coached couldn't possibly fit into this dress—they simply didn't have the curves.

———

Much of the media coverage of women's gymnastics in the last forty years since Olga and Nadia has largely ghettoized the sport from the cultural and athletic mainstream. The focus has been on how separate the female gymnasts are: they are rounded up in kindergarten, shipped off to special sports schools, Dickensian orphanages for the athletically gifted, where they live apart from the "real" world. Or, if we're talking about American gymnasts, the emphasis until recently had been on their hours in the gym, homeschooling, and how childlike they appeared as teens. In a 1988 puff piece on gymnast Chelle Stack, a fifteen-year-old Olympian, the camera panned to the ground to show her feet dangling off the chair, unable to reach the floor, at a mall food court. The point of this shot was to allow the viewers to gawk at how small and young she was. This all gives the impression of a sport and a cohort that functions on the margins of society, in an athletic Twilight Zone.

Roslyn Kerr, however, in her research into the history of women's gymnastics, has argued convincingly that the development of the sport usually went hand in hand with wider cultural trends, be they progressive or reactionary.

Take, for instance, the popularity of Korbut at the 1972 Games. It wasn't just her daring that caught everyone's attention. It was her slight, androgynous body. As Kerr pointed out, this physique was hardly anomalous in the early 1970s, especially in fashion. Twiggy had already made it famous. In Korbut, audiences were responding to a build that had already been deemed "attractive" by the mainstream. Twiggy used hers to model clothes. Korbut deployed hers to perform acrobatics. In this case, gymnastics followed fashion.

When Karolyi defected to the United States in 1981, his first star athletes were Dianne Durham and Mary Lou Retton. Their forms looked markedly different from the Romanian sylphs that he had made famous in the 1970s. Durham and Retton were stocky, powerfully built. Retton, of course, went on to win the 1984 Olympic all-around gold medal in Los Angeles. Her autobiography, *Mary Lou Retton: Creating an Olympic Champion*, made note of her build and how it was a departure from the 1970s stereotype that her own coach had helped popularize. Her cowriter described her thusly: "She is fifty-seven inches tall, and most of her ninety-four pounds appear to be leg and thigh muscle. Her silhouette hardly conforms to the traditional model of a female gymnast, which is ponytailed and spindly thin. Mary Lou is constructed like a cast-iron toy truck."

In his memoir, *Feel No Fear*, Karolyi wrote about how he wished to create a new kind of gymnastics in the United States: "I had introduced a new powerful style of gymnastics to the American community, which was more proper and accessible for American kids in general," he said of Durham's win at the 1983 National Championships, which was a first for an African American gymnast.

Though Karolyi may have believed he was reinventing the wheel, he might have simply been influenced by the culture of the 1980s. "The 1980s were a period in which female 'power' was being emphasized in all aspects of Western society. Physically fit women such as Madonna and Jane Fonda were the icons of this period," Kerr wrote. "Therefore, it appears more likely that Karolyi, possibly unconsciously, was reacting to changes American society was experiencing and initiating these changes into the sport."

Women's gymnastics didn't just adhere to cultural trends; it followed the laws of physics. As the sport increasingly prioritized acrobatics, it has also conferred an advantage to gymnasts who were shorter and smaller. In the post-Comaneci era, gymnasts' bodies were progressively specialized to be more aerodynamic. In that way, elite gymnastics was following the same playbook as basketball, track and field, swimming, and several other sports. In all cases, the best athletes in these sports possessed bodies whose proportions were vastly different from those of the average person. In short, basketball players were getting taller, football players were getting bigger, and gymnasts were getting shorter.

David Epstein wrote about the phenomenon of "body specialization" in his book *The Sports Gene*. He pointed out that from the classical period until the first half of the twentieth century, the body with the most average proportions was considered the most beautiful. This sort of body was also thought to be eminently suitable for all athletic pursuits. (Of course, the writers and philosophers from this age were dealing exclusively with the male form. The female body wasn't deemed suitable for anything more taxing than childbirth.)

The evidence in this belief in the athletic everyman can be found in the proportions of the athletes in the early twentieth century. "In 1925," he writes, "an average elite volleyball player and discus thrower were the same size, as were a world-class high jumper and shot putter."

So what changed in the sports world that affected the size of the competitors? Epstein postulated "as winner-take-all markets emerged, the early-twentieth-century paradigm of the singular, perfect athletic body faded in favor of more rare and highly specialized bodies that the fit like finches' beaks into their athletic niches."

Though the trend in most sports has been to bigger, taller athletes, the shortest of the short have an advantage in the more acrobatic sports and long-distance running. "Compared with all of humanity, elite distance runners are getting shorter. So are athletes who have to rotate in the air—divers, figure skaters, and gymnasts. In the last thirty years, elite female gymnasts have shrunk from five feet three on average to four feet nine."

Epstein presented this information without any judgment. He offered no commentary about whether these changes were good or bad, simply that they were. And for the most part, most of these changes are not judged. Being freakishly tall to play basketball is seen as merely a fact of the game. *You have to be this tall to ride.* There is no emotional valence attached to this fact. Few seem to be nostalgic for the day when shorter Jewish men dominated the game.

But this increasing body specialization in women's gymnastics has not been viewed apathetically. Much of the writing about women's gymnastics in the '80s and '90s has taken a critical stance regarding the size of female gymnasts, taking their diminutiveness as unhealthy at best and abusive at worst. Most prominent among those critics was Joan Ryan, author of the 1995 bestseller *Little Girls in Pretty Boxes*. Ryan collected stories from many elite gymnasts who admitted to starving themselves or going to other extremes— bulimia, laxatives, anorexia—to maintain a small shape.

Ryan wondered why. "Is gymnastics simply attracting tiny girls? Or does the intensive training required of today's gymnastics stunt their growth?" she wrote. Her conclusion was that it was a little bit of both. While she briefly acknowledged the force of body specialization in sports, which by the early '90s was already in full swing, she also cited a 1993 study in the *Journal of Pediatrics* that found that female gymnasts who trained more than eighteen hours a week— which is far below the number the average elite trains—may not reach their full adult heights. According to this study, the sport wasn't merely finding short athletes in a Darwinian type of selection process; it was creating them through rigorous training that permanently stunted their growth.

But not all studies have replicated this finding. In the past decade, the Scientific Commission of the International Gymnastics Federation reexamined the same question: Does intense training before and during puberty prevent female gymnasts from reaching their full adult heights?

Insofar as it is possible even to study these things, the FIG Scientific Commission found that though gymnasts' development may be delayed when compared to the mean in the general population, their timetables tended to overlap with those of other nonathletic, small late bloomers. The gymnasts were at the edges of the bell curve, but still within normal range.

Which brings us back to Nadia. By the time she competed in her final Olympic Games in 1980, she was by no means the little girl she had appeared to be in 1976. Though still angular and thin, she was just over five feet three and, as Ottum noted, she had breasts. She was defeated, somewhat controversially, by Yelena Davydova of the USSR for the Olympic all-around gold. But Davydova, though noticeably smaller than Comaneci, was only three months younger, making her roughly the same age as the Romanian in 1980. She had actually competed at the 1976 American Cup, placing third behind Comaneci, but was not named to the Soviet team in Montreal, which had favored their older stars instead of young upstarts like Davydova. Comaneci's defeat in Moscow wasn't the result of youth trumping experience.

Like Mukhina had done before her tragic injury, Davydova upped the athletic ante by bringing skills from the men's side of the sport. On the uneven bars, she performed a release move called a Tkatchev. To do this, the gymnast swings down from the handstand and then, when her body is stretched and parallel to the floor, she releases up and over the bar, regrasping by counter-rotating her hips and reaching through straddled legs. This was much harder and far more technical than Comaneci's release move, which had been the first same-bar release for a woman back in the mid-'70s. Davydova was also credited with having performed the first front tuck and the side somersault on the balance beam. And on floor exercises, she performed a rollout tumbling move similar to the one that Mukhina had so grievously injured herself practicing. (Rollout tumbling skills are now banned for women on floor exercise, though the men are still permitted to perform them.)

Typically, it took a few years, a generation in gymnastics time, for an innovation to take hold. You had to wait until the old guard retired. It wasn't so easy for Kim's and Comaneci's full-grown peers simply to go back to the gym and learn the new skills they had intro-duced with older, larger bodies.

But after 1980, nearly all of those gymnasts, including Kim and Comaneci, had retired. It was time for the young, daring gymnasts Goodson had observed in Moscow to take over. The era of the mini-monsters would begin in earnest.

PEAK 10:
HOW GYMNASTICS' MOST POPULAR SCORE
REACHED ITS BREAKING POINT

If the 1988 Olympics were turned into a Nancy Drew mystery, it would be called *The Case of Too Many 10s*. In the years between Nadia and Seoul, the Perfect 10 went from rare occurrence to practically commonplace in high-level competition. And at the 1988 Olympics in South Korea, gymnastics hit "Peak 10." As *Sports Illustrated*'s E. M. Swift pointed out, "A total of 40 'Perfect 10s' were awarded to fourteen gymnasts during the week, many for performances containing flaws that could be spotted from thirty-five rows back in the Olympic Gymnastics Hall."

In the all-around contest, Romania's Daniela Silivas scored two perfect marks. She was matched in this feat by the USSR's Yelena Shushunova, who edged the Romanian for the overall title, since she carried in a slightly higher point total from the team competition. In the event finals, the parade of 10s continued. The uneven bar finals featured three separate perfect marks—one apiece for Silivas and Shushunova and the third for Dagmar Kersten of East Germany.

Throughout the competition, the commentators noted the pro liferation of 10s, especially when they seemed to be incongruent with the performances. Dick Enberg, a member of ABC's commentary team, pointed out that though the USSR's Olga Strazheva clearly hopped on her beam dismount during the compulsory competition, the Soviet and Dutch judges each gave her 10s, prompting his co-commentator, Bart Conner, to ask, "How can they possibly give a 10 when they saw a hop on the landing?"

In the event finals, Kersten visibly hopped on her bar dismount and got a 10 while Boginskaya hit her entire routine perfectly and ended up with a 9.987. "I think these kind of scores are bad for gymnastics," Conner observed. "It doesn't make sense." But as he also noted, Comaneci had slid forward on the dismount on her first "perfect" performance in Montreal, similar to the one he was pointing out in Kersten's routine on the uneven bars. Yet Comaneci's 10 was more or less accepted orthodoxy within gymnastics, but Kersten's and others' were somehow suspect.

Why were these other, "imperfect 10s," as Enberg called them, being called into question? Was it simply that there were so many of them? That could be it. In Montreal, Comaneci received seven in total, same as Silivas and Shushunova, who maxed out at seven 10s each, too. Or was the problem that the 10s were spread around among so many gymnasts? Perhaps it was easier to believe that one person could be perfect the way monotheists believe in one deity than to accept that so many individuals in a given time and space could be so. That might have strained credulity and forced the viewers and commentators to start asking questions. Or maybe the standards of perfection changed in the ten years since Nadia competed?

Yes and yes and yes. It was all of these things—the sheer number of 10s, the way in which they were spread among so many gymnasts, and the fact that the standard of perfection had changed in the sport and audiences had grown savvy to that.

For instance, sticking the landing. You might think there is just one way to skin a cat or stick a landing: land a vault or a beam dismount without moving your feet. But the definition of "sticking" in gymnastics, well, hasn't quite *stuck* over the years. A slide back or forward, if accompanied by the salute, was often seen as a stylistic choice. Then there are the hard sticks where the gymnast's legs are so far apart their knees don't even touch, but from the side where the judges sit this might not be visible as it is to the TV audience, which can watch a vault from multiple camera angles. The judges see it as a 10, but the viewers don't.

After gymnastics competition in Seoul, Mike Jacki, the executive director of the U.S. Gymnastics Federation, said, "No question about it. We have the worst judging in any sport." Of course, the list for this dubious distinction is rather short—most sports don't rely exclusively on judging to determine outcomes.

Swift, in his article, took aim at a different target—not the adjudicators, but the rules that they're supposed to be applying. "The scoring system doesn't do anyone in the sport justice," he wrote. Or, to paraphrase Al Pacino in *And Justice for All*, "The whole system is out of order!"

But there is a way to view the proliferation of 10s other than through the lens of incompetence or corruption. All of those 10s could also be read as a sign that Comaneci and her gymnastics descendants had mastered and surpassed the rules. And so started the cycle of rule revisions. Every four years (and occasionally during the intermediate ones), the rules that govern gymnastics were modified to steer gymnasts away from the magical 10. Too many gymnasts scoring at or near perfection means that the rules had become obsolete, at least for the top tier of athlete. These changes were gymnastics' way of establishing a grading curve.

"The 10 was too easy for the best and too hard for the rest," Hardy Fink, a former Canadian gymnast and coach, and the chief architect of open-ended scoring, observed. He repeated this so often that it took on the feel of a mantra or the chorus to a Top 40 song. Fink began judging in 1969, seven years before Comaneci made her big splash and three before Korbut rebranded women's gymnastics as a sport for pixies. He has been philosophizing about the nature of judging and gymnastics evaluation ever since. And for him, the biggest problem with gymnastics evaluation has been the Perfect 10.

"It was an ongoing series of observations that this isn't making sense," he told me when we met at the 2014 World Gymnastics Championships in Nanning, China. We were at the edge of the growing Chinese city in a multisport complex that could support a full range of swimming and diving activities and soccer in addition to gymnastics—a complex that hadn't even been there just a few years before.

At a time when Western democratic countries were opting out of hosting the Olympic Games—just before I arrived at the competition venue, Norway withdrew its candidacy for the 2022 Winter Olympic Games, leaving only Beijing and Almaty, Kazakhstan, in the running—Nanning, like several other Chinese cities, was proving that it could host an Olympic-level sporting event with just a couple years' notice. The international airport terminal had been renovated just in time for the start of the World Championships, and a light rail was under construction. There were dedicated bus lanes for shuttles running to and from the competition venue, training halls, and athlete hotels. The city was plastered with advertising for the championships. And there was a small army of volunteers, numbering around eight hundred, to help address the athletes', judges', officials', and media's every need. When at the end of the championships Bruno Grandi, the president of the International Gymnastics Federation, compared the flawless organization behind this competition to that of an Olympic Games, the Italian bureaucrat wasn't exaggerating at all. It was the only time he used the word *perfect* during the thirty-minute press conference. In 2014, eight years into open-ended scoring, *perfect* was used to describe not athletes' but the host city's administrative performance. Not exactly the stuff inspirational sports movies are made of.

But there was once a time when "perfection," at least as represented by the 10, was abundant. For Fink, every single one of these 10s was politically motivated.

Even Nadia's. He cited his theory about what he believes happened at the 1976 Olympics, with the caveat that it is impossible to prove. "Clearly in '76, the scores were just pushed to the limit. I think the Dutch girls had 9.6 averages or something like that. Everybody was up so high."

When I looked into the scores—at least those that were searchable—I found that though the Dutch team was not averaging 9.6s across the board, more than a few were in that range. This is still relatively high considering the fact that the Netherlands was ranked eleventh out of twelve teams in the competition. The teams just a few notches above them, yet also out of the medal range, were averaging in the 9.6s and 9.7s, which was pretty high for that era.

Compare these averages (for just the average teams) with the marks half a generation earlier. In 1972, Tourischeva, the all-around gold medalist from that competition, recorded two scores in the 9.6 range, one 9.4, and only one 9.9. Her team's marks on the balance beam averaged to just 9.41. And they won the team title. In 1976, when the stately Soviet won the bronze, her scores were significantly higher than they had been when she won gold.

Abie Grossfeld also brought up the scoring inflation he observed in 1976 as a spectator. He had been sitting next to a Canadian judge during the competition. After one of the hometown girls received a 9.6, Grossfeld remembered the same woman saying, "I gave her an 8.6 in the [Canadian Olympic] Trials for the same routine done the same way."

Fink suspects that the Soviets, through their control of the judging panels, inflated everyone's scores in 1976, banking on the fact that, though seemingly stoic and preternaturally composed, Comaneci was just fourteen years old and would crack, at least a little bit, under the pressure of the Olympics. Objectively, she was more than a full—or half a point—better than her nearest competition. She should have been able to count a large mistake and still win the overall title. The Soviets, by bringing the rest of the field closer to Comaneci in the scoring, might have been hoping to make it impossible for the Romanian to absorb a fall and still win. "If she made one mistake, boom, she's done," Fink explained.

Of course, this plan (if such a plan existed) backfired. Comaneci didn't crack under the Olympic pressure. As Nellie Kim, her closest Soviet rival of that era, said in a Sky Sports documentary, "Nadia was prepared better psychologically. That's why she won." And since the rest of her competitors' marks had been high—and she was demonstrably better—the judges had no choice but to give her 10s.

When I asked him how the Soviets could have possibly pulled this scheme off, Fink practically laughed at my naïveté. It sounded like a conspiracy theory to me, the gymnastics version of a second shooter on the grassy knoll in Dallas. But apparently I had missed out on decades of gymnastics' most flagrant and egregious examples of judging scandals.

In a 1998 interview in *International Gymnast*, retired American judge Delene Darst, who evaluated routines domestically and internationally from 1967 to 1992, confirmed Fink's assertion of rampant judging corruption. Of the early years of United States participation in international competitions, she said, "Basically years ago, when the Eastern bloc ruled gymnastics, and we were fighting and scrounging to get recognized, our gymnasts used to do good work—not great but good work—and they got scored terribly. The first World Championships that we went to, we couldn't get a 9.0. . . . We'd hit a routine and get an 8.6. Then Hungary would do a routine with a fall and get a 9.0."

Darst recalled other instances of judging violations that she witnessed throughout her career. At the 1987 World Championships in Rotterdam, "We got pieces of paper from the Romanians with scores on them for their gymnasts. Those were the scores they hoped their gymnasts would get if they hit their routines," Darst said.

Greg Marsden, head coach of the University of Utah's women's gymnastics team, had been selected as the coach for the United States' 1987 World Championship squad. This was his first and only foray into the world of elite international gymnastics, and he was not quite ready for the level of gamesmanship he encountered. "I wasn't prepared for how much it was about the grown-ups and it wasn't about the gymnasts," he recalled.

Each team, he told me, hosted socials where their country's judges would mingle among other country's judges. At first, it was friendly, but eventually they would get down to brass tacks and discuss the scores they could plausibly hope to receive if their gymnast hit. "It probably sounds worse than it was. The gymnast had to do the job on the floor first," Marsden noted, before scoring bonuses could be applied.

Marsden quickly departed the elite gymnastics scene after the 1987 Worlds. "My one-year experience with international gymnastics was like when you're young and you find out there isn't a Santa Claus. I thought the Olympics was this pure thing. It is not that at all."

And, as Fink described, it wouldn't have taken an evil mastermind to orchestrate the scoring inflation he noticed at the 1976 Games or at any other major competition, for that matter. It just takes a few judges and officials willing to prey on the insecurity of their fellow judges. "It's easy to lead, easy to do because most judges are insecure," he explained. "They don't have the confidence in their score. It's not a problem of competence. It's not even so much a problem of conscience nowadays at least. It's a problem of confidence. Like, everybody's giving her a 9.8, and you think it's 9.1—are you going to give a 9.1? You'll give a 9.75 or whatever the hell so you're not too far away."

And it's not as if anyone would complain about this sort of scoring manipulation. No one was getting lowballed. "Holland was happy. Every country that was there had their best ever results. And so I sensed that that was a deliberate strategy because that was the only way," he said.

That said, it seems that Fink believes that Comaneci's 10s, even if they were politically motivated, were the most legitimate of the bunch. She was technically superior in almost every way to her peers, and the rules had no way of rewarding her prowess. Had there been no scoring manipulation, "She [still] would have [won] by a large amount," Fink said. The margin between her and Kim, the all-around silver medalist, was just over six tenths. Nadia could have fallen and won after all.

Despite the seeming scoring inflation, Fink conceded that Comaneci's 10s were special. "That was a unique moment in time. Almost every 10 after that was suspect."

But the problem wasn't simply the 10 itself but all of the contortions (if you will) that the rules underwent over the years to keep all of the components—the acrobatics, the artistry, the execution—under the "10."

"Every cycle, they would change the difficulty requirements. They change the values of the difficulty elements. They change the number of difficulty elements," Fink observed. And sometimes, the technical committees would make adjustments midcycle to address problems that had arisen, usually due to the changes made at the start of the cycle. "No one could do any long-term planning because it was not stable. You [a coach] couldn't plan for the future of your gymnast because the next cycle everything started all over."

Two women's judges from New Zealand I spoke to while in China acknowledged that one of their jobs while they're at a major competition is not simply to evaluate routines (if they're lucky enough to draw one of the judging slots) but to gather information for the coaches back home about which way the wind is blowing, gymnastically speaking: which skills and combinations will be emphasized in a couple of years when the new *Code* is approved.

"One of our jobs is to get all of the information. When we come away overseas, we pass it on to the coaches," Esther Hyde said. "You get to hear quite a lot when you go to the meetings about things that may not be the rules now but may be the rules in the next years." Armed with this information, Hyde is able to go home and tell the juniors (and their coaches), "Don't work on this. Work on this [skill category instead] because this is going to be important in a few years' time."

Karen Bevins, another Kiwi judge, recalled the rumors she heard at competitions in the early '90s that front tumbling—where the gymnast flips and rotates forward—would be more highly rewarded in the 1993–1996 *Code of Points*. (Virtually no one did any front tumbling passes at the 1992 Olympics because it wasn't worth much.) So she went home and told the coaches to start training those elements. And lo and behold, in 1993, Natalia Bobrova, a Russian gymnast, won the bronze medal on floor exercise with two front tumbling passes (out of four total). The 1996 Olympic champion Lilia Podkopayeva one-upped her, winning her title with three forward rotating lines out of her four.

"If we don't start with our five-year-olds, with the right techniques, the right emphasis on specific skills, by the time they're fourteen, it's too late to change. We get that info from networking," Bevins said.

These comments make Fink's point more concrete—an ever-shifting set of rules makes it hard for coaches to mold young talent and put together multiyear development plans for their athletes.

And if an evolving rulebook is difficult for judges, coaches, and athletes to keep up with, how much harder must it be for the uneducated viewer to understand?

Jim Holt, a coach who has known Fink for decades, explained how incomprehensible gymnastics is to a mass audience, due to its continual cycle of changes. "With the exception of the designated hitter rule, which I hate, when was the last significant rule change that baseball had?" he asked me. I shook my head. "When the pitching mound was moved back from fifty feet to sixty feet six inches in 1893," he answered. "If we had a time machine and went to see St. Louis play Cincinnati in 1896, the uniforms would be funny, but it would be a game we could completely follow," Holt said. "These sports have had a sustained, knowable set of regulations."

Holt's right. Despite the fact that I know very little about baseball, whatever I do know—bits and pieces I've picked up over the years attending the occasional game in the Bronx or catching an inning or two here and there on television—likely will never become obsolete. The touchdown you see at a Super Bowl party, which is the only time a year many of us ever watch a football game, will always be worth six points. But the value of the two-and-a-half twister vault that Maroney made famous in 2012 will not remain static—in London it was worth 6.5 points, but after the Olympics, it was downgraded to 6.3.

"We haven't had the same rules for at least fifty years. We change it year after year after year. And then we tweak it in between with all of these newsletters," Holt added, referring to the short communiqués that FIG sends out to member federations informing of small rule changes between the big ones that occur at the beginning of each new cycle.

Holt first met Fink all the way back in 1981, when Fink owned a gymnasium in British Columbia and ran an annual meet. At the time, Holt was a coach at the University of Washington. Shortly thereafter, Fink sold his gym and moved to Vancouver, where Holt became an intermittent houseguest. "He's got the world's best gymnastics library. He's got stuff that's staggering," Holt recalled. "I'd go up and we'd talk gymnastics for the entire weekend."

"I don't know when the [open-ended] code first occurred to him, but we started having conversations about it in '82 or '83," he said. "I was there while Hardy was formulating it in his basement."

That's when Jeff Thomson, a men's judge and fellow Canadian, also recalled first hearing about an open-ended code from Fink. "Probably sometime in the early '80s," he told me. "That's when I first remember him starting to talk about it . . . It sounded good to me. It did seem unfair at times . . . two great routines but one had more difficulty, but wasn't recognized in some way."

Or at least not within the bounds of the rules. As Thomson wrote in an essay about judging in an anthology,

> I remember clearly the first time I saw Valeri Liukin perform his triple back somersault on floor exercise and this Tkachev with a full twist on high bar [movements now named in his honor]. In both instances, the aesthetic performances were not perfect. However, the recognition that these movements were exceptional for their technical preparation and were clearly pushing forward the boundaries of difficulty allowed one, with a clear conscience, to say, "It is not only acceptable but perhaps necessary to 'forgive' these small aesthetic shortcomings in favor of pushing the sport forward."

What Thomson did there—by looking the other way when it comes to small deductions when you're confronted with exceptional difficulty and risk—was something of a common practice among judges during the 10.0 years. While most of the gymnasts struggled to keep pace with the changing rules and requirements, the top echelon often surpassed them quite easily and very early into a new cycle. They were the elites among the elites. They performed routines that were worth more than ten points because they could.

"I think the nature of human endeavor, the nature of the sport, is to keep competing. So for us to say that it [the difficulty] was capped [under the 10] didn't make sense anyway," Fink said.

It is tempting to view judges as simply referees—calling the shots as they see them, enforcing the previously agreed-upon rules—but Thomson's statements indicate a much more complicated relationship between athlete and judge, between performance and evaluation. "As a judge, I strive to present myself as someone the coaches and gymnasts could rely on for an accurate assessment of their work." In this configuration, judges are an important part of the gymnastics feedback loop. As much as you want the judges to look kindly on your athletes, you also need them to be brutal at times, to show you where your weaknesses are.

Many fans faulted judges for not deducting World and Olympic champion Aliya Mustafina harshly enough on her Amanar vault (the same one that Maroney performed to perfection) back in 2010. She performed the skill with "helicopter legs," with her legs splayed and separated like the blade of a helicopter, not straight like an arrow. This was not only poor form and aesthetically unappealing—it was potentially dangerous should she land short of rotation. And at the 2011 European Championships, she did just that, twisting into the ground and tearing her ACL. When this happened, the gymternet exploded with blame for the judges and, to a lesser extent, her coach: the latter for allowing her to compete an element that she clearly had not mastered and the former for not deducting her so harshly that she would abandon the skill. As for the gymnast herself, most recognized that there was no way that Mustafina, who is über-competitive, would stop doing this skill if she could win with it. It would take an act of judging or injury to get her to stop. And since the former didn't happen, it took the latter to sideline that skill. Mustafina hasn't competed that vault since her devastating injury. Steve Butcher, the current president of the Men's Technical Committee, said, "Taking deductions makes things, in my opinion, safer for the gymnast." But it seems that even with the new open-ended code in place, something of the old attitude among judges remains. They sometimes give the benefit of the doubt to a gymnast performing a skill of surpassing difficulty and don't penalize her as harshly for faults in it.

"We need a code applicable to all levels," said Holt. One "that could be tweaked but is more or less permanent." And once those values were set, they would not be changed unless there was a compelling reason to do so. When you downgrade elements, you risk seeing them disappear from the sport, since they do not amass points. That skill becomes a word that has slipped from daily usage; when elements are devalued, the overall gymnastics vocabulary shrinks. In this way, the rules push the gymnast and the sport, but back in Olga's and Nadia's day, it was the other way around—the gymnasts innovated and pushed the sport forward, and the rules had to constantly play catch-up.

———

Though Fink had started toying with the idea of an open-ended code in the early '80s, it wasn't until the early '90s—after the 10-laden 1988 Olympics and 1989 World Championships—that he was allowed to start testing his ideas. By 1991, Fink was given the go-ahead to draft his proposed *Code*. And at this point, he was no longer working alone. He had partnered with Jörg Fetzer of Germany to write and distribute this new scoring paradigm.

Fink set out to design a system that was not only open-ended but also universal, eternal even. It would include every skill ever performed, from the simplest to the most difficult, so it could be used at every level of competition. And this rulebook would also be anticipatory—it would not only catalog what had already been done but would predict what might be done.

This is not as hard as you'd think. You don't necessarily need a crystal ball to know what comes next in the sport—double twists become triples become quads becomes quintuples (though the last would entail a massive leap in either human evolution or orthopedic ACL repair or both). This part of the code-writing process actually sounded like fun to me. I imagined sitting around, daydreaming up heretofore unheard-of skills such as the ones I had my Barbies perform when I was younger and playing "the Olympic Games" in my bedroom.

Also, as Fink pointed out, many gymnasts train at greater difficulty than they will ever use in a competition. Those skills, which are often recorded and uploaded to YouTube, could also be given values and added to the rulebook. He saw no reason to wait for someone to do it in competition before putting it into the *Code*. And once an athlete debuted it in a meet, the *Code* could be amended so that the skill would bear her name.

Fink's vision of a new gymnastics rulebook was downright utopian—a *Code* that could be used by all, that would last forever, that would never need to be changed. It was to be the renewable energy source of sports rulebooks. Or as Holt put it, "The code that Hardy was envisioning was a unified field theory of our sport."

"Hardy Fink is one of the most remarkable and visionary people in the history of gymnastics," Holt told me. "I'm in awe that with all of the baggage that the sport has, that someone would try to attempt this."

To hear him speak about Fink so effusively was something of a surprise to me. Though he had once been close to Fink, the traveling coach, in Nanning working with the Indian men's team, had been introduced to me as someone who fiercely opposed the changes made to the scoring system. And he certainly is. But it seems that for Holt, his disappointment with Fink's code is how it fell short of its creator's goal, that the Canadian elder statesman didn't have the political chops to push his vision through. "He made poor decisions on the timing [and] on how to convince the gymnastics community to do it. Complicating that was a whole other level of political machinations," Holt said.

Doug Hills, an American coach and judge, seemed to agree about Fink's lack of political acumen. "I have not been able to figure this [man] out. He is the least political guy at the highest levels of politics I've ever met or heard of. I think that's a real testament to that guy," he told me.

But without a political skill set, Fink was ill equipped to counter the opposition to his proposed rule change. Many in the gymnastics community opposed the proposed elimination of the Perfect 10. Grandi commented to me via email that the initial measures to push through open-ended scoring in the '90s were defeated, "basically for political reasons."

The most strenuous resistance to the change came from the American camp. Philippe Salacci, who was then the FIG press officer, confirmed that the United States had been the most opposed. One American judge told me that in the '90s he had been given a copy of the proposed *Code* and told to find ways to punch holes in it. "I was asked by a judge here how to attack that code, because USA Gymnastics didn't want it. I asked if I could borrow the *Code*, and I read it and I got it. I understood why he [Fink] was doing what he was doing," he said.

"Here's the basic logic behind it: if you have a 10.0 cap, the athletes are going to do the easiest exercises they can do to hit the 10.0 cap and then no more. They should be doing their best stuff. And so Hardy system's was you do your ten best skills, no repeats." This judge, though mostly on board with the concept, didn't fully agree with it. "I happened to think, Mozart liked repeats. Why shouldn't the gymnasts?"

Perhaps the fiercest opponent of the scoring change was Jackie Fie, who was then the president of the Women's Technical Committee. Fie, who did not agree to be interviewed for this book, held the same position in women's gymnastics as Fink did on the men's side of the aisle.

In addition to Fie, few were more outspoken than Ziert. "Of course, everybody says, 'You love the ten,' " he told me in his Oklahoma office. The room, like the rest of the building, was a veritable trove of gymnastics memorabilia, from framed artwork to sculpture to novelty items such as Perfect 10 wine. Comaneci's office was across from his. I was in Perfect 10 Central.

"Yes I do," he continued, "because you get a lot out of this new code, but the price you pay is in people understanding what you're doing, people liking gymnastics." Ziert felt that the concerns of rewarding difficulty and distinguishing between routines of greater and middling complexity could have been addressed while maintaining the sport's iconic score. "With the way of computers in this age, you could have this code and still have it concealed under the 10, and I think the public would be much happier," he said.

But gymnastics had already tried to keep it all in the 10 like the mafia tries to keep it all in the family. In 1997, the judging panels for each event were increased from one to two—the head judge of the apparatus and an assistant would evaluate the start value, or SV, which could not exceed 10, and the other judges would tally up the deductions. The latter would be subtracted from the former, say a 0.5 taken from 9.9, which was how you arrive at the final score: a 9.4.

What this meant, in practice, is that not every routine started from a 10. Now, when a gymnast mounted the apparatus, you didn't just watch to see how she did, appreciate good execution, and notice mistakes; you also had to wonder if all her skills added up to a 10. Or had she skipped something or missed a connection, which forced it to drop to a 9.9. The 10 as an appreciative score, as an evaluation of a whole performance, was gone. It was now simply a start value.

And as before, there were some gymnasts who could master the rules easily and reach the potential 10.0, but most could not. This led to confusion among the lay viewership. I remember back in 2004 a friend querying me about the beam score of Mohini Bhardwaj, an American gymnast. In team finals, she was a last-minute sub for an injured teammate and performed quite heroically on the beam without any warm-up. But the routine she did just didn't have the technical complexity to qualify for a Perfect 10, even if she had indeed executed it perfectly.

Bhardwaj performed admirably, if not flawlessly. In the end, her score was a 9.4. Had she done it to perfection, the highest she could've scored was a 9.8—that would have been a "perfect" score for that given routine. Confused yet? A lot of people were.

In 2005, Dwight Normile complained about the incomprehensibility of the scores still under the 10.0 ceiling. "Years ago," he wrote, "we understood the significance of a 9.4 or a 9.5, but what do we really make of a 9.237 or a 9.812?"

But despite all of these acknowledged problems with the 10, Fink just couldn't get the traction he needed to pass his new scoring *Code*.

As the debate around the new *Code* raged in the gymnastics world, the rules were being tested in Fink's native country, Canada, among the male age group competitors. It was very much still a work in progress.

Rick McCharles, a Canadian men's gymnastics coach and blogger, recalled this period of experimentation. "I had mixed feelings about the Fink *Code* when it was first piloted with age group [boys] in Canada," he wrote to me in an email. The biggest problem he could recall was on a vault where one gymnast scored higher with a fall, ahead of a gymnast who had performed an easier skill. "It sent the wrong message," McCharles noted.

Fink was still working on the math behind his new scoring plan. But he needed more than time to tinker with the formula—he needed some political know-how to convince the voting members of the gymnastics community to buy into the plan. And that wasn't proving easy.

"At the time Hardy talked about adjusting the weighting of difficulty versus execution until he had the right balance," as a chef in a test kitchen would try to find the right balance of ingredients in a new recipe. "No other person has spent as much time weighing the pros and cons. Hardy is a Mensa [member] with very strong math. If he had enough time, it could have worked well," McCharles said.

Trying to explain to people that the thing they intuited and believed was true—that the 10 was essential to the sport—wasn't necessarily true was an uphill battle, especially since Fink did not speak the language of those he was trying to convince. In all of our conversations about the sport, he was passionate about gymnastics but not besotted by it. Fink, as a rule, does not seem to be a nostalgic sort of man. He loves gymnastics but may not be *in love* with the

sport. Fink's dissection of its failings was academic, practically clini-
cal. He was suggesting amputating the beloved 10 with the bedside
manner of a Civil War field surgeon.

When Fink attempted to persuade the community, as he once
did in an online message board, he made academic arguments. "No
other sport uses the 10.0 as a final score. Perhaps this uniqueness
should not be tampered with. But I submit the public doesn't understand a 10.0 that includes performance and content factors," he
wrote. This, while true, is not exactly a rousing rallying cry.

In 1999, the FIG voted open-ended scoring down. Fink's grand
experiment was over. Gymnastics would retain the 10 and all of the
machinations needed to maintain it. Fink blamed the defeat largely
on the Americans who, with Fie at the helm, had fought vehemently
against his new system.

After his *Code* was voted down, Fink faded somewhat. He didn't
run for reelection as the president of the Men's Technical Committee when it became apparent that he didn't have the requisite votes
and support to win. Instead, he was appointed as the head of the FIG
Academies, a position that Ziert characterized as a "pushing aside."
The Fink *Code*, as it was called by many, was also pushed aside. Many
in gymnastics assumed that that's where it would stay.

But then 2004 happened. As Rahm Emanuel said, "You never
want a serious crisis to go to waste. And what I mean by that—it's
an opportunity to do things you think you could not do before." For
gymnastics that meant changing the rules and ridding the sport of
the Perfect 10.

4

BLAME IT ON THE MEN:
THE 2004 OLYMPICS AND THE END OF THE 10

In 2004, Paul Hamm entered the Olympic Games as the defending World all-around champion, a feat he accomplished the year before in Anaheim, California, at the 2003 World Championships. Typically, U.S. victories in gymnastics that occur on home soil are largely regarded as suspect—Mary Lou Retton's 1984 gold medal in the all-around at the Los Angeles Games, Kim Zmeskal's World Championship win in 1991 in Indianapolis, the Magnificent Seven's team title in Atlanta in 1996.

There are frequently grumblings about judging bias when American athletes win at home, as though judging panels are subject to the whim of the crowd. And perhaps there is some credence to those ideas. Many of the United States's major gymnastics breakthroughs took place where charity is supposed to begin—at home.

But by the time the early 2000s rolled around, U.S. gymnastics' home field advantage seemed increasingly less necessary to win. The American women were starting to assert themselves as the future of the sport. And in the case of Hamm's 2003 win at the Anaheim World Championships, few took issue with it. He was something of

75

a gymnast's gymnast—performed some of the highest difficulty of the day with clean form and pure technique. The complexity of his skills didn't exceed his grasp. And it's not like his 2003 win had come out of left field. He had been poised to win—or at least medal—in 2001 at the World Championships in Ghent as a nineteen-year-old until he fell while re-grasping a release move on the high bar, coming in so close to the apparatus that he hit his nose and bloodied his face and uniform in the process. Hamm's Anaheim win was almost overdue. It meant that he was finally starting to live up to his potential and become the greatest U.S. male gymnast of all time.

Hamm started his Olympic gold medal run on floor exercise, an event on which he was the defending World Champion, taking an early lead over his biggest rival, China's Yang Wei. Yang and Hamm volleyed the lead back and forth over the next two rotations, with the former grabbing it after the second rotation, and the latter taking it back at the halfway point.

Then Hamm went over to vault, an apparatus that always feels somewhat safe to gymnastics spectators. The vault is basically a single skill. You either land on your feet or you don't. It's not much more complicated than that. This also means you only have one chance to make a ghastly mistake, whereas the screw-up potential on the other events is seemingly limitless. On balance beam and pommel horse, the gymnast always seems to be teetering on the brink of disaster for seventy to ninety seconds. But vault is over much faster than that.

All of this to say that what happened next on vault was shocking. The vault should have been easy for Hamm, a stroll down the runway. Everything seemed fine on the approach. Hamm ran toward the table, jumped onto the springboard, and turned his body 180 degrees to meet the apparatus with his hands before blocking off and launching into two-and-a-half twists off. Hamm landed on his feet—and this is an important fact because if he hadn't stood it up, he wouldn't have received credit for the skill—but then lurched to the side, crossing his left foot in front of his right. And then more steps to the side and off the landing mats until he was almost off the podium.

"He's on the judges' table!" the Australian commentator Liz Chetkovich exclaimed when he finally stopped moving, helped by a judge who stuck his arm out to break his fall. "That's going to blow it for him," she added. The slo-mo revealed that although it looked nice and clean in the air—he got good height off the table and had enough time to complete his rotations—he was off side from the get-go. He planted in the mats skewed to his right, his shoulder dipping to the side, landing with so much force and momentum that he couldn't help but stumble sideways. "I wonder if there is a special deduction for sitting on the judges' table," Chetkovich mused.

It turns out, there wasn't. A score of 9.137 flashed. Even though this was the third-lowest mark on the event in the twenty-four-athlete field, it still struck me (and many other observers), who didn't expect to see a mark above a 9.0 for a vault with a fall of that magnitude, as a bit high. After all, he didn't merely sit it down. He took several out-of-control steps and practically landed on a judge's face.

The extra tenths could've constituted the "World Champion's bonus," a sort of scoring "benefit of the doubt" for those with a track record of competitive success. This was not unheard of in international competition, even if this "bonus" was never written into the *Code of Points*. As Nellie Kim said of Nadia Comaneci's post-1976 wins, "First, you work for your name. And then the name works for you." You first had to win a big title to get it.

Either way, it seemed that the all-around contest was over, at least for Hamm. A medal seemed highly unlikely. The gold, impossible. There were only two rotations left—not a lot of opportunity to make up that kind of scoring ground. Besides, gymnasts with falls didn't win all-around medals. Not only was that sort of comeback next to impossible, it's not even considered desirable by gymnastics fans.

Comeback stories in gymnastics are about comebacks from injuries. Or coming back in one competition after you biffed it in the previous one. Had Hamm's subsequent flawless routines on parallel bars and high bar netted him a merely respectable finish—say, fifth place—then this would be the sort of comeback that gymnastics fans could applaud. *He made a mistake but didn't give up*, they would have said.

Sports fans of the more mainstream variety, however, love a good comeback story. And the greater the mistake at the start, the better it is in the end when the athlete ends up on top. Serena Williams double faulting, dropping one set to her opponent only to storm back and win the tournament? Fantastic. A marathoner tripping early in a race but making up the lost ground and then punching through the winner's tape at mile 26.2 before his opponents? Inspirational.

But in gymnastics, we don't want to see the sort of comebacks that crowds eat up in other sports. We want to see mastery from start to finish. It doesn't matter how superb the rest of your competition. In gymnastics, winning with a fall shouldn't be possible.

Yet after his final event, Hamm found himself in first place, ahead of two South Korean gymnasts by a slim margin. Everyone was shocked, and no one more than the American himself. After receiving a 9.837 for a flawless high-bar performance, Hamm shook his head in disbelief as his coach told him he had completed the most improbable of sports comebacks—winning the Olympic all-around after a fall. He kept saying, "No, no, no." He didn't think it was possible.

And as the scoring controversy that engulfed Hamm demonstrated, it actually wasn't. It was later revealed that the South Koreans had submitted a petition—albeit too late—to inquire about the start value on the parallel bars of Yang Tae Young. The panel had credited him with a 9.9 start score instead of the 10.0 he had been assigned during the team competition. Had that tenth been applied, Yang would have been the gold medalist instead of the bronze medalist. (That's how tight the rankings were—it only took one tenth to jump from third to first.) This error resulted in the suspension of three judges, including American George Beckstead. Hamm's gold medal was contested all the way to the Court of Arbitration for Sport, which ultimately found in favor of the American gymnast, allowing him to retain his title. Their decision, however, did nothing to remove the taint the controversy had left behind. There would be no Wheaties box for him as there was for his fellow all-around winner Carly Patterson, who won the ladies' title on the following night, becoming the first American woman to win the all-around since Retton did in 1984. The corporate sponsors want your gold medal to be decided in the competition arena, not by barristers in a courtroom.

The scoring issues continued into event finals where Marian Dragalescu, the bronze medalist, counted a fall among his two vaults. But before he fell, Dragalescu had performed what was arguably the best vault of the Games. He stuck his eponymous skill—a double front somersault with an extra half-twist kick out—cold. For this first vault, he received a 9.9, which was the highest score of the Olympics. The vault, however, was seemingly without flaw. NBC commentator Al Trautwig said with exasperation, "They can't do it," of the judges. The "it" in question was hand out a perfect score. The judges in Athens seemed more comfortable inflating the score of flawed vaults by a tenth or two than they did with handing out that final tenth to an exceptional performance.

But there may have been more than lack of courage at play. As the New Zealand and Canadian judges explained, the better the gymnasts get, the more likely they are to be scrutinized more closely because the judges have the luxury of time—they're not busy taking a litany of deductions. Chris Grabowecky, a Canadian judge, offered an example from men's gymnastics. "Think of a rings routine where a gymnast is making multiple errors on every skill—he's got an overgrip, his arms are bent, his toes aren't pointed, he's got bad body position—you're trying to see all of this on one element, get all of those errors down. It's almost impossible in gymnasts that have so many errors, you can't record them all," he explained.

In 1985, Fink published a paper in the gymnastics federation's journal about just how much is required of the human brain to evaluate a performance accurately in the short amount of time allotted. "More and more research and experiential evidence is accumulating that suggests judging or evaluation of gymnastics performances is extremely difficult and may, in fact, be impossible." Fink, who specialized in men's gymnastics, used the men's side of the sport to point out the difficulties judges face in coming up with a score. "My investigations reveal that a full competitive performance [all six of the men's apparatuses] requires, typically, some two hundred seconds and presents some eighty to one hundred distinct skills, an average of one new skill every two seconds." And that was back in the mid-'80s, when the skill level was substantially lower and the gymnasts did far fewer elements in any given routine.

But not every gymnast makes several major errors on any given skill. "Then you have a gymnast that's almost perfect, but his grip is a bit off. So he gets a one-tenth deduction, but the terrible gymnast gets four tenths. When really the difference should've been one tenth and a full point," Grabowecky said. The terrible gymnast may not even get penalized for an off grip or any small number of slight errors because the judge has bigger fish to fry. But when evaluating a spectacular gymnast, say, someone like McKayla Maroney on vault, the judge has the opportunity to notice and deduct for all of the small stuff. "It's easy to find small problems when there aren't big problems," Grabowecky pointed out.

In the slow-motion replay, you can find an error in Maroney's vault—her legs came slightly apart on her preflight. That was a fair deduction. But was it fairly and consistently applied? If the judges had given Maroney a 10 for the execution part of her score, it would have been like Nadia's first perfect score—it wouldn't necessarily have signified "perfection"; it simply would have meant "better than." And in Maroney's case, it would have been about ensuring that her score adequately reflected the true distance between her and her nearest competitors on that event. Fink said of her vault, "That was a chance to give a 10."

The last judge to throw out a 10 was Grabowecky the year before the scandal-ridden 2004 Olympics. He had been a judge at the World Championships on the pommel horse and had awarded a perfect score, the last ever seen in World or Olympic competition. He did this during the preliminary round at the 2003 World Championships. The recipient was Xiao Qin, a Chinese gymnast who specialized on the pommel horse. "I didn't really reward a 10," he cautioned me when we sat down in a Nanning hotel lobby to discuss it. "I rewarded 'no deduction.' If the score had been out of five hundred, I would've awarded 'no deduction.' " By 2003, the judging panels had already been split into two—one to evaluate the "start value" of the exercise, the other to determine how well the skills were performed. The former would hand in numbers like 9.8 or 9.9 or 10.0; the latter would submit deductions such as 0.5 or 0.3. Grabowecky was tasked with taking the deductions in that competition.

"I remember watching this Chinese gymnast during the warm-ups, and I remember thinking about how perfect he looked. I had never seen anyone that could perform on this apparatus like he could," Grabowecky told me. "The entire gym would stop and watch him. That kind of beauty."

The judge in him fretted about where he'd find deductions when this gymnast mounted the pommel horse for his competitive routine. "When you're normally judging, you'd script what element they did and then what the deduction was so if somebody asked, you could say, 'On this element, I took this amount.' " This way the judge had a record if his score was challenged or subject to review.

But after watching Xiao practice and warm up, Grabowecky decided to employ a different strategy for this gymnast's competition performance. He wouldn't script Xiao's entire routine. Instead, he'd just record the mistakes and resultant deductions.

"I just decided to sit and watch. Really watch. I'm going to watch his toes and his ankles. I would watch his entire routine, and if I saw anything, I'd put a mark down." After Xiao spun in his handstand atop the pommel horse and saluted the judges, Grabowecky looked down at his paper. "It was blank," he said.

When he saw that he had no deductions, Grabowecky panicked. "I was sitting there and going, 'What do I do now? I knew—

I suspected—that nobody else was going to have no deductions. It just doesn't happen."

"I was trying to think, 'What do I do? Should I invent a deduction and just give him a 9.9?' " After brief deliberation, Grabowecky thought, "It was perfect. Why not give it to him? Give the guy the credit he deserves."

"It was as perfect as any routine I had ever seen in my life," he added. "There were a lot of perfect scores given out in the seventies and eighties that were nowhere near perfect. This was *perfect*," he emphasized.

"I knew when I put the score in, I was going to be 'wrong.' And sure enough, the final score ended up being a 9.75 or something," he said. In fact, his final score had been a 9.812. Grabowecky's perfect mark had been an outlier.

The way Grabowecky described the judging process—half evaluation of what you see, half trying to guess what the other judges see—reminded me of *The Newlywed Game*. The game is supposed to test one spouse's knowledge of the other, so in order to win, you're not necessarily trying to get to the right answer but predict the answer your partner wrote down on that placard. Gymnastics judges, in their quest to remain in range with their colleagues, are playing a similar game.

After that preliminary round of competition was over, Grabowecky went to the head judge. "Did I miss something?" he asked, worried about what this might mean for his future as an elite-level judge. At the time, Grabowecky was relatively new to high-level international judging, having made his World Championship debut in that capacity only in 2001.

The head judge reassured Grabowecky. "He said, 'No, it was a good routine. Don't worry about it.' " After the competition,

Grabowecky then asked his fellow judges what they had deducted for on Xiao's routine. "No one could come up with an answer that was clear," he said.

Yet just a year later, Grabowecky, the judge who found no fault, was called out for finding excessive fault, this time at the Olympic Games, where he was a judge during the men's high-bar final.

After so much uncertainty during those 2004 Games—a men's all-around title in doubt, questionable ethics of the parallel-bar judges, a dubious vault bronze medal—it seemed that everyone was on edge. The judges, the gymnasts, and even the audience. This was the atmosphere in which Russian legend Alexei Nemov mounted the podium. Nemov was competing in his third and final Olympics. Despite winning twelve medals at his first two Games, he was medal-less thus far in Athens. This would be the last chance to add to his career haul. He jumped up and grabbed the bar to start his routine.

Nemov performed a crowd-pleasing style of gymnastics. His routine was chock full of spectacular release moves—four of which were performed consecutively. This is the kind of difficulty that is comprehensible to an audience. Swing, let go, flip, regrasp. Release moves on the high bar are the SEO-friendly headlines of gymnastics. They jump out at you, grab your attention. They are not subtle. And the crowd's cheering seemed to be proportional to the height of his release moves. As Dwight Normile noted in *International Gymnast*, "He was in the air as much as on the bar, avoiding the tedious pirouetting combinations that can put fans to sleep."

The commentators also got swept up in Nemov's performance. Elfi Schlegel, one-third of the NBC commentariat, said, "This is what the audience appreciates. And what they understand, more importantly. Release skills like this. They think this is big-time gymnastics."

When Nemov's score came up—a 9.725—he was in third place, or last, since only three gymnasts had performed. There were five more in the final, and it was practically assured that at least one of them would outscore Nemov and push him out of the medals.

As un-luck would have it, Paul Hamm was the next athlete up. He was standing on the podium with his coach, Miles Avery, chalking up when Nemov's score flashed. And that's when the booing and whistling started. The cameras panned the audience to show many of them on their feet, jeering, thumbs down in disapproval of Nemov's high-bar score.

On the sidelines, the good-natured Russian gymnast seemed utterly bemused and grateful, bowing to the audience several times. For Hamm, who had been the subject of much scorn in the days since he dubiously won the all-around, it must have all felt a tad personal, that the audience wasn't merely booing the judges' score but the next gymnast up, the one who was the beneficiary of another judging mistake. Here he was, ready to salute the judges and pounce on another medal opportunity, leaving nothing for the crowd favorite.

Hamm and Avery waited for the green light from the judges, who were waiting for the jeering to subside. But it didn't. Instead, it grew louder and more insistent. The head judge, Japanese gymnastics legend Sawao Kato, the 1968 and 1972 Olympic champion, motioned for the two judges who had given the lowest marks—a Malaysian and the Canadian Grabowecky—to approach. Per the rules, the Malay's score hadn't even factored into the final mark since his was the lowest of the bunch (just as Grabowecky's 10 had been dropped the year before). His 9.6 had been tossed. But Grabowecky's 9.65

had been included and had pulled Nemov's overall average down. Kato's instructions to these judges were inaudible in the din, but after a few moments, they returned to their stations to reevaluate their deductions.

With Xiao's routine, he couldn't find a tenth to deduct and didn't have to. But with Nemov, he was forced to find a tenth of a point to add to appease the restive audience. Which he did, raising his mark to a 9.75. Nemov's adjusted score was a 9.762, but he was still in third place. His medal prospects hadn't changed. And neither did the tenor of the crowd. They continued to boo this new result, too.

It was now time for Hamm to go. He had dismounted the podium while Nemov's mark was being reviewed and remounted once the new one had been issued. But the judges hadn't yet given him the green light to mount the high bar. The jeers were still too loud.

By now, the competition had been delayed for nearly ten minutes. Hamm and Avery motioned to Nemov on the sidelines. Nemov jumped up on the podium and gestured for the crowd to calm down so Hamm could compete. Only then did the arena begin to quiet, though not completely. A few stray whistles echoed in the rafters as Hamm completed his first swing. He scored 9.812, bumping Nemov off the podium.

Grabowecky defended his initial appraisal of Nemov's routine to me. "He [Nemov] had errors in the routine that the public doesn't recognize as errors because they're not judges. But he had these beautiful release skills, and they go, 'Wow, that guy should win.' But they don't see that he's catching his release close, bending his knees here, taking a step on the landing," Grabowecky noted.

His dissection of Nemov's exercise down to its components underscores the difference between the way judges and spectators watch routines. The viewers, especially the lay viewers, are looking to be moved in some way—excited by a release move, captivated by a beautiful leap, even horrified by a scary fall. They also tend to view routines holistically, as complete exercises rather than mere compilations of skills that you can pick and choose from. To put it in music-biz lingo, viewers buy complete albums, but judges download the tracks one at a time from iTunes. And given the division of the judging panels between start value and execution, none of the judges was tasked with looking at the routine as a total package as they had during Nadia's heyday. (In fact, all of the 10s ever awarded in men's and women's gymnastics were given out before the judges were divided into separate panels. Dividing the judging labor had made the 10 obsolete long before it was formally eliminated.) Had Nemov fallen off the bar or committed an overt, egregious error, the crowd wouldn't have protested. But they didn't notice his small mistakes because they weren't looking for them.

But Grabowecky was, just as he was when he studied Xiao's routine intently, looking for something to deduct. That's his job. He doesn't, however, fault the fans for their misunderstanding. Rather, he sees it as a problem with gymnastics evaluation. "This is the problem with the sport. It's almost too technical," he said.

It isn't simply the complexity of the rules that Grabowecky faults for the scandals and mistakes at the 2004 Olympics. He also cites the scandals of figure skating two years prior and at the 2002 Salt Lake City Games. There, a French judge and a Russian judge allegedly colluded to give a Russian skating pair the gold over a Canadian pair. The controversy resulted in waves of bad press for the sport, suspensions for judges, duplicate gold medals for the Canadians, and ultimately, a new evaluation system that eliminated figure skating's own iconic perfect mark—the 6.0.

Two years later in Athens, the gymnastics judges were on edge. "I even remember the discussion pre-Games," Grabowecky recalled. " 'We can't be the figure skating of the Summer Olympics.' " The gymnastics judges and officials were uptight in Athens, worried that something similar might befall them. "When there's so much focus on not being something, then you end up being it. It's comical," Grabowecky said.

Philippe Silacci recalled that before the start of the men's all-around, Grandi addressed the judges. "President Grandi met the judges and asked them to do their job. Nothing else. Two hours later, a big mess," he recalled with a laugh.

Speaking of funny, before Grabowecky departed for Greece, "One of my good friends jokingly before I left said, 'Don't create any international scandals.' " When Grabowecky returned to Canada, his friend apologized.

Taken individually, the different scandals that plagued the men's gymnastics at the Athens Olympics—the all-around final, the vault final, and the high-bar final—might have been weathered. But together, they brought the sport and its opaque scoring system to the breaking point. "It was especially evident at the Athens Olympic Games in 2004, when I saw all the difficulty being done on the high bar that couldn't be judged in the correct manner," Grandi commented. Unlike the all-around fiasco, which hinged on judging errors that no system can fully prevent, the scores on the high bar were just according to the rules. According to Silacci, after the competition several judges admitted, " 'I do not have the right tools to do my job.' I think it was the best understanding we had after this problem in Athens that the best judges did not have the best tools in their hands to do their job."

When the crisis arose after the 2004 Olympics, FIG had to spring into "do something" mode to prove to the public and the IOC that it was handling the situation, and quickly. Grandi canceled the judging courses and scrapped the *Code of Points* that had been planned for the new cycle.

Fink's code—the one that had been proposed, tested, and then rejected unceremoniously just a few years before—was the only alternative plan that was close to being ready. It's not as if anyone else had spent more than a decade trying to come up with a completely new system of evaluating gymnastics. The rest of the community had spent its time fighting his agenda. When Grandi, who had been supportive of the idea of an open-ended scoring system, went grasping for a solution, Fink's code was the only thing he found.

This time, however, there wouldn't be lengthy debates and years of voting on resolutions and principles. There would be no further experimentation or trial periods. This was a bigger problem for the women than for the men, since the women never had the opportunity to play around with the open-ended scoring as the men did. As in the earlier eras of sport, the women would be forced to adapt to something that had been created with mostly men in mind. For them, the change to open-ended scoring would be a much bigger conceptual leap. Ziert recalled Fie lamenting the fact that the women were essentially being "punished" for the problems with the men's competition. "This was our cleanest Games," Ziert remembered her saying of the women's results in 2004. After Athens, Fie retired as president of the Women's Technical Committee.

Two years after the debacles of 2004, a new open-ended *Code of*

Points was implemented. When I asked Fink if the new *Code of Points* would have been adopted had the judging fiascos of 2004 not happened, he replied, "It would've taken another cycle. It was falling under its own weight. It just couldn't last."

"If you went back and judged the entire competition [the 2004 Olympics], you'd have found dozens of mistakes," Grabowecky said. "Why? Because that's the nature of the sport. It's human beings. You make mistakes because you're human. You can't be perfect," he said. It seems that in that respect, the athletes and judges have something in common. Neither can be perfect.

This plea for understanding, however, is not one we usually entertain from competition officials. We don't show mercy to the referee whom we believe made the wrong call; we jeer him. Gymnasts who are performing herculean acrobatic feats are given the benefit of the doubt. But judges, though just as human and as fallible, are not. Maybe we forgive the athletes because they're accountable—they suffer extreme consequences for their mistakes, be it injury or missed titles or dashed dreams. The judges are not held responsible in such an extreme way. They may lose their positions on international panels, but that doesn't seem as steep a price as a ruined Olympic dream or bodily harm.

"I want you to understand that I'm not anti–this system," Ziert said, "but I think that whether you like it or not, the one thing is the public likes it [the Perfect 10]. It's simpler to them." Though scores could be difficult to parse at times even in the 10 era, everyone understood that the closer a gymnast scored to 10, the better he or she had performed. Even when the 10 had been reduced to mere start value, this still held true.

The open-ended scoring approach abolished this frame of reference. Now the gymnasts were receiving marks like 13.667 or 14.825, and you had no way of knowing if these were good or bad scores. I'll admit that during the first year or two of the new system, I couldn't tell you that either. Eventually, I got used to seeing these bizarre strings of numbers and learned how to interpret them. But I'm an über-fan. What about the more casual viewers? Those are the folks that Ziert is most worried about.

In debating the rules with Fink and Ziert, it becomes clear that the two men disagree about more than point values and rankings—they have different worldviews. Fink possesses more of an elitist perspective. Though he wants a unified rulebook that could be used at all levels of the sport, he seems primarily concerned with distinguishing between gymnasts at the uppermost echelons (which makes sense, given his former office as president of the Men's Technical Committee). Whereas Ziert is something of a gymnastics populist. He's more concerned with the popularity and image of the sport, especially since part of his business is selling gymnastics as entertainment. And, like virtually everyone else I spoke to, he invoked figure skating's post-scandal fortunes as a cautionary tale to talk about everything that can go wrong when you eliminate your iconic score.

Since 2002, skating has suffered a marked decrease in television viewership—if you can even find it on TV at all. The 2013 World Championships weren't even broadcast in the United States. The competition purses and prizes in figure skating have also dropped significantly from their heyday in the wake of the Nancy Kerrigan–Tonya Harding era. Many of the touring ice shows either have shut down or make fewer stops. Long gone are the days when figure skating at the Olympics challenged the TV ratings of the Super Bowl or World Series.

In many articles, skating's sliding popularity and decline in viability has been blamed on the new scoring system. The complaints about it are the same as they are about gymnastics' scoring change: the fans don't understand it, the sport has lost its artistic edge, skating has given up an iconic score and all of the memories attached to it.

While it's debatable whether the change in scoring addressed the problems of the 2002 Olympics—judges are even less accountable now since their marks were anonymized—it is highly simplistic to blame skating's downturn solely on a scoring change. The 6.0 didn't make figure skating hugely popular in the mid-'90s. Nancy Kerrigan and Tonya Harding did.

The women's figure skating competition at the 1994 Olympics remains one of the most-watched television events in history. And after the Games, the hits kept coming. The Kerrigan and Harding soap opera came at a time when American singles skating was at its peak with medalists on both the men's and women's side. The "whack heard 'round the world" may have brought a lot of new eyeballs to the ice, but the bevy of stars kept them coming back. And none shone brighter than Michelle Kwan, who went on to dominate the sport for nearly a decade after being bumped from the 1994 Olympic team in favor of Harding.

For the next ten years, Kwan remained in the spotlight, at or near the top of the heap. She won two Olympic medals and five World titles. Kwan was a bona fide celebrity and a big draw to crowds and television audiences.

And domestically, Kwan wasn't skating alone. She always had an almost equally talented challenger for the top spot—first, Tara Lipinski, then Sarah Hughes, and then Sasha Cohen. Kwan was certainly the biggest star in U.S. women's figure skating firmament but by no means the only one. A good rivalry drives media attention and TV ratings.

Since Kwan retired, U.S. figure skating has not found another star of even half her magnitude. For viewers who came to the sport because of the larger-than-life personalities of Kerrigan, Harding, and Kwan and were excited by the string of American victories in major events, there wasn't any reason to stick around and keep watching. Figure skating's popularity in the United States after the 1994 Olympics and Kwan's decade-long reign were in a sense artificial, inflated like the real estate bubble of 2007. It simply could not last.

Gymnastics never experienced skating's popularity bubble—not even during the aftermath of the Magnificent Seven's win in 1996—so it hasn't seen its fortunes drop off quite so precipitously. Also, U.S. women's gymnastics has produced something figure skating hasn't had in a very long time: gold medalists. As long as U.S. gymnasts keep winning and club enrollments remain up in this country, gymnastics is not in danger of sharing skating's fate.

It's not just the scoring that has changed since the heydays of Nadia and Mary Lou. The world of sports has been completely reshuffled with the addition of events that draw on the same acrobatic foundation as gymnastics. Gymnastics has lost market share to the extreme sports, which feel much more modern and far less fusty than a discipline that has roots in nineteenth-century military training. "We're competing against the X Games," Steve Butcher admitted. "If we think of execution and artistry only, we won't be able to compete against [those sports] . . . We have to have a little bit of the element of excitement. I don't like saying this, but it needs the 'extreme factor.' "

Also, there are simply more athletic opportunities available to women across an ever-expanding range of sports. It is no longer necessary to do a sport with feminine connotations to be accepted as a mainstream female athlete. (Though it still helps to be really, really hot.)

"I tell people all the time, we have to be careful with gymnastics now because there are a lot of sports out there that are available to women and have a bigger pot of gold at the end if you do well," Ziert said. He told me that if he had had a daughter, he might have nudged her toward something like tennis, not gymnastics.

That most discussions of the new scoring system with major actors usually became about the past popularity and long-term viability of gymnastics really underscores how vulnerable those devoted to Olympic sports—even the most popular of Olympic sports—feel about their own survival. To hear Ziert or even Fink talk, gymnastics is eternally on shaky ground, under siege from the IOC that wants to reduce the number of competitors and medal categories or ignored by an uncomprehending public with too many options and channels. The scoring system change wasn't just about introducing a new method of evaluation. It was an existential crisis.

"If you reduce gymnastics to its numerical evaluations, you lose its essence," Brian Cazeneuve, a sports journalist, said about gymnastics' big change. But a scoring system is a means of ranking and determining outcomes, not for measuring or capturing the essence of the thing. Scoring more points than the other team is not the essence of basketball, but it is how you win a game.

And culturally we've taken to reducing everything to numbers. Blame it on Nate Silver if you must, but *everything* has become data driven—from test scores to predicting the outcome of electoral campaigns and sporting events. That gymnastics would adopt a model that lent itself to easier number crunching was in keeping with larger societal trends. The sport is a part of the culture, not cordoned off from it.

Butcher also referred to Athens when we spoke. Back in 2004, the current president of the Men's Technical Committee was home in the United States watching the Olympics, judging every routine from the comfort of his living room. "I was really upset with a lot of scores that I saw. There was no separation between two gymnasts that had extremely different routines," he said. He felt that everyone was scoring far too high, that the judges then weren't properly educated on how to take deductions the way the present ones are.

"If all those gymnasts that were in those Olympic Games, they all had their 10.0 or 9.9 SVs, and the judges were trained in how to take deductions by the current standard, it would have made a big separation in those gymnasts," Butcher said. In his estimation, this would have given the exceptionally clean Hamm the gold medal even if Yang's start value had been properly assigned during the all-around competition. "Some of Paul's routines were five tenths better than some of the other routines," he pointed out.

Though he believes that the judging is better in the present than it was in 2004, Butcher is nostalgic for the 10 like just about everyone else. "For me, of course, in my heart I've always said that I want the 10.0 back, but I'm not sure it's possible," Butcher said for the very same reasons he believes Hamm would have won in 2004 if current standards had been applied—the judges are deducting a lot more. To get back to the 10, even just on the execution side, would entail the judges changing their mind-set once again to be less nitpicky or the *Code* would have to be emended to weigh the execution deductions differently. "Now that we take these heavier deductions, how do you mitigate deductions to bring yourself closer to the 10.0?" Butcher asked. "Twenty years ago, ten years ago, they didn't take many deductions. Now we take deductions like there's no tomorrow."

Yet this was not what Fink said he envisioned when he started campaigning for a scoring change. "The concept I put together, the paradigm, came back to Perfect 10 but the 10 that the public could understand," he said. Meaning the 10 for execution. The 10 never meant content to the general public; it only meant perfection in terms of how well a routine was done. He had hoped that gymnastics could showcase the execution score the way diving highlights the marks of the judges instead of the difficulty rating of the dive. But in most instances, the audience doesn't even see the breakdown. All they get to see is the string of incomprehensible digits. "The FIG has done a poor job of showing the audience that 10.0," Butcher said.

Ziert doesn't buy the excuses. "People who were reluctant bought into this code because, 'Oh yes, you can score a 10. There are going to be 10s. I guarantee you.' Bruno Grandi said, 'I guarantee you we're going to see 10s, it's going to be in execution though.' What's the closest? Have we seen a 9.8 yet?" Maroney's 9.733 in London has, thus far, been the closest anyone has gotten to the iconic 10 in Olympic competition.

Even Fink isn't particularly pleased with the outcome. It was not the complete scoring revolution that he had been envisioning while brainstorming with Holt in his basement all those years ago. "In my estimation, when they were forced to go into the separation of difficulty from execution, they jumped halfway across the stream. That whole paradigm shift didn't happen," he said. Instead of challenging the gymnasts to present their eight or ten best skills on each apparatus and fulfill a minimum of requirements, the technical committees maintained the complicated bonus systems of the 10.0 years. The equations have only gotten clunkier, not simpler.

When I mentioned to Holt that his old friend wasn't thrilled with how the *Code of Points* turned out, he waxed biblical. "This *Code* should be an abomination to him," he said.

But Fink remains optimistic that gymnastics will be able to get it right eventually. "Every cycle they're getting a little closer," he observed. The New Zealand judges I spoke to seemed to agree—if fewer changes every year means that we're approaching some sort of endpoint of reform. Bevins said, "The changes in the last three cycles have been fairly minor since they've gone to the open-ended." Both judges seemed to believe that there has been less cheating under this system, too.

Grandi, in his closing remarks at the end of the 2014 World Championships, was critical of the *Code* but stopped short of suggesting another complete overhaul or a return to the 10. "For the future, I don't ask the technical member to change the *Code of Points*. I don't want to change another time," he said, with a touch of weariness. Grandi was near the end of his final term as president. He was not seeking reelection in 2016. The scoring change, for better or worse, would be his legacy to the sport.

In my conversations with Fink, I frequently likened his *Code of Points* to Obamacare. It may not be the single payer system many hoped for, but it's a start.

"Didn't the Republicans try to repeal that a bunch of times?" Fink asked in the bemused manner of all Canadians who just don't understand their southern neighbors.

"Yes, but it passed muster. Executive, legislative, and judicial review." Well, at least so far.

His brainchild seemed to have withstood similar trials and scrutiny. And it has endured for nearly a decade. It's an imperfect 10.

5

NEW *CODE*, NEW GYMNAST: THE RISE OF SIMONE BILES

Simone Biles had a cold when I showed up to watch her train at World Champions Centre in Conroe, Texas. The then-two-time World Champion had been feeling poorly for nearly a week, her coaches told me, and it was taking a toll on her during the second workout of the day. It seems that it takes a virus—not her rivals and certainly not the complexity of high-level gymnastics elements—to defeat the female gymnast many have hailed as the most talented of all time. During the late-afternoon hours on a Thursday in December, I saw her balk at vaults; sometimes she skipped the skill entirely. Other times, she performed fewer twists than anticipated. I also witnessed her crashing to her knees on at least one skill that is typically simple for her, the Lopez. This vault is Biles's second, the one she pulls out almost as an afterthought during event finals.

Shortly after her botched vault, Aimee Boorman, her longtime coach, approached me to say that Biles was heading home early. "She has a cold," she said.

Perhaps I wasn't seeing a cold at work but just a run-of-the-mill gymnastics practice early into the season. By the time I visited Biles's gym, I had observed several elite practices. Falls, even among the best, are hardly uncommon, especially when a gymnast is several months away from competition. The science of peaking, if it can be called a science at all, teaches coaches and athletes not to be in optimal shape all of the time, not to go for stuck landings on hard, competition mats until you need to.

"We're given a plan of when you should be at sixty percent, seventy percent, eighty percent, ninety percent, so that by Worlds it is one hundred percent," Boorman had told me over the phone in September shortly before the 2014 World Championships team had been selected. Biles was on it, of course, and she went on to win four gold medals and one silver at that competition. In doing so, she bested Shannon Miller for most World Championship gold medals won by an American gymnast, six to the Oklahoman's five back in the early 1990s.

It was December, a couple of months after that golden competition, and Biles wasn't scheduled to perform again until March at the American Cup, which was being held a straight shot up I-45 in Dallas. This is why Biles is allowed to have her cold now but not later, not right before a competition or during the meet itself. There was no reason for her to be operating at or near her peak. It was probably foolish of me to expect polish at this practice, even from the world champion.

But the last time I had watched her do gymnastics in person, Biles had been polished. I, along with much of the media, had been situated vault-side with a front-row seat to Biles's silver-medal-winning performance at the World Championships in 2014 during the event final. Though Biles had been edged by the 2008 Olympic champion, Hong Un-jong, the North Korean didn't have Biles's ease in flight. She defeated the compact American by gunning it on the difficulty and was almost a point ahead of Biles before either had saluted the judges—though she was only half a tenth ahead of Biles when it was over. Biles almost made up an eight-tenth deficit in potential start value by flying higher and cleaner than Hong had.

Biles's vaulting is simultaneously fast and slow. Slow because she allows herself time to lift off before wrapping in twists; fast because once she hits the peak of her somersault, she has only half of the rotational time to wrap in all of those delayed twists. And slow seeming once again because she spends more time in the air than almost anyone else does.

Coughing, Biles headed over to the floor mats to stretch and wind down her workout. Boorman mothered her with some cold-fighting wisdom, advising her to take a hot shower and drink tea with lemon. The other coaches and her teammates chimed in with some of their own recommendations. "Do you know what a neti pot is?" one of the coaches asked. As the explanation of what it is and what it did to your sinuses and nasal passages grew more explicit, Biles began shaking her head and clasped her hands over her nose in horror. She would apply Boorman's less nostrilly invasive remedy.

Biles left the gym with her younger sister, Adria, also a gymnast, in tow and drove home in her new car, a black Cadillac CTS purchased on the Monday of the same week. It was the seventeen-year-old's second car in as many years of driving. Neither automobile, however, had been purchased with endorsement money. A few weeks before my arrival, Biles had committed to compete for the UCLA women's gymnastics team. In order to maintain her NCAA eligibility, she could not accept any cash or prizes. The money that bought her car was the same that was financing the construction of World Champions Centre, or WCC, in nearby Spring, Texas. The gym I visited in Conroe—two converted warehouse suites just over the railroad tracks—was a temporary location. "This is our J. C. Penney," Boorman explained of their current bare-bones situation. "We're building our Neiman Marcus." The "we" referred to the Biles family, which was constructing WCC. Gymnastics had become the family business. But unlike the gymnasium built by Dominique Moceanu's family after her Olympic gold medal in 1996, this gym's operating budget was not going to come from Biles's earnings, because at that point there were none.

But about seven months after my visit, just inside a year before Rio, Simone Biles did what everyone predicted she would do—signed with an agent to take full advantage of sponsorship opportunities that would surely come her way as the heavy favorite a year before the Olympics.

Biles's MFA vs. New York City–style dilemma was similar to the one faced by 2012 swimming star Missy Franklin when trying to decide whether to accept the lucrative endorsement deals or compete as a college swimmer. Ultimately, she decided on the latter, knowing full well that unless her swimming career unexpectedly ends early, she will have many years to swim professionally and make money after competing for the University of California Berkeley for a couple of seasons. But for female gymnasts like Biles, the proposition is typically either/or. Either you compete in college or you take the money while it's on the table—which is right before the Games and right after. For most elite gymnasts, there is no after-college competitive career.

But you can't blame UCLA for trying to recruit Biles. The teenage Texan is a once-in-a-lifetime sort of gymnast, the kind of athlete that supporters of open-ended scoring must have had in mind when they pushed their initiative through the FIG's executive committee after the Olympic judging scandals of 2004. She is preternaturally talented. She can do heretofore-unthinkable skills cleanly. The *Code*, with its "sky's the limit" tolerance for difficulty, incentivizes Biles's daredevil brand of gymnastics.

And in keeping with the sport's narrative since Nadia, Biles makes the extraordinarily difficult look effortless. When I watch Biles do gymnastics, I can't help but think of the lyrics from "The Daring Young Man on the Flying Trapeze."

> *He'd fly through the air with the greatest of ease,*
> *That daring young man on the flying trapeze.*

———

Biles was just a little kid getting started in gymnastics when the open-ended *Code of Points* was adopted in 2006. The first competition conducted with this new system was the 2006 Commonwealth Games. And the first female gymnast to enjoy significant success under the new rules was the Italian Vanessa Ferrari. In 2006, she became one of just a few world champions in the post-Nadia era to hail from a country that was not one of the Big Four: Russia, Romania, China, and the United States. Technically, Ukraine's Lilia Podkopayeva, the 1995 World and 1996 Olympic champion, also accomplished this feat, but since her senior elite career began shortly after the dissolution of the USSR, it can be argued that she was actually a product of the Soviet system. Lilia didn't exactly seem like an underdog.

The first time I became aware of Ferrari was shortly before the World Championships in Aarhus, Denmark, in 2006. A video of her floor routine from the Italian National Championships that year was getting a lot of play from gymnastics fans on YouTube. Two things stood out to me about this performance.

First, she experienced a major hairstyle malfunction. On her third pass, her ponytail started to come apart. The elastic's grip had clearly slackened on her straight brown hair. By the time she landed her fourth tumbling pass, Ferrari's hair was practically wild. She finished her routine that way, tumbling into her fifth pass, a double-pike somersault, with her hair loose, hanging down around her shoulders, obscuring her vision on her flips. I don't know if she was deducted for this, though I assume she was, since women's gymnastics has deductions for everything. It's a shame, though, because it actually made her tumbling seem all the more impressive.

The second thing I noticed was that fifth tumbling pass. Namely, that there was one. At that time, four was something of a global standard for the number of passes in women's floor exercise, but in that routine, Ferrari had upped the ante to five. She had been freed by the newly introduced open-ended code to load up on tumbling skills and increase the difficulty level or "D-score" of her routine. In other words, without the 10.0 scoring cap, a fifth tumbling pass now had real value. She arrived at the 2006 World Championships with an Italian national title, a European title, and more difficulty in her routines than most of her competitors.

Her coach, Enrico Casella, had been confident when addressing the media heading into that meet. " 'We [will] go for a medal in the all-around,' and people think I'm crazy because no one Italian ever had," Casella told me in a hotel suite in Nanning, China. It was just a few hours before the 2014 women's all-around final, and I was shocked that he had given me time so close to when his athlete was set to compete. But Ferrari was just shy of her twenty-fourth birthday, an old hat when it came to World Championships finals. She was a long ways away from the teen gymnast who won her first and only World title in 2006. She no longer needed her coach by her side at every moment.

The hotel room where I interviewed Casella doubled as the Italian's team therapeutic suite. Gymnastics teams often bring along their own entourage of physical therapists and other caregivers to major FIG competitions. Most teams end up booking an extra hotel room where treatments are administered to athletes between training sessions. In the Italian therapy suite, a massage table was open next to the bed, and one of the coaches or trainers was being treated while I spoke with the Italian head coach. Her shirt was pulled up to her bra, and a man manipulated the flesh on her back with his hands. I wondered if the pains were residual, from her past life as a gymnast. (So many coaches had once been high-level gymnasts. They often have the scars and early-onset arthritis to prove it.) Or if her aches came from the act of coaching itself.

Coaching, especially spotting gymnasts, can be physically grueling and dangerous work. All gymnastics coaches have their own war stories. A coach at Biles's gym told me about his wounds, a broken hand and nose among them, good naturedly calling out the gymnasts who had accidentally injured him. That day, I saw a gymnast take him down with her when attempting a full twisting double back somersault on the floor. Fortunately, neither he nor the athlete was hurt. At Texas Dreams outside of Dallas, I watched as a female coach's fingernail was ripped off while she was guiding a little girl through a skill on bars. "Can't have nice things as a gymnastics coach," she said laughing, holding up her bandaged finger when she returned to the gym floor. Her only concern was that the nail would grow back before her wedding in a couple of months.

Despite the doubters in the Italian camp in 2006, Casella knew he had a potential winner on his hands in Ferrari, and he was willing to exploit the new rules to her advantage. "I used the *Code*. The *Code* gave me this chance, and I started. I have in my hands a gymnast that is a talented one, different from the others. Then I had the *Code*. What can I do with this gymnast? I can make five [tumbling] runs. She can and so I use it. I use this *Code*. I use it all I can."

And she needed all five of those passes to win the 2006 all-around title after she fell off the balance beam in the previous rotation. Ferrari had been leading the field by nearly half a point when she hopped off the beam on a back handspring to a full twisting back tuck, an incredibly difficult maneuver. "That was likely the gold medal slipping through her hands," said Bart Conner in the Universal Sports commentary on the competition.

Ferrari seemed to agree with Conner's assessment, later telling *International Gymnast*, "At that moment I thought, of course, that everything was over." She had good reason to think her title run was dead. In the new rulebook, the deduction for a fall had just been raised from 0.5 to 0.8. It more than swallowed up the lead she brought with her to the third event. Besides, gymnasts don't win all-around titles with falls unless egregious judging errors are involved. (See: 2004 Olympic men's all-around.)

But for Casella, not all hope was lost. Ferrari said that her longtime coach "told me to stay calm, that nothing bad has happened." He felt that his protégée could still win this thing with her jampacked floor routine. Which she did, besting the stolid American Jana Bieger for the title.

At the time, Casella acknowledged that Ferrari was able to win with a significant error, in part, because the two top Americans were out with injuries. Nastia Liukin, who would go on to win the 2008 Olympic all-around title, was limited to one apparatus due to an ankle injury, and Chellsie Memmel, the defending world champion, had to withdraw from the all-around finals after tearing her labrum during the team competition. "I think with Memmel and Liukin in good condition, it would be difficult to win with a big mistake." But he also believed that their presence might have helped his athlete sharpen her focus. "Maybe with Memmel and Liukin competing, Vanessa wouldn't have made a mistake." If you play "What if?" with the results of major gymnastics competitions, you can't assume that everything else would've remained the same when you change a single variable. If that one thing changes, then so can everything else. In that parallel universe, Ferrari might have stayed on the beam. If anything is possible in this game, then surely that is also possible.

By winning the all-around title with a fall, Ferrari had confirmed gymnastics fans' worst nightmares about the new scoring system: that a gymnast could simply load up on difficulty, fall off the apparatus, and still win. In its header for the article about the women's all-around, *International Gymnast* editorialized this belief. "Formula Won," it read. It was the new math behind the sport—not Ferrari—that had won on that day.

Romanian head coach Nicolae Forminte was critical of Ferrari's win over Bieger and his own athlete, Sandra Izbasa, neither of whom had absorbed a fall in their all-around totals. But as writer John Crumlish noted, "Neither Bieger nor Izbasa had a perfect meet, either, and under the new rules, Ferrari's content and execution proved to be adequate enough to overcome the deduction for a fall." Subsequent to the 2006 World Championships, the deduction for a fall would be raised from 0.8 to a full point. Yet even if Ferrari had received the new penalty, she still would have won with a slimmer margin of victory, 0.275 to 0.075. (And that margin wouldn't have even been the slimmest in World or Olympic all-around history. That distinction belonged to the 2005 final, the last World All-Around Competition under the 10.0, where Memmel and Liukin tied for the gold. The federation reached down to four digits after the decimal point to pull the two apart. The official difference between the two was 0.0001.)

In concluding that Ferrari was undeserving of the all-around title based on her fall from the beam, Forminte was thinking of the all-around in piecemeal fashion, skill by skill, instead of more holistically. Because a holistic perspective would have required taking into account Izbasa's bars, which in the great Romanian tradition on that event were terrible, practically an eyesore. Her swing was lax, her arms were frequently bent, her legs were apart on elementary moves. The *most* you could say for her on that event was that she didn't fall. But does the simple fact of hanging on make her a more worthy gold medalist than Ferrari, who showed superior form, technique, and difficulty throughout but fell on a single element? If it's a crime for a gymnast to win the all-around title with a fall on one event out of four, what do you say about a gymnast who wins a medal with one event out of four that's so weak that she placed seventeenth on it in a twenty-four-person field? Is that kind of leap up the standings a more appropriate comeback than nailing a floor performance in the final rotation after a fall from the beam to win the title?

Crumlish's words, while not exactly a ringing endorsement of Ferrari's gold medal, acknowledged a certain truth about that competition: even with a mistake, Ferrari had done enough to win. Her work, in his words, was "adequate." And falling off the beam isn't the same as falling into molten hot lava. It's a mistake, to be sure, but must it also be a catastrophe? Is the all-around a game of sudden death? Should it be?

"Okay, she faulted, but what happened? She fell and then got on the beam and went on as if nothing happened," Casella pointed out. "Only a very talented champion can do this."

Andre Agassi talked about the scourge of perfectionism in his memoir *Open* and how it ruined many a match for him until a new coach talked him out of his need to be perfect all the time. "You don't have to be the best in the world every time you go out there," he explained to the tennis star. "You just have to be better than one guy." For gymnastics, 2006 was the year they first started grasping this basic lesson of athletic competition. Just be better than your competitors are on the day.

This shift in the rhetoric about gymnastics—from the artistic, almost transcendent to merely athletic—is something Elizabeth Booth, the founder of Rewriting Russian Gymnastics and the *Guardian*'s Olympic gymnastics expert in 2012, pointed out to me in an email about the before and after of the rule changes. "Gymnasts have become athletes. They perform solid routines, work hard, and go out there and enjoy themselves," she said. "Power, explosion, and solidity have become the defining characteristic of medal-winning teams rather than artistry, virtuosity, originality, and amplitude." Casella made no apologies for the way Ferrari won her title. As Agassi finally learned, he was playing the game, point by point, set by set, match by match. For him, as for Casella, a win was a win was a win.

Biles, like the younger version of Ferrari, can also win a competition with a fall. At the 2014 National Championships, she won her second consecutive title with a four-point margin over the rest of the field. It would've been five points had she not fallen from the beam during the last routine of the competition. (The following year she won her third consecutive national title by an almost five-point margin against a much stronger field, again with a fall.) This show of dominance—and isn't it truly more dominant to be able to win on an off day than it is when you're at your absolute best?—led many to speculate that she'd be able to do the same six weeks later in China at the World Championships. Her eventual triumph seemed to be in little doubt.

When I first spoke to Boorman shortly before the 2014 selection camp, she was less sanguine about her star pupil. "Nothing is ever guaranteed," she said about naming Biles to the team. I didn't believe she truly doubted Biles's inclusion but was being understandably circumspect in the "anything can happen" world of elite gymnastics. And by "anything," we typically mean "an ill-timed injury."

Boorman, however, doesn't seem to be as neurotic as her athlete's fans. "She's durable," Boorman said of Biles and her body. True, she's been injured, but so far has managed to avoid significant injuries that require a lot of time off and out of the gym. After getting home from the 2013 World Championships, she had minor surgery on her ankle, which kept her out of the gym for a few weeks. And throughout the 2014 season, she and her coaches coddled a "loose" shoulder. They reduced her difficulty on the uneven bars to protect it from further damage. The shoulder, Boorman assured me, was doing fine when I visited. Biles had restored all of the complexity to her bar routine. To prevent a recurrence, she spent time every week treating the joint with physical therapy activities during the Friday-morning practice. For an elite gymnast who's competed through two consecutive senior seasons at the highest level, she was almost shockingly healthy. Except for that cold, of course.

But Biles's body is more than simply durable. It's the sort of body that seems to have been made for a *Code of Points* that demands power and complexity. Or maybe it's the sort of body that's created by those rules. It's something of a "chicken or egg" question. Which came first: the rules or the body that satisfies them?

What is clear, at least from anecdotal evidence and observation, is that the physique of the female gymnast has changed over the last decade, from the slim-hipped, feather-light body to something more substantial, more powerful. To something that looks more like Biles.

Even before Biles made her senior debut, the shift was evident. Just take a look at the 2012 Olympic gymnastics team. Aly Raisman and Jordyn Wieber were the most obviously muscular of the five. Both had defined shoulders that tapered into practically nothing, as far as hips were concerned, but their legs added some heft, with quad muscles clearly outlined above their knees. Super vaulter Maroney seemed leaner than Raisman or Wieber but at five feet four stood above them in terms of height. Kyla Ross, the youngest at just fifteen, had a physique similar to Maroney's—long legs and lines and strong shoulders. The smallest among them was Gabrielle Douglas, who was just four feet eleven at the time. But even she didn't look wispy.

That Biles is strong is obvious even in repose. There's an incredible broadness, expansiveness even, to her shoulders and upper-body musculature. When she stands casually in the corner of the floor exercise mat with her hands on her hips, her muscles bulge. Just standing there, waiting for her turn at practice.

The narrative around gymnasts and their bodies for years had been focused on their smallness and slightness. Young gymnasts' physiques were supposed to belie their physical abilities—she's so small *yet* she's strong. It was supposed to surprise us that these little naïfs can hold planches on the beam and flip over the vault with speed and velocity. We were supposed to think, *I can't believe she can do that*. She's not butter. She's margarine. But she flips like butter. Biles is butter in both appearance and ability. She appears to be capable, just from looking at her, of all of the acrobatics and feats of strength she performs.

And yet despite this expectation, it is still astounding to see what Biles can do. Terry Walker, one of the other coaches at WCC, pulled out his phone to show me a video of Biles from the previous week practicing on the floor exercise. She was performing her eponymous skill, a double somersault in the straight body position with a half turn at the end, which she performs almost as an afterthought—just a small dip of the shoulder and her body swivels 180 degrees to face the corner of the floor exercise mat. But in this video, the sequence didn't end there. Biles had tacked on a punch front somersault. Like the double layout, like the half turn, like everything she does, at least in competition, it seemed so easy.

I responded with a "What the what?" doing my best Liz Lemon impression. I then started mentally tabulating what this new combination would mean to Biles's already hefty start value on floor exercise when Walker told me that Karolyi and the rest of the national team staff probably won't let her compete that combination. She didn't need it to win. The team didn't need it to win. Combo passes, especially those that involve any sort of twisting, carry increased risk of injury. Yet when I later mentioned this impressive pass to another elite coach, she laughed. "That's what they told them about the Biles," she said of the double layout half now named for the Texan. The national team staff didn't want her to chance that skill either. This gave me hope that maybe I would see this combination in competition someday.

———

That Biles would dominate international competition was by no means a given, not even in 2013, the year she won her first World title. During her debut meet as a senior at the 2013 American Cup, Biles placed second to Katelyn Ohashi from Plano, Texas, who had also just aged into the grown-up leagues. It was Ohashi's arrival that everyone had been waiting for. Ohashi had won the Junior National Championship in 2011 and several event gold medals. She had also competed internationally several times from 2010 to 2012, racking up even more wins. In particular, she was known for her beam routine so loaded with difficult elements that as a junior, she competed with as much complexity as her senior counterparts. Many expected her to lay waste to the senior field once she arrived.

Biles, by contrast, did not have a standout junior career. Until late in 2012, she managed middling results, at best, winning medals here or there that were almost exclusively of the pewter variety. That she possessed superior athletic ability was widely known. A video of her attempting a double back somersault from a complete standstill—no run, no hurdle, no round-off, no momentum—had been circulated among gymnastics fans. Biles landed the skill on her face, but the fact that she got so close to fully rotating it, almost to her feet, seemed to point toward an innate talent. But this raw talent wasn't enough to win competitions or even get sent abroad to compete.

Boorman, who has been coaching Biles since the athlete's second year in gymnastics, said that her physical gifts were spotted almost immediately. "We said, 'This kid's got talent, and we believe she's going to learn things really fast,'" she told me. The qualities that she and the other coaches noticed off the bat were her brute strength, her bounciness, her hyperactivity, and of course, her fearlessness. "She wasn't afraid to try anything," Boorman recalled.

So far, the story that Boorman was telling me about Biles could be told about a thousand preternaturally gifted little girls who are enrolled in recreational gymnastics classes across the country. This is how virtually every article or NBC puff piece about an elite gymnast starts. *Once upon a time, there was a little girl who was fearless, strong, and so hyperactive that she destroyed the family furniture, so her parents decided to enroll her in gymnastics instead of treating her for AD/HD.*

After evaluating Biles's physical abilities, the coaches at Bannon's Gymnastix decided to fast-track the young gymnast toward the higher competitive levels. "Our goal was to do one meet, score out, and move to the next level," Boorman explained, though her explanation could probably use a little bit of an explainer of its own. The majority of the competitive gymnasts in the United States compete in the Junior Olympic, or JO, program. Each level in this track—which runs from 1 to 10—has a minimum all-around score that has to be attained or surpassed—or "score out," in gym parlance—in order to progress to the next level. Some gymnasts spend an entire season or more competing at the same level; others, especially those that go on to become elites, might compete at only one meet at a given level before moving onward and upward. Often, future elites and Olympians bypass entire levels in the JO program altogether.

But things did not progress as planned with Biles. "She was so rough that it took us two meets to score out because she would just fall. The meets that we went to score out the first time, she fell, like, six times," Boorman said. This slower competitive development explains why Biles did not become an elite until she was nearly fourteen, whereas Ohashi, who is the same age, wasn't even a teenager when she started representing the United States at international competitions.

And even when Biles finally entered the elite ranks, her results weren't immediately impressive. Though she could do the hard skills, she couldn't do them with anything approaching clean execution, especially on the uneven bars, which requires strength but also finesse and patience. As an interloper at many elite practices, I've never heard coaches remind athletes to "Wait for it" more than on the uneven bars. Gymnasts who really know how to swing on that event are the most patient—they pull down on the bar and then let it push them up instead of trying to muscle through it.

When I rewatched her performances at the Junior National Championships, I understood why I had paid scant attention to the fourteen-year-old Biles. Her work on bars had been rudimentary and sloppy. She took extra swings between skills and flexed her feet. Her legs rarely came together on any element. Her swing seemed to stall like a sputtering car, as if with fear and worry, before she tapped into big skills and release moves. On beam, she showed more nerviness than amplitude and fell or very nearly came to grief. On floor and vault, she demonstrated the same power and height that she would become internationally known for but none of the control. She bounced up and back several feet upon landing her passes. In 2011, she placed seventeenth in the all-around and was not even named to the Junior National Team.

Boorman and her fellow coaches were well aware of Biles's shortcomings as a gymnast back in 2011, yet they didn't push her to correct them immediately. They were more concerned with simply keeping her in gymnastics. "I guess my whole philosophy with her from kind of raising and nurturing her was I always knew that it had to be fun. It had to remain fun in order to keep her in the sport," Boorman said.

When I interviewed Biles for ESPN in late 2014, the word *fun* or some variation thereof was mentioned a dozen times in our rather brief conversation. Boorman clearly had a good read on the mentality of her young charge.

Maggie Haney, a New Jersey coach with two prominent elites—2014 Junior National champion Jazmyn Foberg and 2015 Junior National Champion Laurie Hernandez—commended Boorman for the job she's done with Biles. Specifically, for the patience she has shown in developing Biles from a rough-and-tumble young gymnast to a polished world champion. "She's a perfect coach for her [Biles]. She's kept her in the sport." Haney acknowledged that many coaches—herself included—would have forced her to conform to their programs and expectations, which would have likely driven her from the gym given her unique emotional temperament. "She's a regular kid, not a gym head," Haney said of Biles.

Boorman has heard the same thing from other elite coaches in the United States over the years. "Other coaches would tell me, 'Aimee, you're the only coach that could have managed that kid,' " she recalled. "Not 'coached' but 'managed,' " Boorman emphasized. Given Biles's immense physical gifts, her natural coordination, and her air sense, it's not particularly difficult to teach this athlete new skills, something that Boorman often noted. Training Biles up to this level has been more about emotional management and less about technique.

"Another gym would break her. They would push her and make her do things she didn't want to do. She's not going to spend hours on flexibility at eleven years old. She's just not going to do it. I know this kid. Her parents understood that, and I understood that."

"It's a perfect match," Ziert said of Boorman and Biles. "I watched them and I thought, 'Dear God, Simone's success lies in the fact that luckily she has a match. They found each other.' "

His words echo Boorman's own description of hers and Biles's partnership. "We were lucky to find each other. With my coaching style, and that's what she needed. I learned from her because of her natural talent, and we're just kind of on a journey together, I guess." Boorman had been a relatively young, inexperienced coach when Biles entered the gym. The coach has learned a lot simply by working with Biles. And Biles, of course, has learned from her.

But eventually Biles started to improve and refine, to work on things that were less enjoyable in the moment but produced the results she wanted for herself. "I think there was a switch in her that was like, 'This isn't always going to be fun, but I'm going to keep doing it. Some things are going to be fun and some aren't, but being an elite and getting to do this stuff is fun in itself.' So right there her attitude started changing a little bit. She started maturing. She started growing up because obviously she was getting older," Boorman commented.

By the end of 2012, Biles had been added to the U.S. Junior National Team and had a podium finish—third place—at the National Championships, ahead of Ohashi, who had dropped from first to fifth a year after her win. The fortunes of Biles and Ohashi, the upstart and the prodigal, had seemingly flipped. Ohashi, who seemed to have left the womb with pointed toes and straight legs, was slipping while Biles was on the rise.

The American Cup would be Ohashi's last elite meet. She would spend the next two years sidelined by injury, reemerging in late 2015 to pursue a college scholarship and eventually earning one to UCLA. The Olympics were no longer her goal. One of the most promising juniors of the last quad was out of the running for the ultimate prize.

Biles, of course, would go on to win, win, win in a scoring system seemingly made for her. As Booth wrote in a post on her website, "Biles is the only true protagonist of the new acrobatic gymnastics that now rules the world, her audacious and spectacular acrobatics at the center of a unique style that exploits her daring and explosive movements to the full."

Booth had written these words after Biles won her second World all-around title. By this time, the international gymnastics community had all but conceded defeat to the powerful American teen, acknowledging that she might be the most talented gymnast who has ever lived. And after Biles won her third consecutive World title in 2015, becoming the first female gymnast to win three in a row and shattering the record for most World titles won, Nellie Kim told me, "She comes here already with plus two points ahead of everybody."

But after Biles's first win in 2013, the international gymnastics jury was still out on the gymnast. First of all, she didn't enter the competition with a "mandate" from her win at U.S. Nationals. There, she only narrowly defeated 2012 Olympic team gold medalist Kyla Ross, who is something of Biles's polar opposite. Tall for a gymnast at over five foot four, Ross has struggled to add difficulty to her routines since leaving the junior ranks but managed to get by on extremely clean execution. And during the all-around finals in Antwerp, Ross had been leading the Texan heading into the final rotation where Biles had a nearly a point on her in difficulty. Biles won, but she didn't exactly run away with it.

After the all-around award ceremony, one athlete suggested a baser, more racist explanation for the sixteen-year-old's beginner's luck. Italian gymnast Carlotta Ferlito addressed the Italian media, remarking, "I told Vanessa [Ferrari] that next time we should also paint our skin black, so then we could win, too."

In the age of the internet, nothing a gymnast says remains confined to her native tongue for too long. Her comments were quickly translated into English, and the online fallout ensued. To her credit, Ferlito quickly apologized on Twitter. (Where else?) But the scandal didn't end there. David Ciaralli, the spokesman for the Italian Gymnastics Federation, attempted to rationalize Ferlito's remarks in a post on Facebook. As you can imagine, rationalizing racist comments did not go well.

"Carlotta was talking about what she thinks is the current gymnastics trend: the *Code of Points* is opening chances for colored people (known to be more powerful) and penalizing the typical Eastern European elegance, which, when gymnastics was more artistic and less acrobatic, allowed Russia and Romania to dominate the field," he wrote.

Powerful and *artistic* not only describe types and quality of movements but also are coded language for body type, and in this instance, race. Gymnasts who are long and lean tend to be called "artistic" regardless of how well they move or engage with the audience. *Artistic* is a code word for *thin* at a time when it is no longer acceptable to publish the weights of elite gymnasts.

The use of *powerful* and *artistic* in gymnastics is similar to how certain code words are used for African American athletes in other sports. White players, since they're not considered innately physically gifted, are talked about in terms of their mental capabilities and hard work—they have "grit," they "hustle," they're "scrappy." A study that analyzed announcer comments from 1,156 men's and women's college basketball games found that black players were characterized as "athletic" and "physically powerful" and "possessing great jumping abilities." The language of intelligence and leadership was used to describe the white players.

Swap out *intelligence* for *artistry* and you've got exactly what Ciaralli was saying in his statement about Biles and black gymnasts.

And though the trigger for Ferlito's offhand remarks and Ciaralli's defense of them was Biles's win in the all-around at Antwerp, they clearly also had another gymnast in mind when they spoke—2012 Olympic champion Gabrielle Douglas. Biles's victory made it back-to-back wins for gymnasts of color in World and Olympic all-around competition. It was this seeming "trend" of black gymnasts winning major titles that prompted the Italians' comments on race, not Biles's win alone.

But Douglas and Biles, as Ferlito and Ciaralli failed to note, actually performed different styles of gymnastics despite a shared racial affiliation. (Imagine that—two black women actually being distinct from each other.) Douglas is lithe and flexible, excelling on bars and beam while being noticeably weaker on the other two more dynamic apparatuses. And Biles is most certainly the power gymnast—performing explosively on the two leg events.

But perhaps more significantly, the language of inevitability, of "best ever–ness," has never been applied to Douglas. She was seen as being imbued with the same degree of natural ability that all elite gymnasts possess—much more than the average person, more than even the average NCAA athlete—but not more than her fellow top-notch elites. Russia's Viktoria Komova, silver medalist behind Douglas in London, was arguably the most naturally gifted gymnast at the 2012 Games. Komova is the daughter of a Russian champion and entered the senior ranks after a stellar junior career. She was the 2011 World all-around silver medalist and the World champion on the uneven bars. Douglas had competed in that same uneven bar final in Tokyo but had placed fifth. In 2012, Komova entered the

Games with a bag full of new tricks and was the top qualifier to the all-around final.

Komova seemingly had it all: she had the highest collective degree of difficulty in the competition, and she performed with a refinement honed through years of careful study and ballet. Douglas was next in line, in terms of difficulty. After watching the Russian during the qualifying rounds, I wrote to a friend, "This [gold medal] is Komova's to lose." It was. And she did. Douglas needed Komova to give her an inch. Or, as it turned out, several wayward steps on her vault landing. Douglas won in 2012 by capitalizing on her opponent's errors, which is a perfectly respectable way to win an athletic competition. But she was by no means dominant. Her win in 2012 was hardly a given. Her gold medal was not inevitable; her gymnastics was not effortless as Biles's performance is frequently characterized.

A note on the word *effortless*: it is perhaps one of the most frequently deployed adjectives when it comes to Biles and her brand of gymnastics. (I've already used it several times in this chapter.) It can mean either "requiring or involving no effort" or "displaying no signs of effort." After watching Biles practice in her home gym for two days, I couldn't decide which definition worked better. Was it that she wasn't working as hard as her teammates? Or was it that she was putting in the same amount of effort as the others, but hard work simply looked different on her? Biles was taking the same number of turns as her fellow gymnasts, doing the assignments as ordered by Boorman, yet her practice struck me as lackadaisical at times. Maybe that's because she was so much better than her compatriots that *effortless* even described maximum effort.

Or maybe the fact that she doesn't have to struggle quite as much is the trick—Biles doesn't have to push herself to the breaking point to win. It's as Comaneci recalled Karolyi saying of her when she was young, "I was the only gymnast he could never break." It's a risky business trying to stay on the right side of the breaking point, to know just how hard to throttle and when to back off. That Karolyi didn't know Comaneci's limit was, in part, the secret of her success. He didn't know how to crack Comaneci. (At least the 1976 Comaneci—it was an entirely different story when she came back to train with him in 1978.) And with Biles's limits seemingly nowhere in sight, perhaps she won't break either. Excellence, for both Biles and Comaneci, has been about not showing your work as you would on a math test.

Not that Boorman is trying to break her star pupil. "It's just gymnastics," she repeatedly announced as her guiding philosophy about the sport. This laid-back attitude sort of upends the narrative of "hard work" that plays a prominent role in athletic training and in women's gymnastics in particular. So that to admit that sometimes you and your athlete cut out of practice in the middle of a bad day for a cup of coffee—which Boorman did in the mixed zone after the 2014 National Championships—probably rankles some folks. It also undermines the story that gymnastics tells itself when looking into the mirror—that it's the hardest, the toughest, and, doggone it, people like it that way.

———

Timing is said to be everything. But in gymnastics, timing is called peaking. It's considered less a matter of good luck and fate and more the result of optimal planning and coaching. Douglas is an example of an athlete who was "perfectly peaked." In London, she competed at the edge of her physical and mental abilities at exactly the right moment—the Olympic Games. She rode the momentum all the way to an all-around gold, her only significant individual international title as a senior gymnast until that point.

The 2011 World Champion Jordyn Wieber was seen as being imperfectly peaked. She won the World title and national title the year before the Olympics, which is a bad omen for winning the Olympic all-around. Wieber failed to qualify to the individual all-around finals in London.

"Is she peaking too soon?" is another way of asking "Is she winning the wrong titles?" as though a top gymnast and coach have total control over when and where to excel, when to be injured, when to turn sixteen, when to be ready. Before the 2014 World Championships, I asked Boorman about the fear that many have about Biles, that she is winning too soon and will have a tough time staying on top until the Olympics. Implied in that concern is that maybe something can be done to change the narrative, to keep her from winning until Rio. And then, this thinking implies, you can just flip the winning switch again.

Boorman has heard this all before, even from inside her own gym back in 2013. "I know that, this was last year, the other coach I was working with at the time said, 'We need to hold her back. We don't want her to win this year. We don't want her to win Nationals. We don't want her to win Worlds because she's going to peak way too early.' I said, 'You know what—what if this is all she ever gets to do? What if this is her hurrah moment? That she's the national champion and gets to go to Worlds. What if it's all done after that? Are we going to hold her back because we're thinking about Rio? Or are we going to let her shine now and then just try to keep her healthy and keep her shiny?' "

Opportunities to win major titles aren't like party invites—you can't turn down one and then simply decide to win the next. So many things need to go right for a gymnast to win an Olympic gold medal or a World title—physical health, mental preparedness, age—that to believe you can control all of the variables verges on magical thinking.

I'll admit, however, that like the coach who had suggested that Biles "try" not to win in 2013, I had given some serious thought to this idea before Biles competed at the 2014 World Championships. Would it be so terrible for her to win the silver? I wondered. Can a gymnast even throw a competition in the same way that a boxer throws a fight? Should Biles have hopped off the beam or slipped intentionally from the uneven bars? What would "not peaking" even have looked like for her?

It probably would have looked like the World Championships Biles had in Nanning. During the preliminary round, she made a significant error on bars (though she didn't fall). She wobbled badly during the team final, though the United States still won the title by a hefty margin. During the all-around final, Biles was quite nervy on beam, performing tentatively. It was by no means a peak performance. Her competition at the World Championships in 2015 was also less than perfect. In the all-around final, she almost fell off the beam and bounced out of bounds on floor. No matter—she still won her third consecutive all-around title, the first female gymnast ever to accomplish that feat. By the final day of competition, when she repeated as World champion on beam and floor, she broke the record for most gold medals won by any female gymnast. Ever. And yet, her 2015 competition was also not a peak performance. After her win in the all-around, Biles told the media that "Martha [Karolyi] said this was a bad meet for me." In some ways, this is reassuring. It means she can still go up from there.

To watch Biles compete and train, of the ease of her trying hard, reminded me of a David Foster Wallace line from one of his several essays about tennis. He described the experience of watching two pros nonchalantly practice on the courts before a match. "The suggestion is one of a very powerful engine in low gear," he wrote of the two tennis players hitting balls back and forth. Biles seems to be operating consistently in low gear, which makes you wonder—what would it look like to see her perform in high gear?

Perhaps it would mean seeing her do skills such as the ones she unveils in practice videos she posts online. In one from four years ago, she performed a double twisting double somersault from the balance beam. For most gymnasts, this skill is the most difficult you can do on the floor exercise. I asked Boorman about this astonishing dismount. "How that transpired is she's doing these huge full ins [full twisting double backs] one day, and I was like, 'You know, you can double double that.' We had, for months, been kind of joking about her doing a double double off beam."

Biles, at first, had refused. " 'I'm never going to do that. I'm going to die,' " she supposedly told her coach. During the WCC training session I had watched, I had seen her fall from the uneven bars. On the way down to the mats, she cried out, "I'm going to die!" It had been in jest as it had been when she said the same to Boorman about that crazy dismount. Everyone, including Biles, laughed. In Biles's vernacular, "die" seems to be synonymous with "fall."

"Then that day [the video was shot] I said, 'You know, you could double double that,' " Boorman continued. "She goes, 'Yeah, I know I could.' I leave it at that. I wait for her to say, 'I'm going to do it.' She walks over and she says, 'Go get your iPad because I'm only doing it once and if I die, I want it on video.' " This is the video that has been circulating ever since.

I told Casella about the video of this skill when he brought the conversation around to Biles. (Everyone I interviewed in China wanted to talk about her.) Despite the Italian delegation's fraught history with the American gymnast, he had nothing but praise for her. And he seemed to understand why Boorman would put Biles up to this move in the gym even if it never left their training base. Casella said, "Sometimes they need to try something new because sometimes it becomes boring to repeat the routine." The need to innovate and increase difficulty isn't always borne out of the desire to win but from something much more mundane—boredom. Biles went for that dismount from the beam, not because she needed to but to relieve the monotony of the daily grind, to get a jolt as one does from a cup of coffee. This is how she plays. It's just that her level of play, Boorman explained to me, is so far above that of her nearest competitors.

Knowing that Biles can do an extra twist on that skill changes the way you watch her do the comparatively easy dismount. That missing revolution is like a phantom limb—you can feel its presence by the additional height she gets off the edge of the beam. Ever since seeing that training video of her doing the more complex dismount, I mentally insert the extra twist when I watch her.

I have a feeling that's what her fans do when they watch her do her incredibly difficult gymnastics—they wonder what else is possible. Biles doesn't impress so much with what she can do but with what she might do.

———

When talking about Biles, Nadia Comaneci said, "She's a talent that's born once in a while. You have somebody who can do something we cannot even design on a paper."

Kim told me, "When we created *Code of Points*, we couldn't even think that a girl like her will show up. She's unique."

At its best, the open-ended scoring system is supposed to inspire and reward the Simone Bileses of the world to train and master extreme skills. But if Comaneci's assertion is correct—that Biles exemplifies the best in the new rulebook but is also a unicorn who possesses a style unlikely to be replicated—what does that mean for this *Code of Points*? Is it inherently flawed if only one athlete can fully embody its noblest aims, to push the envelope on difficulty while also performing with virtuosity, verve, and form?

In 1976, Comaneci raised the bar for all the other female gymnasts in the world, but within a couple of years they had caught up. There were more 10s after she retired, more performances of stunning technical accuracy, mastery, and a high degree of difficulty. The first-ness of Comaneci's perfect marks was not repeatable, but the quality and content of her routines were. With Biles, however, it doesn't seem like she's spearheading new trends. Her style can't be replicated.

Comaneci had come to symbolize the Perfect 10, so her rivals were chasing the athlete, a score, and the idea that the score represented. Without a symbolically meaningful score, it's just Biles herself that everyone is chasing.

PART II

NEW WAYS
TO TRAIN

THE GUINEA PIG GENERATION:
THE 2000 OLYMPIC TEAM AND THE BLUEPRINT
FOR AMERICAN GYMNASTICS SUCCESS

In 2010 at the National Championships in Hartford, Connecticut, a most peculiar award ceremony took place. Before the best gymnasts in the country—all teenagers in leotards and track suits—took to the floor, the lights in the arena were dimmed. Out marched six women, all in their twenties and thirties, seemingly dressed for the corporate office. They were in heels and dressy flats, pressed pants and dresses. Their faces were lightly etched with age, their cheeks suctioned of the baby fat that had lingered during their teenage years. They did not look like they had vaulted right off a Wheaties box. In fact, many of them hadn't vaulted in nearly a decade.

This was the 2000 Olympic team, the team that nearly everyone had forgotten. In Sydney, they placed fourth behind dominant Romanian, Russian, and Chinese squads. At those Games, the American men and women finished the competition without any medals, but the women were judged more harshly for this result. After all, just four years earlier, the U.S. women had won their historic team gold in dramatic fashion, with Kerri Strug vaulting on a sprained ankle as Bela Karolyi chanted "You can do it" from the sidelines. This triumph, coupled with the dissolution of the Soviet Union and the dismantling of their legendary training programs, was supposed to mean the beginning of American dominance in the sport of gymnastics.

Yet success did not beget success. The years after 1996 were devoid of medals for the Americans on the international stage. The team placed sixth at World Championships in 1997 and 1999. No individual gymnasts won medals. At the Olympics in 2000, the United States walked away empty-handed once again, to much derision in the media and from the national team coordinator, Karolyi. He accused the team members of not working hard enough.

With the exception of the youngest team member, Tasha Schwikert, who had been only fifteen at the Games, every other 2000 team member retired from elite gymnastics immediately after the Olympics. Amy Chow went to medical school. Dominique Dawes resumed her tour of promotional speaking duties, which eventually led to a stint as the president of the Women's Sports Foundation. The remaining three gymnasts—Jamie Dantzscher, Elise Ray, and Kristen Maloney—went on to college and competed for top-notch NCAA teams. After graduation, every one of them hung up her grips. They would never compete in another Olympic Games.

But in 2010, here they were, back at the elite National Championships, together again for the first time in a decade. The reason: they were being awarded the Olympic bronze medal in the team competition after the International Olympic Committee found the 2000 Chinese Olympic team guilty of age falsification for using an underage athlete. (The Chinese were also stripped of their team bronze from the 1999 World Championships for using the same underage gymnast. This medal was subsequently awarded to the Ukrainians, who had placed fourth at that meet.)

As Anita DeFrantz, an IOC representative, presented the 2000 team members with their medals and bouquets of flowers, the women's faces shone brightly with joy. They raised their flowers overhead and turned to face the different sides of the arena. The crowd cheered appreciatively and gave them a standing ovation.

But before all of the fanfare out in front of the crowd, the retired gymnasts sat in front of microphones, answering media questions about their surprise bronze ten years after the fact. You'd think there would've been anger, or at least frustration, directed toward the Chinese for lying about their gymnasts' ages, a practice they were widely assumed to engage in anyway; but no one blamed Dong Fangxiao, the gymnast the IOC determined was underage in Sydney. The Americans understood that it wasn't her fault. Dawes even described Dong as "the forgotten victim."

Back in 2000, the Chinese had claimed that Dong was seventeen, one year above the relatively new age minimum. But in 2008, Dong applied to work as a technical official at that year's Olympics in Beijing and listed a birthdate that would have made her fourteen in Sydney, two years too young to compete. The IOC immediately took notice of the discrepancy. Dong tried to recant, but the IOC concluded that she had indeed been underage as a competitor. Apparently, no one had explained to Dong that she had to go through the rest of her life fudging her age upward, that she'd have to enter middle age prematurely in order to cover up the decisions made by Chinese officials before she was thirteen. Dong was promptly abandoned by the Chinese federation, with one official even accusing her of forging her own passport after her competitive career ended. Dong and her husband relocated to New Zealand after the fiasco.

Ironically, the 2000 team being awarded the bronze in the Chinese's stead was one of the oldest teams at those Games. In 2000,

Dawes was twenty-three and a veteran of three Olympics. Chow was twenty-two and in Australia for her second Olympic go-round. Maloney was nineteen and had deferred college for a year in order to make a run for the Olympics after missing out in 1996. Ray and Dantzscher were both eighteen and university bound after the Games. Only Schwikert, the last-minute replacement athlete, fit the stereotype of the teenage gymnast at fifteen. In Sydney, they had been one of the oldest teams out on the floor and were beaten by one of the youngest. (Another Chinese gymnast, Yang Yun, confessed on Chinese television to being underage in Sydney but quickly recanted. Fortunately for her, she didn't leave a trail of contradictory paperwork with the IOC, so her case was dropped and she kept the individual medal she earned on the uneven bars in the apparatus final.)

As juicy and soap-opera-worthy as this story was, no one on the press conference dais seemed the least bit interested in discussing these details in 2010, even though it was ostensibly the reason they were all reunited, the reason that the Olympic record books had been revisited and rewritten. Rather, the story to come out of that pressroom wasn't about the conduct of the Chinese but that of the Americans—of the gymnasts, the coaches, and the officials who were testing a new system of training and selection out on the girls in 2000. As Dantzscher noted that night, "We were definitely the guinea pigs of a new system they were trying."

In order to understand how the 2000 team had come to be guinea pigs of a new semicentralized training system, you have to go back to the early 1990s in U.S. gymnastics. During those years, the Americans were beginning to enjoy their first bits of sustained success, with multiple medal winners at every competition. Unlike Mary Lou Retton's victory in 1984, which can be viewed retroactively as an aberration and not necessarily a harbinger of things very soon to come, the American medal gains in the early 1990s seemed to create momentum and expectation. In 1991, Kim Zmeskal won the World all-around title, the first for an American woman. Earlier that week she had led a very young squad—averaging at around fourteen years old—to the silver medal at the World Championships behind the Soviet Union, their highest-ever team finish in a fully contested international competition. Shannon Miller and Betty Okino added to the medal tally with a silver on bars and a bronze on beam, respectively.

Things continued apace for the next few years, with a team bronze in Barcelona and a huge medal haul for Miller, making her the most decorated American Olympian in 1992. Miller, Kerri Strug, and Dominique Dawes soldiered on after those Games and became the backbone of American gymnastics. The United States medaled at every World Championships between 1992 and 1996. They didn't always take first place, but they always walked away with something. By contrast, in the '80s, each U.S. medal was heralded as a lifetime achievement because they were so few and far between.

And then there was the Atlanta Olympics in 1996. That year, the U.S. women won their first gold medal in gymnastics for the country at a non-boycotted Olympic Games. They accomplished this feat by putting together a team of superstars. First, there was Miller, who at the time was the most successful gymnast in U.S. history. She had already won five Olympic medals and back-to-back World all-around titles before 1996. Then there was Dawes, who often threatened Miller's dominance after 1992, nearly winning the World title a couple of times herself and becoming the only gymnast in U.S. history to sweep all of the golds at nationals in 1994. There was the stalwart Strug, a veteran of five World Championship teams and one Olympics. Team captain Amanda Borden had been in the mix in 1992. Amy Chow was a prodigy on the uneven bars, Jaycie Phelps was a veteran of three World teams, and Dominique Moceanu was the youngest gymnast ever to win the senior national title at the age of thirteen. Add to all of that, they were competing on home soil in front of a boisterous, supportive crowd that got so loud at times that it drowned out the floor exercise music of the Americans' rivals. This was no ordinary team—it was an experienced team of superstar gymnasts. Their win was the pinnacle of years of hard work, but it shouldn't have necessarily been taken as a sign of things to come.

After 1996, the entire Olympic team with the exception of Moceanu moved on. The Karolyis retired yet again. (They had done the same after the 1992 Games.) Almost immediately, the gymnasts and coaches who had played an outsized role in the past half decade of success were all out of the picture. Yet because of the team's results, the expectations on the next generation of gymnasts had never been higher. This was akin to expecting the Chicago Bulls to win the NBA title *after* Michael Jordan retired because they had won it so many times with him playing at shooting guard.

At the 1997 World Championships, the defending U.S. Olympic team champions dropped all the way down to sixth place. Kristen Maloney was the highest all-around finisher for the Americans, landing in thirteenth place. Moceanu wound up in fourteenth place after having spent the year after the Olympics on tour with her 1996 teammates and away from serious training. The closest the Americans came to a podium finish was the fifth place earned by Mohini

Bhardwaj on the vault. The United States left Lausanne in 1997 without any medals.

The absence of medals, however, wasn't as troubling as the missed competitive opportunity for Vanessa Atler, the über-talented gymnast from California, who, despite tying for the national title that year, was unable to compete due to the new age minimum imposed in 1997, moving the bar from fifteen to sixteen. Despite her ineligibility for major senior competition, the blond, spunky Atler had already been turned into a star by the media. She had cultivated a large, young fan base through regular entries in her online diary about her life as a gymnast. Atler also already had an agent, Sheryl Shade, and had done a commercial for Reese's three years before she had a chance to prove herself in major international competition. Her christening as "the One" back in 1997 had as much, if not more, to do with her personal charisma than with competitive outcomes.

Despite the United States's weak finish in 1997, things seemed to be turning around in 1998. Atler, now a senior, was at the top of her game. She won two gold medals—for floor and vault—at the Goodwill Games. Moceanu was also back in peak form and won the overall title at that competition in what was probably the best year of her gymnastics career. Moceanu was taller, leaner, and more mature. She showcased high levels of difficulty on all four events, even challenging the naturally explosive Atler for the national title on vault.

In 1998, the 2000 Olympic team seemed to be starting to take shape in many people's minds with Atler and Moceanu in key leadership roles and gymnasts such as Maloney and Dantzscher pitching in on their best events. Things seem to be pointed toward a brighter, more successful future. If only the World Championships had been held that year.

By 1999, however, things had started falling apart. Moceanu had stopped training after running away from her father and legally emancipating herself from her parents. And Atler left her coaches in Covina, California, after two years spent falling off the uneven bars, which had become a mental trap for the talented gymnast. She kept peeling off on one particular move, the Comaneci salto. More than twenty years after Comaneci introduced this to the sport, it was still a highly valued skill.

Atler would go on to call the uneven bars "the devil" in her online diary. As Atler's grip slipped more and more, the media story around her shifted from her Olympic inevitability to her crisis of confidence on the uneven bars. Every time she approached the event in competition, the cameras hovered nearby while the commentators added to the sense of impending doom with dire prognostications. In 1998 and 1999, Atler rarely completed a routine without a major mistake on this apparatus. Yet she still managed consistent top three all-around finishes, so strong were her other events. Beam follows bars in the Olympic rotation order, and after every missed bar routine, Atler managed to refocus on beam and hit her aggressive, difficult set.

But at the 1999 National Championships, after Atler fell off the bars yet again on the same release move, her coach, Steve Rybacki, harshly rebuked her when she walked toward him after the routine. The exchange, though muted, was caught on camera. Atler bit her lip and slumped her shoulders as she took in the criticism. Though Steve's wife and coaching partner, Beth, hugged the young gymnast supportively, Atler made the decision to stop training with them shortly after that competition.

Atler gave no notice to her coaches or longtime training partner, Dantzscher. "There was no phone call, there was no nothing. She just left one day and moved to Texas, like, Beth and Steve had no idea. None of us had any idea," Dantzscher recalled.

America's most promising gymnast of the era arrived at her first World Championships in 1999 without a coach and with an ankle injury, a shell of the gymnast she had been in 1997 when she was too young to make the team. She performed disastrously. Atler left the mat in tears, limping, her future on the Olympic team in doubt for the first time since her senior debut.

The rest of the team did not fare much better. Once again, the Americans finished in sixth place, proving that the result in 1997 had not been a fluke. They were headed to the Olympics with a full team—the top twelve teams at the pre-Olympic World Championships received full team berths to the Games—but without any clear medal prospects. They were seeded behind a team from Australia, which had never won a major international medal but would be competing on their home turf in Sydney just as the Americans had in 1996. It seemed that the United States was regressing to the '80s, when each medal seemed like an unexpected gift from above.

Dantzscher said that she and the rest of the team overheard the coaches at the 1999 Worlds maligning the team in the next room over. "They didn't know that we could hear them, and they were saying that we were rebellious, and that we were fat, and all this stuff," she said. "I don't know if they were having some beverages in there, or what, but they were going off on us, you know? And we're, like, seventeen."

But the coaches weren't the only ones looking for solutions or where to place the blame. Within the American gymnastics community, there was soul-searching, recriminations, and questions. *How did we end up at the bottom of the pack after so many years of success, after a historic Olympic team gold medal, after so many World Championship medals?*

It didn't seem to be a problem of ability. The talent was certainly there. In addition to Atler and Dantzscher, Elise Ray had begun to make her move up the standings. She was a gymnast in the classical mold—perfect extension, beautiful toe point, and the upright carriage that rivaled the Russians. She also swung a silky set of bars, moving with the rhythm of the apparatus instead of fighting against it. Everything she did on the bars seemed easier than it had any right to. She performed some of the most difficult moves on that event, innovating several skills including a dismount that would come to bear her name. Ray seemed to be the perfect antidote to Atler's bar woes.

There was also Kristen Maloney, who did the most difficult tumbling program of any female gymnast in the world. And then there were the 1996 Olympic veterans who were creeping out of retirement to make another run at the Games. Shannon Miller was back in training as was Jaycie Phelps, Dominique Dawes, and Amy Chow. It was Chow who looked to be the most promising of the returning veterans—her difficulty level had been staggeringly high when she competed in 1996. She could do the same exercises four years later with few, if any, modifications and still start from the vaunted 10.0.

So talent was not the problem; organization was. The Americans' problem was that there was no strategy and no cohesion. It was each gymnast and coach for her- and himself. USA Gymnastics had mistakenly believed that winning medals meant that the system was working when, in fact, there was no system. The presence of superstars in the early '90s had papered over the inadequacies of the American arrangement.

Bob Colarossi became president of USA Gymnastics in 1998, right in the middle of the country's downward spiral, and decided to revamp the system after the 1999 World Championships yielded yet another medal-less result. He brought Karolyi out of retirement to be the national team coordinator and gave him free rein to reshape the gymnastics landscape in the United States as he saw fit.

Karolyi believed that some centralization was needed. All of the top teams at the time worked out together—the Russians trained at Round Lake outside of Moscow, the Chinese brought their best to Beijing, and the Romanians had a facility in Deva. These training programs fostered team camaraderie and uniform athletic standards for the gymnasts.

This sort of centralization, however, was simply not feasible in the United States where there were many gyms and coaches. It was preposterous to think that coaches would cede their athletes to the national governing body, especially less than a year before the Olympics, or that parents would just let their children move away from home for the next nine months.

Instead, Karolyi instituted monthly mandatory weeklong training camps for national team members down at his ranch in Texas. They would be accompanied by their personal coaches and would continue to train with them but under Karolyi's and the national team staff's watchful eye. The girls would have to prove readiness in their physical and skill preparation. They would have to verify routines in order to be given international assignments. Those that could not keep up would find themselves off the team.

And perhaps the most important change—the team would no longer be decided by the scores and rankings at Olympic Trials. Up until 2000, the World Championship and Olympic teams were put together by taking the top six or seven, depending on team size that year, at trials or nationals. Occasionally, special petitions were accepted for injured athletes who couldn't compete at the selection. Such was the case with Miller and Moceanu in 1996, and so it was with Okino in 1992.

Though selecting the team based solely on scores seems to be the fairest, most straightforward, and transparent, it doesn't always yield the best results. In 1988, the American men left their best gymnast, Dan Hayden, at home because he had a bad meet at Olympic Trials. He fell twice from the high bar while attempting a very difficult maneuver. Rick McCharles, a longtime Canadian judge and coach, recalled the international community's reaction to this result. "We all knew that Hayden was the best American guy. We couldn't believe that he wasn't on the Olympic team," he said.

Karolyi's ideas were good ones—semicentralized training, monthly evaluations, teams decided by committee instead of solely by competition rankings. The execution of these ideas, however, left much to be desired. The new system disrupted the coaches' longstanding training plans less than a year before the Olympics. And the strategy was instituted with little to no regard as to the thoughts and feelings of the coaches and athletes. It was the least democratic implementation of an already undemocratic system.

"After '99 Worlds, it was brought to our attention that we would now have a national team coach/coordinator in Bela Karolyi and we were restructuring. It was one year out of the Olympic Games," Kelli Hill, 2000 Olympic team head coach, recalled in an episode of *Behind the Team*, a USA Gymnastics–produced series. She spoke without emotional affect, but Hill's passive phrasing, "It was brought to our attention," tells the story: they were told, not consulted.

"We had a year, and we were given this situation with Bela, and that was it," recalled Mary Lee Tracy in the same video.

And it wasn't just a problem of when the system was implemented but also of who was put in charge. "It was not the right person in that position," Hill asserted.

Karolyi agreed with Hill's assessment of his performance. "What I did not have and I never did before is the diplomacy," he said. "I was never very good dealing with people that were going on their own agenda," he noted in the video.

To understand why Karolyi was not the best person for the job, you need to know what role he played in gymnastics in his heyday as a personal coach. As many in the community openly discuss, Karolyi's forte was not teaching high-level skills. "Bela's brilliance lies in his boldness, not in his ability to teach," Dr. William Sands, a sports scientist and former elite gymnastics coach, said.

With more than a decade of perspective, Dantzscher believes that Bela's role in the whole process had been overstated to the team. "I think it was more for the media," she said of his involvement. "Even at training camp, you know, Martha did a lot of the coaching, and you heard Martha's voice more, and Bela would stand there and do the lineup, the warm-ups, and when I think back, I think he wasn't really doing a lot of the giving assignments and making corrections. He was kind of there, you know?"

What Karolyi brought to the table was media attention, charisma, and the ability to motivate. His athletes repeatedly talked about how no one made you feel more ready to compete than he did. His gymnasts were often the best physically conditioned gymnasts. Svetlana Boginskaya, who trained with him for the 1996 Olympics, described him as practically brimming with intensity. "Just his presence in the gym gave me a huge surge of energy. Bela could stand there without speaking a word, but a wave of assurance radiated from him," she told Russian reporter Elena Vaitsekhovskaya.

None of Karolyi's strengths as a coach, however, would be called into play as the national team coordinator. He wouldn't be motivating the athletes on a daily basis. This time around, Karolyi would be an administrator. He wouldn't be on the floor during competitions, mugging for the camera and encouraging the gymnasts. By the time the press would have arrived for a meet, his job would essentially be over. All of his work was supposed to be done when no one was watching.

"Bela was the charismatic motivator on the outside," said Mary Lee Tracy in the video, "but as a national team leader, really their responsibility is a little bit more behind the scenes."

And as the training camp system was just getting off the ground in 1999, there was strife behind the scenes. It wasn't just the coaches who were unhappy. The athletes were, too.

"We felt like we were almost like animals in a cage. Everyone was watching every little thing you do and taking notes. If you happen to mess up a little bit, it was a huge deal. That's what it felt like," said Kristen Maloney in an interview with GymCastic.

Sands, who was brought in early in the process in 1999 by then–USA Gymnastics vice president Kathy Kelly, felt that the real problem was that it was started too late; simply, it was a rush job. "If he had started six months earlier, the picture of gymnastics from that era would've been very different," he told me. "If they had started sooner, I think Bela would've come out looking like the hero, not the villain."

Gymnasts like Atler wondered why they didn't bother waiting until the next Olympic cycle. "I think the timing was bad too. Like right before the Olympics? Why would you do that?" she asked. "Why don't you wait until that quad is over and then let's make a change so we have some time? I think they just had so much panic about the Olympics."

The real culprit for Sands, other than the late start, was the lack of physical preparedness exhibited by many of the gymnasts. "They couldn't do a press to handstand. Bela and I were talking, 'My god, my kids back in Chicago from a decade ago would cream these kids in fitness.' "

Gymnasts like Ray, Maloney, and Dantzscher don't agree that they were out of shape or improperly conditioned; the problem was that the national team staff was demanding far more from them than they had any right to. "The amount of the work and the amount of conditioning that they were expecting us to do was just impossible, and every single person knew it," Ray said. "I mean, even when I talk to Kelli about it, she remembers hoisting my body through a million cast handstands."

The other gymnasts' accounts of their own experiences in the training camps corroborate Ray's. "You felt like you had to do everything they asked you to do, no matter what, no matter how injured you were," Maloney, who had been recovering from multiple injuries and surgery during that period, said. "I remember a time I had to come crawling back on the vault runway because my shin was hurting so bad, but you had to keep going." Maloney and others said that there was no individuation in the training plans in those early camps—everyone had to do the same exact thing, regardless of ability or injury status.

Dantzscher remembered one time, after running through a long gamut of upper-body conditioning, being told that she had to start doing full routines on the uneven bars. "I'm, like, looking at Steve [Rybacki], like, 'I can't feel my arms right now, I don't know how I'm going to hang on the bar.' " Dantzscher's coach negotiated the assignment down a bit to full routines but sans competitive dismounts, which was more manageable for her. Of course, Dantzscher worried what the selection committee thought about her reduced load. She remembered thinking, *I'm not going to make the Olympic team because I can't get through five bar routines right now.*

———

After the competition was over at the 2000 Olympic Trials at the Fleet Center in Boston, Karolyi along with Tracee Talavera, a World and Olympic medalist, and Chari Knight-Hunter left the arena to finalize the six members of the team. These three comprised the selection committee. The TV cameras followed them, TMZ-style, as they headed to a private room and closed the door behind them. There was a digital clock at the left side of the screen, keeping track of the time the trio spent trying to figure who to put on the team and who to leave off. They were supposed to be in the room for no more than five minutes but stayed cloistered for more than ten. (Fortunately for them, they did not incur a penalty as a gymnast would if her beam routine went overtime.) In 2000, the selection of the Olympic team was treated as a sporting event unto itself.

As the three deliberated in private, the NBC commentators for the event, the gymnastics perennials Tim Daggett, Elfi Schlegel, and Al Trautwig, filled the time by trying to guess which athletes Karolyi would name to the team. But really, the discussion centered on whether the committee would name Atler to the squad. This seemed to be a continuation of the media narrative at Trials that was geared toward making a case against Atler's inclusion. On the first day of competition after she performed a double twisting Yurchenko—the best among the Americans on vault—Schlegel immediately registered her disgust, commenting on the steps on landing. True, it was not up to Atler's usual standard, but it was clean and powerful. And better than what most of the team could muster on that event.

Atler commented to me that she could sense the shift in the media's, crowd's, and even other coaches' attitudes toward her in 2000. "I was such an emotional and sensitive kid that I could see other coaches mad at me for leaving Beth and Steve," she said. "I felt the media, kind of, they used to always feel so good [about] me. There was this change in mood of the way they looked at me for leaving [the Rybackis]. It was awful."

Unfortunately for Atler, her performance at Trials did little to change the negative slant of the coverage. That first vault would be the highlight of the meet for her. She struggled on bars, which was nothing new. And then on beam, she missed her foot, which caused her to land flat on her back during her double back dismount, a scary mishap that was shown over and over. The following night she had mistakes across all four events. Daggett commented that as far as he was concerned, Atler had gone 0–4 on the second and final day of competition.

Despite all these mistakes, she landed in sixth in the all-around rankings, just a couple of tenths ahead of returning Olympic gold medalist Dominique Dawes. This placement, after so many missed performances, was a real testament to Atler's talent. Her difficulty level on almost all events (except bars) dwarfed that of the other American gymnasts. And had this been a different time in U.S. gymnastics history, that would've been enough for the demoralized gymnast to make the Olympic team. But in this whole new world of closed-door meetings and selection committees, there was virtually nothing a gymnast could do to guarantee herself a place on the squad. Except, of course, winning Trials, which is exactly what Ray had done.

"I was, like, 'I'm not going to let somebody else decide whether or not I'm going to be on the team,'" she told me. "I remember distinctly making a decision, 'I just need to win both of these things [Nationals and Trials] to solidify my spot.' " Though Ray faltered on her last event at Trials, balance beam, she was so far ahead of the field that it didn't affect her ranking or position on the U.S. team. She had, without a doubt, clinched it. There was nothing for the commentators to speculate about when it came to Elise Ray.

Ray was hardly alone when it came to being opposed to the new Olympic team selection procedures. During the previous competition at the National Championships, Beth Ruyak from NBC noted that several of the coaches had registered their disapproval. Waving the papers that outline the selection process, she explained, "It indicates that they understand and agree to those procedures. Donna Strauss has signed it, but she has crossed out the word 'agree.' It's a small protest, but she and others who have also done the same thing feel that it's one way that they can express their dissatisfaction with this selection process." Strauss and her husband, Bill, had been burned once before by closed-door selection. Their gymnast, Kim Kelly, had made the 1992 Olympic team on the basis of her performance at Trials but was dumped after a secret camp in Florida. In 2000, the Strausses' only Olympic prospect was Maloney, who said that she could tell that her coaches were quite nervous about all the changes. "I felt like it was harder on them than it was with me. They just wanted to make sure that nothing happened and that I didn't get taken off the team," she recalled. Not that her coaches had much to worry about. Maloney looked like she was a lock for the team in 2000. The way that Atler had once seemed.

"We have all said among ourselves," Trautwig said, attempting to fill airtime while the committee decided, "that if Vanessa Atler had been handed over at Bela Karolyi at some point, he would've been the one to fix her, to mold her." He wondered aloud if Karolyi's ego would come into play and he would name her to the team, believing that he'd be able to set her straight during the training camp between the Trials and Sydney.

This was not such a preposterous idea. Back in 1999, when the Californian had left her coaches, it had been widely rumored that Karolyi was going to take over her training. Atler herself had heard as much, though she's also quite hazy on a lot of details from that time. "I'll be dead honest with you, Dvora," she said. "There are parts—I don't know if it's a mental thing—there are many parts I don't remember at all." Atler also admitted that a lot of wheeling and dealing had happened without her knowledge. "I was just a teenager and people were telling me things. I wasn't the one making deals with Bela. I just told my parents, 'I want to quit.' " This utterance, coming from the most gifted gymnast in the United States, seemed to have prompted panic in everyone around her. "I get why it was such a big controversy. I couldn't go to the world and say, 'This is too hard for me.' "

Atler said she wished that she had been a bit more like her outspoken training partner, Dantzscher. "She's the type that is able to communicate to people and tell them the truth whether it hurts their feelings or not. She knew that she had to tell them how she felt. In the end, it's one of the best things to do. For me, I was so scared of confrontation, so scared of telling people how I felt, so scared of hurting someone's feelings that often I would lie to them and tell them everything is fine or whatever. I think leaving Beth and Steve was a shock to Beth and Steve. I always put up a front that I was very, very happy."

With more than fifteen years of hindsight, Atler said she regretted not staying with her longtime coaches. "I just wanted someone to give me a hug and say, 'It's okay. We can get through this. Let's go to Steve and Beth and talk it out,'" she said.

Instead, her mother suggested that they look for another coach. "All I got back was, 'Hey, Sheryl Shade [Atler's and Karolyi's agent at the time] said Bela wanted to come out of retirement for you. Isn't that exciting?' I'm like, 'No, I don't want to go with that guy. I don't know him and he scares me.' I was kind of relieved when I found out later that he didn't want to do it or had another job."

Atler ended up moving to Plano, Texas, to train with Valeri Liukin, who was then best known as a Soviet gold medalist from 1988. He had not yet made a name for himself in the United States as a coach. He had been suggested to the Atlers by Karolyi.

She showed up with Liukin at Nationals and then Olympic Trials, where she twice placed behind Dantzscher, whose star was on the rise after being eclipsed by Atler for most of her senior career. At Nationals, Dantzscher had a breakout performance and won the bronze; Atler was off the podium for the first time in four years, placing fourth. And at Trials, Dantzscher landed in fifth, nearly a point ahead of her former teammate.

Both Atler and Dantzscher, while expressing deep affection and admiration for each other, acknowledged that they both probably trained better without the other. "When she left to SCATS, I feel like my workouts got better," Atler recalled, speaking about a time when Dantzscher had left for several months to train at Don Peters's gym. "And I'm sure that when I left to Valeri her workouts got better. I think she got more attention from Beth and Steve because when we were both there together, they tended to be with me a lot more."

"I think we both should've been on that team together, ideally, but also had she stayed, too, I don't think I would've made it," Dantzscher admitted.

But Dantzscher was ultimately named to the team after more than ten minutes of deliberation behind closed doors. Atler knew right away where she stood. Colarossi read off the gymnasts' names in alphabetical order. If she had been chosen, Atler's name would've been announced first. The committee reached below her, to the seventh and eighth places, to name the final team member and alternate. Despite amassing higher point totals than Dawes, Beckerman, or Schwikert (who would be named later as the second replacement athlete), Atler was excluded from the team. It was clear from her performance at Trials that she was on the downslope and gymnasts like Dawes and Schwikert were on the rise. The committee chose forward momentum instead of regression. Atler, at the time, acknowledged that this was probably the right call. "Deep down in my heart, I knew I wasn't prepared," she told the reporters in Boston. "When I read the names, it was almost a sense of relief." No one had let Atler quit gymnastics, but she found a way out anyway.

The drama didn't end with the team selection. After the Trials, the team and alternates traveled to the Karolyi Ranch for their pre-Olympic training camp, where then-team doctor, Larry Nassar, joined them. Dr. Nassar, who was quietly dismissed from his position with USA Gymnastics in 2015 has, since the first publication of this book, been accused of sexual abuse by eighty gymnasts who have filed criminal and civil complaints. Shortly after he arrived at the ranch, he discovered that Morgan White was nursing a foot injury. "When I was allowed to show up at the selection camp, it was already too late. Her foot was injured, but they were letting her do too much in the gym," he maintained on a podcast.

The time to rest it would have been in the months leading up to the Trials, to let it heal before the big push for the Olympics. Though he said White stayed off her foot during the remainder of her time in Texas, it was of no use. "When we got to Australia when it was time to test it, she couldn't do it," he lamented. Nassar explained the unique challenges that the new selection procedures presented when it came to athletes and coaches disclosing injuries to the national team staff. Previously, when competition results determined team composition, a gymnast didn't have to worry about being kept off a squad due to an injury unless she wasn't able to do the work. But in the age of selection where injury status—regardless of ability to perform—could be a factor in making a team, there was incentive for gymnasts and coaches to not be completely honest with the national team staff.

"They'll do whatever they can do to avoid showing the injury, because that may displace them from the selection," Nassar told GymCastic. "You're setting them up to lie and deceive. We don't want them to hide injuries, working beyond what they're capable of doing and make a small injury worse because they're hiding it," he added. "If they trust us, they do not have to hide the injury."

But trust, like uninjured gymnasts, was in short supply leading up to the 2000 Olympics. "It was exceedingly hard to get the coaches, athletes, and administration to gain their trust," Nassar said. "Athletes have to be able to trust and be able to talk to their coaches and tell what the injury is. Coaches have to be able to trust that the administration won't use the information against them."

White was removed from the team roster in Sydney and had to pack up and leave the Olympic Village. Her removal left a vacancy in the roster that everyone assumed would be filled by Alyssa Beckerman, who had been the highest-ranked alternate after Trials, but Karolyi selected Schwikert for that role and didn't bother explaining it to the team. "It was not communicated to us athletes," Maloney recalled to GymCastic. "We didn't know until she was leaving that that's what happened, that she was injured and that she was off the team."

In addition to not communicating with the athletes, Karolyi seemed to make decisions without discussion or consensus. He handed out the rotations—the order in which the gymnasts would compete on each apparatus—shortly before the team marched out onto the competition floor. He took Dantzscher off bars for preliminaries after she rolled her ankle in practice. For Dantzscher, this was a difficult decision to understand because it was one of her best events. It was also the one least affected by her lightly injured ankle. "Even though I made every single beam routine and every single verification, I could not argue them taking me off beam because of my history competing on beam," Dantzscher said, acknowledging her inconsistent competitive past on the apparatus. "I totally got that. I would've loved the opportunity to compete all-around, but I knew why [I wasn't]." But pulling her from bars was inexplicable. "Bars are a really good event of mine, and then finding out in warm-ups, the day of the competition . . . they tried to say because of my ankle, but they had me on vault and floor," two lower-body-intensive events. And a couple of days later she found herself in the bars lineup for team finals, competing in the anchor position. "It just didn't make sense."

Maloney, now a college gymnastics coach, noted that it's important for athletes to understand the strategy and decisions. "I feel like in order to get the best out of your athletes, they have to know what you're expecting of them, otherwise how else are they going to train and work the best for you?" she observed.

But Karolyi's selection of Schwikert, the neophyte, demonstrated some of his genius. The gymnast performed remarkably well at the

Olympics. She was the most consistent gymnast on the team. "Bela and Martha are very good—Martha in particular—at recognizing who's going to be there in the decisive moment and who isn't," Sands told me. Of course, that sort of decision making is the result of instinct. It's kind of hard to seek consensus over a gut feeling. It's also hard to explain a feeling to your gymnasts.

After the upheavals of the days preceding the start of the Olympics—losing a team member, losing Tracy, the assistant coach—the team marched into preliminaries demoralized. To make matters worse, the United States had drawn the first morning session, which meant the scores would be lower and the arena would be emptier than it would be later in the day. Their performances reflected the energy in the arena. They were sluggish, lackluster, and riddled with mistakes. On floor exercise, national champion Ray's shoulder popped out of the joint. She finished her routine but was in visible distress and received an uncharacteristically low mark. Chow, the defending Olympic silver medalist on the uneven bars, made a substantial error on that event, and didn't make event finals. Dantzscher also fell on floor exercise, an event where she had a good shot at making the finals. The only gymnast to qualify for an individual event final was Ray on the balance beam, an apparatus on which she was not favored to medal. After all of the teams competed, the U.S. women were in sixth place once again, a ranking that had become all too familiar. It looked like the American women would be leaving another major international competition without a podium finish.

Karolyi wasted no time distancing himself from the team, complaining to the media about how this group of girls was unfocused and unmotivated. Hill didn't say much in the press conferences. She was more concerned with picking up the team. "The girls had come in very down and disappointed," she recalled in 2010. "They were getting reamed in the press, and they were working so hard. Our national team coordinator kind of gave them a hard time, and everyone was coming down on them."

Hill gathered the girls after the preliminaries for a team meeting without any of the national team staff present. "This is the Olympic Games. You're looking scared. We're not scared. We can take this," she told them. "You guys have done these routines a thousand times. Let's do them one more [time]." She taped little American flags to their doors that night, which they brought with them into the finals two days later. They entered the arena laughing and cheering.

"It wasn't meant to be any earth-shaking thing," she said of her speech to the girls that many cited later in interviews. "It was just me trying to pick up the kids. I didn't want them to walk away from the Olympic Games so disheartened."

Karolyi may have been renowned for his motivational skills, but in Sydney it was the usually taciturn Hill who got the team to turn things around. "They went in and hit every event. Every kid hit every set," she said with obvious pride. As a result of their strong final performances that last day, the U.S. women placed fourth behind the Romanians, Russians, and Chinese.

It would be nice if the story ended at this moment of uplift, but the anger and resentment that had been building throughout the Olympic selection process came pouring out after the meet ended. Karolyi once again attacked the team. "This generation [of gymnasts] lacks the necessary work ethic," he said about the team he had personally selected.

But given the new age minimums, the gymnasts he was talking about were older than the fourteen-, fifteen-, and sixteen-year-olds he was accustomed to dealing with. They were not the sort of accommodating gymnasts he introduced to the world in 1976.

These gymnasts weren't going to take Karolyi's remarks lying down. Dantzscher responded to Karolyi's comments publicly, calling him a "puppeteer" and added "Bela should not have had so much control."

"The personal coaches were given no credit. He [Karolyi] gets so much credit when we do things right, but everyone else gets blamed when things go wrong," she continued.

USA Gymnastics asked Dantzscher to tone down her comments, but she refused. "I don't regret anything I said," she said at the time. "I believe there are other girls who feel the same as I do. I hope eventually that the people in power will pay attention to what I said and maybe make some changes."

Over a decade after Sydney, Ray admitted as much in an interview, saying, "I love Jamie Dantzscher. She was the only one who said what was on her mind. I was too scared."

Maloney agreed. "I think Jamie Dantzscher got it right when she said [Karolyi] wants to take the credit when we do well, but when we do not so well, it's all on us," she said.

Dantzscher, fifteen years after Sydney, has taken a more nuanced approach to her earlier comments. "I was also told, you know, that it was Bela that, I think, after ten years, and kind of growing up a lot, and that being in the past, and finding out more of the truth, you know, it wasn't all Bela," she said. Still, she doesn't take back what she said. "You're going to get a negative reaction to it when you speak the truth, and I was just trying to tell the truth," Dantzscher noted.

With the exception of the fifteen-year-old Schwikert, the team disbanded and retired after Sydney. "Everybody moved on so quickly. We shot off to college as fast as we could. USAG moved on as fast as they could," Ray said to GymCastic.

Though Ray, who went on to become a Michigan Wolverine, frequently encountered Maloney and Dantzscher, who were competing for UCLA, at college competitions, they never shared their feelings about their 2000 experience. "There was no way we were talking about the Olympics," she said. "It wasn't until we got the medal that we all looked at each other and said—how did you feel about that whole experience? Nobody talked about it. It was pretty remarkable to talk to everyone ten years later."

For Ray, the Olympics got even worse after the team competition. In the women's all-around final, the vault was accidentally set a notch too low and half of the competitors vaulted over it before the officials realized there was a problem. During the warm-up, Ray missed her hands entirely on the horse and landed on her back. During the actual competition, she merely fell. Ray was one of several top gymnasts who took very scary spills on the incorrectly set apparatus, including the favorite to win the all-around title, Russia's statuesque queen, Svetlana Khorkina. "What few people know is that you fall on your first event in a competition, it completely wrecks your mental game," Ray told me. She said that after that disastrous vault, she couldn't even muster the energy to prepare for her next apparatus, the uneven bars. "I was just sitting there with my grips kind of half on my hands and she [Hill, her coach] [said], 'Lucy,' which is what she called me. 'Lucy, you have to get your grips on. You have to keep competing.' Because I was so defeated.

"It took me so many years to kind of come to peace with the fact that that was my Olympic experience because so much of it was just so bad and just really hard. I mean, I had a calendar on my wall, like a countdown calendar of how much longer it was for me to go home," Ray said.

As the members of the 2000 team were doing their best to put the Olympics behind them, the coaches and the national team staff were trying to figure out how to move forward from the competitive and PR debacle that was Sydney. They decided not to throw out the baby with the bathwater. In this scenario, the bathwater was Bela Karolyi. The training camp system, they concluded, was a step in the right direction. That, they would keep with some adjustments and a new person in charge.

"Everybody started thinking that Martha [Karolyi] could do the best job of anybody we had in our country," Tracy said in the USA Gymnastics–produced video. Bela's wife preferred to work behind the scenes and possessed a more diplomatic mien and a greater knowledge of the technical side of gymnastics. Plus, she was perceived as impartial by the athletes. "My own experience with Martha was that she was very fair and she did listen to us," Ray recalled.

The coaches felt the same way. "She asks our opinion, she's very personal," Hill said. One of the primary complaints the coaches had during the first Karolyi regime was that they lost ownership of their gymnasts. They were told what to do and how to train their gymnasts—what exercises to do, which skills to train—by a person who didn't understand their athletes the way that they did. "The personal coaches are now completely in charge of their athletes," Hill noted in an interview with FloGymnastics.

Donna Strauss, former coach of Maloney, said, "Martha will listen to you if your child is injured, if you can't do the same number of reps. She's very understanding about what each kid needs."

In the years since Sydney, the U.S. women have become the undisputed dominant force in women's gymnastics. At the 2001 Worlds, the team won the bronze, and the medals have just kept coming. Since 2005, all but two World all-around champions have been American. They've also won all of the Olympic all-around golds since 2004. There have been World team titles and countless individual apparatus medals, consecutive Olympic team silver medals, and finally, the team gold in 2012.

"Martha is a genius," Sands said.

The quieter Karolyi is not without her critics, but she has demonstrated an ability to grow and evolve. During the first several years of Martha's tenure (2001 to 2004), there were several ill-timed injuries, which some blamed on the camps and their punishing training regimen. But Martha seems to have learned from these early mistakes and softened her approach over time. Nowadays, Nassar said, Martha is one of the first to ask a coach to back off an injured athlete.

"The vast majority of the time after I share the information [about injuries] with Martha, Martha is the one who tries to help get the coaches to decrease," Nassar said. And not just at the ranch and training camps. Karolyi sometimes had Nassar check in with coaches of injured athletes to ensure that they aren't working their gymnasts too hard in their home gyms.

"After the nightmare of 2000 and what happened to poor Morgan White and Alyssa Beckerman, we have not replaced a single athlete at the Olympic Games. I have done whatever I can to keep the team as the team through any injury that they've had," Nassar said. Chellsie Memmel broke her foot during training in Beijing in 2008 but was kept on the team to compete on bars. The 2012 meme star McKayla Maroney was rested throughout most of the training sessions in London due to a broken toe and fractured shin. In team finals, she pulled off one of the greatest vaults of all-time, which galvanized the team on its path to a team gold, its first since the Magnificent Seven won in 1996.

Though neither Ray nor Dantzscher has returned to the Texas training site, both seem to agree that the national team training camps have improved since their time. Dantzscher said she's spoken to coaches who had been with them during that first year and still take students to the ranch, who insist that conditions have gotten better. "I know that Mary Lee had said they're much better," Dantzscher said. "I think the food's probably better."

Atler was proud of the positive changes she's heard about from the athletes and coaches, including her former coach, Steve Rybacki, who spent several years on the selection committee and the national team staff. "They finally figured it out. They really did. The camps are working. They made the camps better where they're more comfortable, they're more homey, they're not so disgusting anymore. They're feeding them better food. They're taking care of them a lot more. And that I think was the thing that was missing the most was it was just not feeling like you were somebody that they cared about," she recalled.

When asked in 2010 if the team's awful experience in 2000 was worth it, Hill quickly and emphatically answered, "Yes. We had to go through 2000 to figure out what we didn't want, and it's been well worth it."

Matt Damon once suggested that the Academy Awards be handed out ten years after a movie's premiere when its long-term impact is fully understood. He told *Parade*, "I think the best way to judge is, like, ten years after they're released." In such a setup, *Crash* probably would not have won the Best Picture Oscar over the elegiac *Brokeback Mountain*, and the frothy comedy *Shakespeare in Love* might not have surpassed the epic war movie *Saving Private Ryan* in the same category.

Ten years after the 2000 Olympic team left Sydney ignominiously, they were awarded their medals. And it took nearly that long for their impact on American gymnastics to become truly apparent. They had been the guinea pigs of a new procedure that had later turned others into gold medalists. And a decade after they had retired, they finally had a medal of their own, as much for their personal sacrifice as for their performances at the Games.

It couldn't have worked out more perfectly than if it had been planned that way.

CAMP KAROLYI:
INSIDE THE NATIONAL TEAM TRAINING CAMP SYSTEM

When the Karolyis defected from Romania to the United States in the early 1980s and set up shop in Houston, it seemed that every high-level gymnast in the country landed on their doorstep. First, there was Dianne Durham, the 1981 and 1982 Junior National Champion, who moved to Texas to train with the famed Romanian coaching duo. The following year, she won the 1983 senior national title with them, becoming the first African American woman to earn the top ranking in U.S. gymnastics.

Then there was Mary Lou Retton, a powerful sprite from West Virginia, who arrived at fourteen in 1982, just two years shy of what would be "her" Olympic Games in Los Angeles. And then in 1984, during the Olympic year itself, Julianne McNamara transferred to the Karolyis' facility. McNamara was already quite established as one of the best gymnasts in the United States—she had been named to the 1980 Olympic team at just fourteen but never competed due to the American boycott of the Moscow Games.

Frank Litsky, writing for the *New York Times* in 1984, described these moves as a "game of musical coaches." When the music stopped, everyone scrambled to get into the handful of gyms in the country, perhaps no more than five at any given time, that trained elite-level gymnasts.

A lot has changed in the three decades since the Karolyis moved to Houston and hung up their shingle. After the dissolution of the former Soviet Union, much of the gymnastics "brain trusts" of those countries—their best coaches—migrated from the Eastern bloc to the West in the 1990s and set up their own shops, just as the Romanians had done in the 1980s. For a gymnast who aspires to train and compete at the highest levels, there are many more gym and coach options to choose from today than there were in Mary Lou Retton's day. Many gymnasts don't even have to leave home to receive top-notch training, whereas in previous generations, moving to find a top gym or coach was a near certainty.

And yet the best gymnasts in the United States are still landing on the Karolyis' doorstep. Every month since late 1999, young Olympic hopefuls have been journeying down to the Sam Houston National Forest in Texas, just outside of Huntsville—or New Waverly, depending on your map—for national team training camps run by Martha Karolyi at the Karolyi Ranch, which has been officially designated a U.S. Olympic Committee training site.

Bela Karolyi, who had retired thrice—first in 1992 and again in 1996 and yet again in 2000—is sort of like Jay-Z: he's never done when he says he's done. And Martha is Beyoncé to his Jay—today, she is more relevant than ever.

The way most people tell it, the story of American women's gymnastics has a before and after: Before the Karolyis and After the Karolyis. BK and AK, if you will.

BK, the story goes, the Americans were not good at gymnastics. Their gymnasts didn't work hard, they weren't fit, and that's why they didn't win any medals.

AK, the Americans were well on their way to becoming an unstoppable force in women's gymnastics, with Retton winning the all-around title at the 1984 Olympics, which the Soviets boycotted, and Kim Zmeskal winning the gold at the 1991 World Championships. According to most histories of U.S. women's gymnastics, the Karolyis have been the engine driving most of the Americans' success.

But the American story in women's gymnastics is a little more complicated than simply BK and AK. First, the Americans were getting better at gymnastics before the Karolyis defected, even if their results internationally didn't always bear that out. American gymnasts were routinely discriminated against by panels of Eastern bloc judges allied against the United States in the 1960s and early 1970s. But by the late 1970s, American male and female gymnasts were starting to be recognized for their performances. In 1978, Marcia Frederick won the World title on the uneven bars, while Kathy Johnson picked up a bronze medal on floor exercise at the World Championships in Strasbourg, France, with a lyrical style that rivaled the balletic Soviets. In 1981, Tracee Talavera won a bronze on the balance beam in the most hostile territory—Moscow. And in 1980, the United States fielded a wildly talented team featuring Johnson, Frederick, and newcomers such as Talavera, McNamara, and Beth Kline. This squad could have made its mark at the Olympics in Moscow had President Jimmy Carter not boycotted those Games in protest of the Soviet invasion of Afghanistan.

All of this is to say that the Americans were getting good not dominant, but good—BK. The Karolyis weren't exactly wandering into a gymnastics wasteland when they opened up their first gym in Houston in 1982.

Their almost immediate success in the United States proves that. No coach, regardless of ability, can build a national champion in less than a year. That Durham, who was already very successful at the junior level, won the senior national title in 1983, less than a year after moving to Houston to train with the Karolyis, is as much a testament to her previous coaches' efforts as it was to the newly arrived Romanians'. With their early athletes in the United States, the Karolyis were clearly building on foundations laid by other coaches who never became household names in their own right.

It's a similar story for McNamara, who went on to tie for the gold medal on the uneven bars at the 1984 Olympics, and Retton, who would become the first female athlete to grace the Wheaties box following her dramatic all-around win at the Games. McNamara had been with the Karolyis for less than a year, Retton for less than two. Durham, Retton, and McNamara were already among the most talented gymnasts in the United States before the Romanians arrived. To suggest a superiority of the Karolyi way based on this early, small sample amounts to a selection bias.

That's not to say that Durham or McNamara or Retton weren't helped by the Karolyis, or that their gymnastics hadn't improved under their tutelage. In Retton's case, the improvement was probably the most dramatic. Always something of a powerhouse, she arrived in Houston with a full bag of tricks but virtually no refinement or consistency. Terry Walker, a U.S. coach who currently works at World Champions Centre, recalled the pre-Bela Mary Lou. "The one thing they did for Mary Lou—Mary Lou had the skills, they really didn't teach her anything—they made her such a great, consistent competitor," he said. "This was a kid who hopped off of beam all the time," before the Karolyis started drilling her on a daily basis. In numerous interviews, both before and after the Olympics, Retton recalled the sheer intensity of her workouts in Texas. "When you get to a meet, it's a relief," she said in 1992, "because you only have to do it once." For the Karolyis, more was almost always better.

At the 1984 Olympics, Retton was one of the most consistent gymnasts, not just on the U.S. team but also in the entire competition. She didn't count a single fall. Even her main competitor, Ecaterina Szabo of Romania, fell at least once in the team competition, face planting on her dismount from the uneven bars. Since back in those days the scores from team competition were carried into the finals, that fall was the difference between gold and silver.

After Retton's victory and resultant fame, more gymnasts started flocking to the Karolyis in Houston. Brandy Johnson made the 1988 Olympic team under the Karolyi banner. She had been with them for approximately six months after moving from Brown's Gymnastics in Orlando. The Karolyis were, in essence, a finishing school for Johnson and many other gymnasts like her who had transferred to their tutelage with the majority of their skill set already established.

Walker recalled that this time—the mid-1980s and 1990s—was one characterized by suspicion among coaches who worried about losing their top pupils. "I will tell you, having been around when Bela and Martha were at their prime, there was a lot of gym hopping going on in the Houston area at the time, and people didn't trust [others] very much at all."

But Walker recognized that being with Bela and Martha conferred certain competitive advantages for a gymnast, especially the lower-ranked ones. "If you're associated with a really good club, everyone automatically assumes that kid is going to be really good. They could be middle-of-the-road, but they get the benefit of the doubt because of who they're being coached by," Walker pointed out.

By virtue of walking out onto the competition floor with Bela and Martha, an unknown might receive the sort of attention typically reserved for a star. This is true not only of the audience but of the judges, too. While that may not be "fair," if you're a coach or athlete, you're going to take every possible advantage you can get. "That's what you do. Most people will not look a gift horse in the mouth and say, 'Take these two extra tenths back. I didn't deserve them,' " he explained. And no one was going to hop on the podium like Kanye to protest your medal: "Imma let your national anthem finish, but Dominique Dawes had the best floor routine of the meet."

That the Karolyis were successful at raising the international profile of American gymnastics and placing gymnasts on the Olympic team did not necessarily make them an immediate favorite among the American gymnastics establishment, then called the USGF (United States Gymnastics Federation). Though he had placed two gymnasts on the 1984 Olympic team, Karolyi wasn't allowed out on the competition floor in Los Angeles and used a baggage handler's credential to get close to the action. This is why when Retton performed her historic vault in the all-around, the one that clinched the title, she had to hug Karolyi across the barricade. Four years later in 1988, U.S. officials tried once again to keep him away from the competition even though it was likely that his athletes—whether recent transplants to his gym or longtime pupils—would account for at least half of the Olympic team. Don Peters, head coach at SCATs in Southern California, was the early choice for the head coach but pulled out when none of his athletes made the team. In the end, Karolyi ended up with three Olympic team members—Johnson,

Phoebe Mills, the only American gymnastics medalist in Seoul, and Chelle Stack and alternate Rhonda Faehn. Karolyi, recently naturalized, was officially named "chief of the American gymnastics federation."

(Don Peters, it should be noted, has been banned for life from all USA Gymnastics activity and coaching after it was revealed that he had sexually abused some of his gymnasts, including Doe Yamashiro, who came forward in 2011.)

In 1991, the year of the Americans' breakthrough at the World Championships—with Zmeskal's win, the team silver, and several other individual medals—every single member of the team was coached either by Martha and Bela or by coaches who had worked with them at some point. Steve Nunno, Shannon Miller's coach, had briefly worked in the Karolyis' gym before opening his own gym in Oklahoma. And Rick Newman, coach of Michelle Campi, had taught at the Houston warehouse for several years before leaving with Campi after getting involved with the gymnast's mother. They moved to California, where Geza Pozsar, the Romanian choreographer who had defected with the Karolyis in 1981, had set up shop. The rest of the gymnasts on the team—Betty Okino, Hilary Grivich, Zmeskal, and Strug—were more straightforwardly Karolyi kids. (At one point, he had a group of six top-ranked elites that were referred to as the "Karolyi six-pack," which seemed to be as much a commentary on their trim, muscular physiques as it was on the number of athletes receiving his instruction.) Just ten years after arriving in the United States, the Karolyis were responsible, at least in part, for every single member of the World Championship team.

At the same time that the Karolyis were climbing to the top of the American gymnastics heap with their athletes, the rumors about their harsh training methods had begun to circulate in the media. In

1992, *Sports Illustrated*'s Richard O'Brien reported on the discontent among the coaching ranks.

> There are plenty of people, other coaches mostly, who see Karolyi as a kind of Coach Dracula, menacing the red-blooded American system ... Talk to some national-level coaches and you will hear Karolyi accused of everything from raging egotism to intimidation of judges to violation of the child labor laws. His peers paint a picture of Karolyi as a ruthless Svengali, overworking his innocent young gymnasts for his own megalomaniacal needs. "You watch Bela on TV and then you watch him in the gym, you see a different man," says one national team coach who insists on anonymity ... "He's used to a totalitarian system," says another coach.

Karolyi brushed those criticisms aside as utterances of those jealous of his success. "I am challenging the system, challenging their sweet mediocrity ... All I am saying is you must push hard. And you must have the highest standards," he said in response to the allegations.

In 1995, Joan Ryan published the bestseller *Little Girls in Pretty Boxes*, which looked at the dark underbelly of elite gymnastics and figure skating. In the gymnastics sections of the book, Ryan's primary target was Bela Karolyi. She accused him of terrorizing his athletes through yelling and insulting them. She claimed that the coach's weight-directed barbs caused many of his gymnasts to develop eating disorders and other body image problems. Ryan also interviewed several athletes who spoke of training through injuries ranging from the moderate to the severe.

Complaints against the coaching duo go all the way back to

their time in Romania. Szabo spoke about the omnipresent hunger. "I truly learned what suffering from hunger means," she recalled. (Szabo was actually an ethnic Hungarian, like the Karolyis. The government changed her first name from Katalin to Ecaterina to make it sound more Romanian.) In response to this declaration, Canadian coach Rick McCharles blogged, "I'll always remember how skinny the Romanian girls were at the 1979 World Championships under the Karolyis. Story was that they were locked in a training camp with no way to beg extra food."

They brought some of their tactics, including the food monitoring, to the States when they defected. Claudia Miller, Shannon Miller's mother, wrote about the food restriction in her memoir, *My Child, My Hero*. Though she wasn't trained by the Karolyis, Miller was under their jurisdiction during the 1992 Olympics and the training camp in France that preceded it. Miller had complained to her mother that she was hungry while working out in France. Claudia put together a food package for her daughter and passed it on to Nunno, Miller's personal coach, who claimed to have not known about the food restrictions. He promised to pass it on to Miller.

There were other Karolyi tactics that raised eyebrows. Ziert, who gave Karolyi his first gymnastics job in the United States as coach of the University of Oklahoma women's team (Ziert was then the head coach of the men's program), recalled an anecdote from an international competition in 1983 in a 1992 profile in *SI*. Bela was already coaching in the United States and, "During warm-ups for the vault, I noticed that [Boriana] Stoyanova of Bulgaria, who three months before had won the World Championships on vault, was using a springboard setup that was against the rules. I told Bela and said we should tell the judges. He'd already spotted it. 'Not yet,' he said. 'Wait till after warm-ups.' Then, right before Stoyanova went up to compete, Bela protested. They changed the board on Stoya-nova, and she wiped out on the vault. Mary Lou won that event."

In this matter, Karolyi's actions demonstrated a certain kind of shrewdness, a penchant for strategic thinking that has been some-thing of a trademark for him throughout his coaching career. He saw his job as more than simply training athletes and preparing them for competitions, but as also managing PR and creating opportunities for them in the highly subjective sport. In his memoir and countless interviews, Karolyi spoke about the strategy he employed in 1976 to get maximum attention for the Romanian team. Karolyi wrote about how when the Romanian team was being introduced for the first time before the start of podium training, he didn't let them go out to greet the audience, which had just welcomed the defending champion Soviet women. "A man ran up to me and yelled, 'It's your turn, you must enter the arena'. . . I pretended I didn't understand what they wanted. We did not move," he wrote. The Romanians were announced two more times, but still, the team did not enter the arena. " 'Sir,' Nadia whispered, 'they are calling us to the floor, shouldn't we go in?' "

"Let them wait for us," he told her. "Let us get the audience's attention." Karolyi was trying to set the stage for his gymnasts, who were largely unknown and came from a country better known for vampires than for flipping. According to his account, by the time the gymnasts—who were dressed identically and perfectly coiffed as though for competition, not practice—entered, the crowd was going nuts. In that training session, they did full routines with all of the elements as opposed to partial ones with watered-down skills. This was a dress rehearsal but with the media and fans present. The Romanians, not the Soviets, had become the center of attention.

Whether this is entirely accurate or partly apocryphal, it shows that the Karolyis bucked the gymnastics maxim that the only strategy for winning is focusing on your own performance. There's more you can do—you can manipulate the crowd to pay attention to you, you can wait until the last minute to point out an equipment problem of an opponent. You just have to be willing to do it this way. Which the Karolyis were.

Some modern-day gymnastics fans might look back on these sorts of tactics with disapproval. After all, the sport is not adversarial in the most basic sense of the word. Gymnasts aren't really supposed to try to impact the performances of their competitors. In theory, what one athlete does on the beam shouldn't affect what the other does on vault or on bars. Gymnastics is not basketball, where one player can block an opposing player's shot. Or football, where you can tackle someone to the ground to prevent him from scoring. In gymnastics, you're supposed to dance like no one's watching, so to speak. Or like you're not competing against anyone. Many gymnasts talk about "competing against themselves" when they are out on the apparatus similar to the way runners talk about beating a time, not a person.

But Karolyi didn't come out of gymnastics. Several of the sports that he participated in—including handball and boxing—were downright adversarial. Even as a coach, he never took his eye off his opponents. And he brought that mentality with him to gymnastics as a coach.

Despite the tough coaching tactics and because of the fierce advocacy he often showed for his gymnasts, many of his former athletes from the 1980s and 1990s have remained close to him and Martha. In 2013, the pair celebrated their fiftieth wedding anniversary, and many of their former gymnasts came down to the ranch to celebrate with them, including a couple who had spoken out against them, such as Kristie Phillips. All these years later, many of these women are now coaches or judges, or in some way still affiliated with the sport. And with the Karolyis.

More than thirty years after the Karolyis' defection, U.S. gymnastics and the Karolyis are basically inseparable. While one could argue that their arrival in the States merely coincided with the rise of American gymnastics—that U.S. gymnasts had already started to climb the international rankings by then—it's too difficult to tease apart the threads and figure out what is and isn't attributable to the Romanian couple. There's no way of knowing how the sport would have progressed in the United States had the Karolyis not defected to come here.

Walker believes that the couple has played a significant role in the development of the sport in the United States. "I attribute a lot of the American success to the Karolyis," he said. "Back in the late 1980s, early 1990s, when they walked on the floor, they normally had the kid to beat. Whether or not it was the number one kid or the number two kid, you knew they were not going to miss." And while there were good coaches and good gymnasts in the United States when they arrived, there wasn't an expectation of success. The Karolyis, fresh off their wins with the Romanians, gave the Americans an expectation that they could and should be winning. (They also were pretty good at spotting trends, predicting the era of the power gymnast, the one we're currently living in, thirty years early.)

Those few years of no medals after their second retirement in 1996 certainly made it seem like the Karolyis were inextricably bound up in U.S. gymnastics success. Walker stated as much. "The problem was Martha and Bela had retired and we didn't have anybody pushing us," he said of the 1997–2000 quadrennium. "There wasn't a driving force."

When the semicentralized national team training camp system was introduced in late 1999, it was heralded as something new, a melting pot approach—taking the Eastern way of centralization combined with the American tradition of independent gyms. But this idea dated all the way back to the '70s, if not earlier.

In 1976, Lars Kolsrud, reporting in *International Gymnast* from a competition between Norway and East Germany, interviewed Helmut Gerschau, one of the East German head coaches, who described the small nation's gymnastics training system, which was second only to the Soviets' at the time. He told Kolsrud that he was one of four head coaches, one for each of the primary gymnastics training centers. Ten times a year—or nearly once a month—all of the coaches and best gymnasts were brought together to ensure they all "pull in the same direction." It also gave the gymnasts the opportunity to work with other coaches and get used to their techniques.

Since 1999, the Americans have experimented with a version of the East German system, with selected athletes (and their coaches) attending monthly national team training camps at the Karolyi Ranch. And it's not just the system organization that is imported from the former Eastern bloc gymnastics powers—the majority of the coaching talent has also been imported from abroad. In addition to the Karolyis, who were among the earliest of the transplanted gymnastics coaches, you have Valeri Liukin, a 1988 Olympic gold medalist for the USSR, who owns two gyms in the Dallas area and is in charge of the developmental programs in USA Gymnastics. (He is also father and coach to 2008 Olympic gold medalist Nastia Liukin.) Liang Chow, a former member of the Chinese national team, coached Shawn Johnson and Gabrielle Douglas to Olympic gold medals for the United States. Mihai and Sylvia Brestyan emigrated from Romania and started a gym outside of Boston where they coached Alicia Sacramone and Aly Raisman to World and Olympic titles. The list of high-level coaches that moved West from the East in the 1990s is seemingly endless and has had a tremendous impact on the recent successes enjoyed by the American women at the international level. The United States, by far, has been the biggest beneficiary of the breakup of the Soviet Union, at least gymnastically speaking.

Overseeing this large system of camps and coaching personalities is Martha Karolyi. She has been the national team coordinator since 2001, when her more famous husband stepped aside. (Or was forced out, depending on who is telling the story.) At times, NBC has made Martha, not the gymnasts, the star of its domestic gymnastics coverage. The commentators frequently wonder on air about what Martha is thinking—*Who does she like? Whom will she choose for the team?* During training sessions at major national competitions, the media and spectators pay nearly as much attention to Karolyi observing the gymnasts as they do the gymnasts themselves. I can't say that I blame them. For some reason, watching a Romanian immigrant in her seventies wearing a warm-up suit walk briskly around the competition floor as though she were part of a morning walk with Jewish seniors in Boca Raton, Florida, is oddly compelling.

But it's not just the Soviet brain drain that's boosting American medal numbers. There's an ever-increasing number of homegrown coaches who are bringing talent up the ranks. And that is also due, in large part, to the training camp system.

Every month, when a select number of gymnasts are invited to the Karolyi Ranch—national team members and some other promising gymnasts—their coaches accompany them to Texas, where they are able to exchange information with other, often more experienced, coaches. To put it into Sheryl Sandberg–ian phrasing, these young coaches are encouraged to "lean in." The camps are the equivalent of "continuing education" for coaches.

Mary Lee Tracy, assistant coach of the 1996 Olympic team and personal coach to gold medalists Amanda Borden and Jaycie Phelps, spoke about how much easier it is for young instructors to learn than it was in her day when she was coming up. "When I was in their position at their age, it wasn't like this," she said. "You had to search and beg for information. Now it's at your fingertips. And everyone is more welcoming. The older coaches are more welcoming."

Back then, it fell to just one or two coaches to figure out everything for a talented gymnast—from drills to progressions to training plans to competition schedules. "Before, it was all up to the individual coach to get the kid where they need to go," Wendy Bruce, a 1992 Olympic bronze medalist, pointed out. "It was on Rita and Kevin [Brown] to produce me. They didn't have a lot of help, nor did they ask for a lot of help, nor did they bring anyone in."

Part of the reluctance to bring anyone in to help had to do with the very reasonable fear that this coach might take the athlete with him when he left for another job or to open his own gym. During Bruce's career, "gym hopping" was rampant, and coaches were trying to hold on to the gymnasts they had spent years developing. If possession is nine-tenths of the law, then the coach who walks into the Olympic arena with a gymnast "owns" more than nine-tenths of the credit. As far as the media and sponsors are concerned, the previous coaches are unimportant.

But nowadays, coaches worry less about losing their top-notch talent because they are able to acquire the requisite knowledge to train an elite athlete from national team staff. "I think the national team training camp is a great system that helps the coaches and athletes," Chow said. And with the frequent changes to the *Code of Points*, which can be difficult even for the coaches to parse at times, the camps help the coaches work through the complex rulebook to help construct routines that are best for their gymnasts. "I think the training camp really delivers wonderful information, valuable information to us."

Kelly Manjak, a Canadian coach with several of the top NCAA gymnasts and Canadian national team members, spoke in admiration of the American system. "All of these coaches are popping out of the woodwork. It's amazing to watch," he said.

And unlike in the bad old days, such as the ones that Bruce, Tracy, and Walker talked about when coaches were worried about losing their athletes to more established programs and instructors, the current system encourages gymnasts to stay put.

"They're telling them [the gymnasts] to stay and 'We'll help you where you are.' That's what Martha told me—they want to build a lot of clubs," Manjak added. The increasing number of clubs and coaches acts as an enormous dragnet on talent, helping USA Gymnastics find that rare prodigy who will become an Olympic champion.

"There are only so many Simone Bileses. The trick is to find them," I said to Manjak.

"And then take care of them," he responded. "In Canada, we're not taking care of them. There's no resource for our Simone Biles. We're not going to fly you out every month and give you homework and you come back and keep showing us."

Biles's own coach agreed. "I just got an incredible amount of education from the national staff," Boorman said. "They see Simone, they see her talent, and they know that I didn't have the tools necessarily to get her where she needed to be. So instead of saying, 'Simone, you need to go to another gym,' they said, 'Aimee, we're going to teach you how to get her where she needs to be.' I will forever be grateful for that because now I feel like I am a coach of a World Champion, not like I was somebody who had talent that I let slip away because I was too afraid to get my hands in there and work for it."

"I think it's way less common than it used to be," Tracy said of the gym hopping that was rampant during the '80s and '90s. But it's not completely past nor will it ever be. "It'll always be there because of personal needs. Some cities don't have the high-level program a kid needs, and sometimes there is just conflict," she added. "But overall because there are more programs developing high-level athletes and doing a really good job, kids just don't find the need to move as much."

The division of labor with the national team staff in charge of management and strategy and the personal coaches responsible for developing athletes is a boon to a coach like Boorman. "That's Martha's thing is to decide who she thinks is going to be able to win because that's how she puts the team together. I, as Simone's coach, just have to keep training her," she said. Boorman has to focus only on her athlete; she is not responsible for larger, strategic decisions.

Though the coaches and athletes put a very positive spin on the camps, Nassar admitted that the early days of these camps was quite rough. First, there were the living conditions. "The gymnasts were quartered in these rustic rooms compared to what they have now," he said. Hilton, a corporate sponsor of USA Gymnastics, has revamped the cabins where the national team gymnasts bunk.

"The social break room was in the middle room where the coaches were at," he added. "We're trying to work out their injuries while the coaches and judges are sitting there playing cards and drinking beer and wine." To expect the gymnasts to be able to relax in this setting, surrounded by the very coaches who had been drilling them just thirty minutes before, was ludicrous. The athletes now have their own break room, apart from the coaches and the other adults. "It was a tough, tough time, those camps. It was very hard from a mental and physical standpoint."

This separation—between coach and athlete during leisure time—is something that 2012 gold medalist McKayla Maroney would like to see applied to mealtime, too. In 2016, when she announced her retirement from the sport in a podcast interview, Maroney spoke of some changes she'd like to see at future camps. "Make a different spot where the gymnasts can eat so we don't have to eat next to our coaches," she suggested. It's hard for the athletes to eat freely and to satisfaction with their coaches around. "We just walk out early 'cause it's not worth eating with them, so we just don't eat," she said.

There were other troubles with food at the early camps. "The kids' luggage would get checked for food in the past. Many coaches did that," Nassar said. "That doesn't happen anymore because we've changed that culture. We have seen that by educating the kids and placing trust in them, giving them a greater sense of self-responsibility, most of the time, they will do the right things." And it's not as if the gymnasts don't understand that their diet and weight are important components to athletic success. They're tested on their physical abilities at the start of every camp. "By physical abilities, we can see if they're out of shape," he said.

If you're going to do well at the physical abilities tests, you must, as Henry David Thoreau once wrote, "Condition, condition, condition!" (I might have paraphrased a little.) The American coaches, who were once in an actual arms race with the Karolyis to have the fittest athletes out on the floor, have redoubled their efforts to strengthen their gymnasts so they can perform difficult elements repeatedly. And, of course, make major teams. Sands noted that the United States had changed the culture to be fanatical about conditioning. "They're strong enough now to do what you ask them to do. You don't have to rely on adrenaline," he said.

Tracy pointed out that a slight downside to this maniacal emphasis on increasing physical conditioning is a commensurate loss of flexibility. "A lot of people are adding yoga and flexibility classes because as these muscles are being developed, we have to spend more time on flexibility and range of motion," she explained. Flexibility, or the lack thereof, has been one of the areas for which American gymnasts have been criticized. From what Tracy said, it seems to stem not just from selection—finding gymnasts who are a little stiffer yet stronger than the rest—but by training design. It's a trade-off. In order to do the more complex acrobatic skills, the Americans have buffed up, but that has compromised the dancerlike flexibility prized by most gymnasts.

It also has changed the look of the modern gymnast. She is hardly the slender naïf of the '70s. Sands is pleased with this shift. "There were the overly skinny kids for a while," he noted. "There was a brief spurt of strong muscular girls—Mary Lou Retton was an example. And then it went back [to skinny]. And now it's kind of gone back [to muscular]. I hope it never goes back. Strong explosive athletes are, indeed, healthier, better able to withstand the rigors."

Kim Zmeskal-Burdette (the 1991 World Champion later married Chris Burdette, changed her name, and opened the respected Texas Dreams Gym) has also noticed the change in body shape and type. "There isn't one way, there isn't one body type," she said. "There's so many ways to put the puzzle together.

"I have to say that I was kind of shocked at it because obviously

I grew up in a system that seemed like we were all very similar. Characteristics of who they had the most success with, not that we're identical, but similar characteristics," she observed. Indeed, if you glanced down the line at the 1992 Olympic team, they all basically looked the same (with the exception of the tallish Okino). All within a few inches of one another, all with slimly muscular physique, all around the same age.

But even as the American gymnasts get stronger and amass difficulty levels that surpass those of their nearest international rivals, they are not recklessly and wantonly throwing skills. Elements are added carefully, incrementally even. Skills that are not properly mastered are taken out of routines. At the 2012 Olympic Trials, Ross had been struggling mightily on her Amanar, crashing it repeatedly. Karolyi advised gymnast and coach to pull it from her program and replace it with the simpler double twisting vault, which she has performed successfully ever since.

This was in keeping with the Karolyis' career-long philosophy about gymnastics. Above all else, they prized not virtuosity but consistency in their gymnasts. "I think the Karolyis were criticized for that quite a bit in the past of 'Oh, but they're not doing the most difficult things,' and I remember us always going 'Does it matter? . . . We're trying to get the highest score,' " Zmeskal-Burdette said. To do that, they did the gymnastics they knew they could, without a doubt, hit day in, day out. No flashy stuff.

Consistency isn't just a trait Martha Karolyi values in her gymnasts; it's one she prizes in herself. When asked about her reputation for being strict in an interview with *International Gymnast* in 2006, she answered, "I don't know if I'd say I'm strict. I'd rather say that I'm very consistent in my expectations."

The closest I got, physically at least, to the national team training camp was the office of Dr. David Toronjo, father of former elite gymnast Macy Toronjo. (My request to visit the training camp and interview the Karolyis was rejected by USA Gymnastics.) Toronjo lives and works in Huntsville, which is just a fifteen-minute drive from the national team gymnastics facility in New Waverly. Toronjo has been there a few times to drop his daughter off and pick her up after stints at the famed facility. Toronjo, however, barely made it past the parking lot during these excursions. He would help his daughter to her cabin and then leave. Five days later, he'd wait in the parking lot for her until she emerged with her gear.

Toronjo did this only a handful of times—Macy, though once elite, was never a member of the national team and has never competed internationally for the United States. For her, the training camps were more infrequent occurrences. She didn't go every month like national team members do, so she never got into the rhythm of them the way that others did.

What Toronjo stressed about his daughter and others like her is her regimentation. These are extremely organized and disciplined young women, more Tracy Flick in *Election* (but a little lighter on the scheming) than slacker, like April Ludgate on *Parks and Recreation*. The camps can take some getting used to for many of the gymnasts, not just the pressure and expectation of them but also the disruption to their daily routines. In order for these athletes to find time for their training and education, they have to be organized practically to the point of OCD. "They can't exist in that unless they can really be regimented," he said. "One of the challenges for Macy going to the ranch is for her to step out of that bubble. It interfered with her normal routine," Toronjo added.

It's not just the company and the surroundings that are different—their workouts are different. "Generally these girls don't do vault and floor twice a day, but when they're at camp, they do it twice a day, every day. Their legs are really sore," Boorman said. On the flip-side, Boorman acknowledged, the training sessions at camp aren't as long as the ones at their home gyms. "At home, they do more conditioning, and at camp they do more skills."

Maroney spoke of the strain that the camps placed on the gymnasts, especially as a major competition like the Olympics loomed. "It's just scary in there," she said. "You feel like every move, this is me making the team or not. And that moment and that amount of pressure had been building up for years."

"The expectation is always very high, especially on beam. Like your feet don't hit the floor except on a dismount," Boorman said.

But the athletes eventually find their way at the camps, creating routines for themselves at the ranch similar to the ones they have at home. And though travel to and from the camps can be disruptive to the gymnasts' routines and schooling, it is a boon to them, socially speaking. Most elite gymnasts in the United States, unless they're fortunate enough to compete on large teams of elites or pre-elites, do not train with many teammates who are at or near their level. "I think for the girls it's important because I would say maybe less than half of them are actually in a public high school or in high school at all," Boorman pointed out. "Most of them are home-schooled, so their interactions are very limited socially. So even if they have friends that are outside of gyms, they're not experiencing homecoming and prom and whatever silly things they're doing in the high school environment. I think one of the best things is they get to go to camp and commiserate on how they miss out on those things. It makes them feel like they're not some kind of social leper because there are other people that are sacrificing the same things as them to achieve the goals that they want."

Zmeskal-Burdette seconded Boorman's point about camaraderie, recalling how different it was from the bad old days. "These kids travel internationally, and it basically is their buddies versus what it was in generations past where you showed up and a lot of times the coaches didn't even have you sit together with the other team [members]. It was very individual," she said.

Elizabeth Price was one of those homeschooled gymnasts who traveled from Pennsylvania down to the ranch during her elite career. She was eleven the first time she was invited to train there. While she didn't speak about the physical and emotional dislocation that Toronjo spoke of, she admitted that it was hard in the beginning. "It was a little intimidating the first time I went, because when I went down there, there were girls who I idolized as a kid. Shayla Worley was there with Ivana Hong," she said, referring to members of the 2007 World Championship team and the 2008 Olympic alternate.

"At the time," she continued, "I was, like, 'There is no way I'm at the same level as these girls.' I felt so out of place." Price would eventually settle into life at camp and would go on to become the 2012 Olympic alternate as well as the 2014 World Cup series all-around champion. As for Hong, the gymnast Price had admired when she first arrived at camp, the two would become teammates on Stanford's gymnastics team.

At camp, one of the messages that the national team staff hammered into the gymnasts was their good fortune at being part of the best team in the world. "They always say that you are training with the best coaches in the world; that is why we're the best," Price said.

"It's inspiring," she continued, "because it means that we have the opportunity, all the girls have the opportunity, to maintain the status of being the best . . . All the girls have been through this and been coached by these people and they were the best, therefore I can be the best."

But camp also can be stressful for the same reason. "It is a little intimidating because you're almost, like, expected to carry on that legacy and maintain the status of being the best in the world." Price's statements demonstrate the primacy of the system over any individual athlete. While the media may be focused on finding the next big superstar, the national team training staff recognizes that any given gymnast can be injured on game day and when that happens, you're only as good as your bench. And the gymnasts might spend just a few years on the national team and in high-level competition. The continuous success of the system is dependent on the continuity in coaching, not on any one individual athlete.

In addition to providing top-notch instruction, the national team training staff encourages competitiveness among the gymnasts. Every camp begins with physical abilities testing, and the girls are ranked according to their strength and speed. "We have physical abilities testing where they test our strength in certain things like rope climbing and cast handstands. At the end of each camp, they award the top three places in those age groups. Those girls receive praise for how well they've done and their strength and everything. Everyone wants to receive that from the national staff and Martha," Price said.

The national team staff also ranks the athletes according to their gymnastics abilities. At the end of each camp, both coach and gymnast know where they stand. When I asked Price whether selection to major international teams comes as a shock to an athlete, she said that although it sometimes comes as a surprise, "more often you can tell based on how well you do at training camps and the feedback you get from Martha and other coaches. You can tell when you have a chance of making the team.

"I knew I was pretty set to make the PacRims [Pacific Rim Championships] team based on how well I had been doing and also how the other seniors were," she continued. "Some of them were hurt. So I knew some of them weren't going to be on the team, and some of them were coming off of competitions, and they had not done all their routines." They're not exactly shocked like Miss America when the tiara is placed on their heads.

These gymnasts, after all, are quite experienced when it comes to monthly evaluations. Even before they started attending the national team training camps, many of the top-ranked gymnasts in the United States were going to the developmental camps, which are the feeder system of the national team camps, the farm team to USA Gymnastics's professional league. None of the gymnasts that attend the development camps is on the national team—junior or senior—and none of them is close to being able to represent the United States in international competition. Some of the gymnasts at the "devo camps," as they are called, are not even elites yet. As the name implies, these camps are for the development of promising athletes. And the man who directs these camps is Liukin.

Walker had one gymnast regularly invited to the devo camps. He described them as mirroring the national team ones in almost all aspects. "The practices are identical. You walk into camp, you line up, whether it's Martha or Valeri," he said. Then Valeri states the purpose of the camp—whether it's a working camp, where they show skills, or a verification camp, where you're expected to show routines or sequences. The coaches, Walker explained, are usually told ahead of time whether it's a verification or a working camp so they know how to best prepare their gymnasts.

"The difference is: mistakes with Valeri are acceptable as long as you're working in the right direction. With Martha, she doesn't want to see mistakes. She wants to see consistency," he said.

There is not just one path to the developmental camps. Some there are kids who were marked early after they did exceptionally well in the Talent Opportunity Programs, better known as TOPs. In Walker's case, Liukin approached him and his gymnast at the Level 9 state championship in Texas. After his athlete successfully performed a handspring-style vault, which requires a lot of lower-body power and is an unusual choice for such a small gymnast, Liukin told Walker, "I want her at camp."

"He tries to find coaches that are doing good things so he can pull them into the system and help develop more kids," Walker said. Liukin and Walker realize that it's a numbers game—to find the five gymnasts who will compose the Olympic team and various World Championship teams, you need to bring as many talented athletes as possible into the fold. And no one has numbers like the United States does.

What the Karolyis had always agitated for was selecting the teams and lineups as close to the Olympics as possible. They felt that choosing a team too far in advance was a mistake. Bela wanted to find the gymnasts who would be the best on the day of the event—not even a month beforehand. If he had been allowed to, he would have named the Olympic team right before they saluted the judges for competition. And with the new training camps and selection procedures, the Karolyis' dreams came true.

The first Olympic team during Martha's tenure as national team coordinator was chosen, not at nationals but at a selection camp held at the ranch less than a month before the Games in 2004. After two consecutive days of competition meant to mirror the schedule the gymnasts would face in Athens, the Olympic prospects sat down on folding chairs and looked toward Karolyi, who on a slip of paper in her hands held their fates. All of this drama was being broadcast on live television.

Hollie Vise, then sixteen, was the defending co–World Champion on the uneven bars in 2003 but had spent the 2004 season enduring a growth spurt and a back injury. She was not yet fully recovered and in prime physical condition. She competed only on her two specialties, bars and beam, and had not done particularly well on one of them. As she sat there waiting for Martha to name the team, she could have only been hoping for the United States national team coordinator to take her past performances into consideration.

"Who will be on Martha Karolyi's Olympic team?" NBC's Andrea Joyce asked, ramping up the drama before the selection committee walked into the gym to tell the thirteen assembled gymnasts and their coaches the outcome. Though there are three members of the selection committee, as far as the media was concerned, Martha's was the most important voice in the room. And 2004 was the first Olympic year that Martha was not sharing the spotlight with her husband. This would be Martha's Olympic team, her first.

As Karolyi began to read off the names of the chosen few in her trademark singsong Hungarian lilt, her voice rising at the end of words and names, NBC's cameras panned the row of girls for their reactions. The network seemed to relish the opportunity to show young women getting their dreams dashed in real time. It was like the "rose ceremony" on *The Bachelor* or like a YA novel set in a dystopian future where kids have to kill each other to survive. But unlike reality TV show contestants, the gymnasts hadn't signed up for this kind of exposure. They were just trying to make the Olympic team—they were not there for any other kind of fame.

The camera lingered on Vise, who was clearly trying to blink back tears. The camera panned to the other girls who were not named—Liz Tricase biting her lip, Carly Janiga shifting uncomfortably—but repeatedly returned to Vise. She was the most decorated gymnast in the lot to have been left off of the team. Even her co–World Champion on the uneven bars, Chellsie Memmel, had been named to one of the three alternate positions.

In 2010, Vise gave an interview to *Inside Gymnastics* at the end of her collegiate gymnastics career. When asked about the Olympic team naming six years prior, she said, "It felt as bad as it looked. Worse probably." Vise said she knew that she was unlikely to make it based on her performance at verification. She had fallen off beam. As Price noted, the gymnasts are not stupid. They often know where they rank even without the officials telling them. She had been hoping that the committee would keep in mind all of her past gymnastics achievements, "but I was a little prepared," she said.

What she was not prepared for was having to keep it together on live TV. "The camera zooming in on me while I just sat there. I was like, 'Go focus on the Olympic team,' and my coaches are trying to hide me by hugging me, but the camera person is [shooting] around them. And seriously? That's evil."

USA Gymnastics learned slowly from that debacle. In 2008, the team selection was announced behind closed doors at camp, and the chosen few were then sent out to greet the limited number of friends and families who journeyed to New Waverly for the announcement. This took place after yet another selection camp, which had followed the Olympic Trials, which came after the National Championships. Before the official announcement, Alicia Sacramone complained to the *New York Times* about the uncertainty of still not knowing, after so much competition, about whether or not she was on the 2008 Olympic team. "It's annoying and nerve-racking and, really, it hurts a lot not to know already," she said.

Karolyi seemed to believe that if a gymnast was named to a team with too much time to spare, she'd relax in her training. "That's why she keeps everybody on edge until the last moment because she doesn't want people to think, 'Oh you're a lock, or you're a shoo-in,' and you're not going to give effort anymore," Dominique Moceanu, a former Karolyi star who has written critically about the pair, surmised. "But that's not the right mentality and the right approach. Once you've made it, you're like, 'Yes, I want to work hard.' "

Sacramone was eventually named to the team as nearly everyone had predicted. That was a dream come true for the twenty-year-old who missed out on her first shot in 2004. Unfortunately, she did not have a dream Olympics. She, like other members of the team, arrived in Beijing seemingly physically and emotionally exhausted. "If you're expected to be, you know, at that top game every single day, all the time, well, the body starts to break down. Not only does the body break down, but the mind breaks down. The mind cannot handle that kind of stress all the time," Moceanu pointed out.

In 2008, there were two significant injuries—one a few days before the competition and one during the last moments of warm-ups before the Americans' first event was set to start. And then Sacramone, the team's captain and emotional core, fell twice during team finals. The media blamed her for the team's silver medal behind China, but in reality, the United States would have lost even if Sacramone had performed perfectly. They had entered the Olympics at a distinct start value disadvantage. They were behind the Chinese, in terms of scoring potential, before the competition had even started. The strategy the Americans were employing in 2008 was to perform perfectly and expect their rivals to falter, which is how they had won their World title over the Chinese in 2007. Maybe the real piece of cruelty that was done to the team was feeding the media's speculation that they were the favorites to win when, in fact, they were never fully in control of their Olympic fate.

Two injuries, uncharacteristic falls in competition, and pictures of unhappy-looking gymnasts, however, are not data; they're anecdote. It's hard to draw causal conclusions from the lengthy, draining selection procedures used in 2008 to the injuries, both physical and emotional, sustained by the team members. "Overtraining," the catchall diagnosis for any of the above, can only be applied after the fact. And at the Olympics, all of the gymnasts, not just the Americans, were beat up due to the hard training it takes to get to that point. But the U.S. gymnasts looked unusually worn out compared to their Chinese rivals. Of course, the Chinese spark could have been due to performing in front of an enthusiastic crowd. They could have been animated by the support the same way that the 1996 Olympic team was spurred on by the boisterous audience in Atlanta.

Still in *International Gymnast*, Dwight Normile questioned the wisdom of the extended selection procedures used by the Americans. "A selection process involving three two-day competitions—two public, one private—within six weeks is a lot to ask from a psychological aspect alone. And it comes at the end of a four-year cycle when just about every gymnast is either coming off of a serious injury or coping with a variety of new ones."

These voices of dissent grew louder both from outside and inside the gymnastics community—even John Geddert, coach to 2011 World Champion Jordyn Wieber, criticized the lack of rest days in the team's preparation schedule for the World Championships in Tokyo. "I would've liked to see a few more strategically assigned rest days," he wrote. "There were none, and thus, this process was simply grueling. I am not saying it is not needed, but I would not be honest if I conveyed that it was paradise. From September 5 through the end of Worlds (if all went according to plan), we were looking at forty-two days and two days off (three if you count the thirteen-hour plane ride travel day as a day off)."

In 2012, USA Gymnastics seemed to get some, if not all, things right. The team was selected behind closed doors right after competition at Olympic Trials was over. The girls who did not make it were allowed to weep and be consoled in private, and the gymnasts who made the cut were sent back out into the arena, tears of joy streaming down their faces, to celebrate in front of the television cameras and a packed house in San Jose. With the exception of Ross, every single one of the team members was ugly-crying like Claire Danes in *Homeland*. The 2012 Olympic team got to enjoy their moment.

Despite this heartwarming display in San Jose, some uncertainty lingered for members of the team that would become known as the "Fierce Five." Maroney said, "They never say that you're on the team. They never say that until you're there and you've competed the first day. They're always like, 'We can switch you out,'" which was not an idle threat in her case since she was very injured in London.

Still, even Maroney admitted that the plan worked even if she sees room for improvement. "We got the gold medal so you can't really argue that that didn't work," she said.

"The 2012 team was closer than a lot of teams I've seen," Nassar said. He attributed their cohesion to what happened in 2011 when Sacramone, the team captain, tore her Achilles' tendon during podium training at the World Championships, just one day before the start of competition. She withdrew and flew back to Boston for surgery. Douglas, a neophyte and quite nervy in competition, was thrown into the meet on all four events and performed very well. Raisman assumed the role of team leader since she was the only one left with World Championships experience, having competed on the 2010 silver-medal-winning team. In Tokyo, the remaining girls seemed to bond over Sacramone's injury and the resultant adversity. They handily defeated the defending-champion Russians. It was the start of a winning streak that hasn't yet been snapped.

After that win, the scoring nucleus of the team stayed connected through digital and social media. These forms of digital outreach made camps easier to endure because the girls were able to remain connected to the outside world, to friends and family.

Social and digital media also helped this cohort remain connected between camps and competition. It wasn't just that they were seeing each other once a month but every day when they checked their Facebook, Twitter, and Instagram feeds. If you follow U.S. women's gymnastics on any social media platform, you can watch the gymnasts communicate with each other in real time, commenting on each other's posts, offering words of encouragement, and sending private jokes in the public square. While I'm wary about speculating about the relationships between teenage girls because I was one a long time ago and remember how volatile they could be—the hot and cold feelings, the feuds that lasted for hours or months or even years, the intensity that felt borderline romantic—I'd venture to say that most of these gymnasts are actually friends outside of the gym and the training camps.

The nucleus of the 2011 team—Wieber, Douglas, Raisman, and Maroney—composed the 2012 team, which also included Ross, who had been too young to compete in Tokyo. The performance of those five young women in London was the crowning moment of Martha Karolyi's career as national team coordinator. Unlike previous teams that had gone through the testing phases in the early aughts or had to transition from the 10 to the open-ended scoring system midway through the cycle like many members of the 2008 team had to, the 2012 team's path was relatively smooth. They progressed in a linear fashion, going from TOPs teams to developmental camps to national team training camps. They won a World team title and then an Olympic gold medal without missing a single routine in team competition. That's sixty hit routines from 2011–2012.

To use Karolyi's favorite word, they were "consistent."

8

A TALE OF TWO GYMS:
THE NEW WAVE OF AMERICAN COACHES

If you only watched women's gymnastics on TV and primarily from the '80s until the mid-'90s and you were asked to draw a caricature of a coach, you'd probably come up with something like: a tall, burly male with a bushy mustache, bear hugging a young girl less than half his size after she finished a routine in Olympic competition.

This portrait fits Bela Karolyi though it could also refer to several other coaches from that time, such as Steve Nunno, who seemed to have fashioned his public persona after the Romanian. Nunno, who coached Shannon Miller, greeted his protégée with the same type of theatrics and sported the same sort of facial hair.

NBC and other broadcasters relished these performances—the coaches', not just the gymnasts'—because they made for great television. The gymnasts tend to be young and shy and at times stoic, which doesn't exactly play well onscreen. They answered questions about the competition and performance with the banal, saying things like, "I just wanted to go out there and do my best," or "I wanted to hit four-for-four," referring to the number of apparatuses.

But the coaches were adults and emotionally demonstrative

where their athletes were reserved. NBC frequently used to leave open microphones on the coaches when their athlete was competing so the audience could hear their moment-to-moment reactions. During the 1996 Olympics as fourteen-year-old Dominique Moceanu was performing on the balance beam, you could hear Karolyi chanting from the sidelines. His mic'd-up excitement was nearly as deafening as the cheers of the sold-out crowd at the Georgia Dome. Even before Moceanu saluted the judges, the camera had already moved to Karolyi, who was celebrating the stuck dismount on the sidelines.

The media's focus on the coaches is understandable. If an elite female gymnast's career seems fruit-fly-lifespan short, then the coach's is "arc of the moral universe bends toward justice" kind of long. The most significant gymnastics coaches have been around the sport upward of thirty years, while several successive generations of gymnasts have competed and retired. As Leonid Arkayev, former Soviet and Russian head coach, wrote, "It is my strong belief that in modern gymnastics, the coach has the primary role and the gymnast, the secondary." The coaches, by virtue of their longevity, are the more influential characters in the sport.

And few had been more influential than Bela, both in training tactics and onscreen demeanor. Back when he was active on the competition floor, the coaches were seemingly larger than life. But the new wave of American coaches, led by Martha, the quieter of the two Karolyis, tend to be background players on the competition floor. There are still high fives and hugs, but the bear hug has seemingly gone extinct.

Also, unlike past top coaches, many of these newer coaches had been high-level gymnasts in their youth, winning World or Olympic gold medals for the United States or their country of origin during the post-Nadia modern era of the sport. They understand what their athletes are going through because they endured the same grueling training, competitive pressures, and injuries themselves. In many cases, they once did the same skills that they're now trying to teach. Sometimes this means that they adopt softer tactics when it comes to their own athletes. But at the very least, they can empathize with them. With these coaches, "I feel your pain" is often more than just a platitude—it's a fact.

The first afternoon I sat in on gymnastics practice at Texas Dreams in Coppell, a suburb just north of the Dallas/Fort Worth International Airport, a preteen in an aquamarine leotard rushed past me carrying an algebra textbook, her lower body dusted in chalk. She had probably just wrapped up her workout and was starting on her schooling hours. But nearly everything in this gym—or really any gym, for that matter—is coated with a sprinkling of magnesium. It's just as likely she could have gotten covered in white stuff by sitting on a mat (as I would later, rueing my decision to wear dark-colored pants). The gymnast headed to the tables and chairs in the rest area, which were set right behind a low barrier between the floor exercise mat and the observation zone where several parents and gymnasts were stationed. There were cupcakes out on the table, leftovers from a birthday party.

The girl in aquamarine was likely a member of the Texas Dreams competitive gymnastics team, which is approximately three hundred strong. And it is probable that she was homeschooled, as are many of the gymnasts that train at the Dallas gym. Some study solo, working through their classes and requirements online. Others attend an abbreviated school day at special academies sympathetic to the needs of the professional child-athlete. But some do their school-work in one of the three classrooms on the other side of the mirrors and the ballet bar. The Texas Dreams school serves approximately seventy students grades one through eight. Maria Froemming, the team coordinator, allowed me to peek into one classroom.

The classroom looked like one you'd find at a comparable lower school. There was a teacher at the helm reading from a book. Her students appeared grade-school age, and the room was colorfully decorated in laminated posters, each emphasizing a different alpha-numeric lesson. Except that in a typical public school, the classroom, not the gymnasium and the extracurriculars, is the focal point.

All of this homeschooling and independent study was a bit of a culture shock to someone from the Northeast, where the traditional school setup still predominates. But, as Froemming pointed out to me, it fits in very well with the culture of the region. "Texas is a big homeschool state," she explained.

And ever since Bela and Martha Karolyi bought their first gym in Houston in the early 1980s, Texas has been a big gymnastics state as well. At the 2015 NCAA Championships, 15 percent of the gym-nasts representing the qualified teams had done their club training in the Lone Star State. If Texas were once again an independent country, it would have no trouble fielding a world-beating Olympic team.

One of the Karolyis' most famous and successful American pro-tégées is one-half of the ownership team of Texas Dreams—Kim Zmeskal-Burdette, the gymnast who in 1991 became the first Amer-ican to win a World all-around title in the sport.

The other half of Texas Dreams is her husband, Chris Burdette. It was Burdette who devised and executed the classroom idea. When we spoke, he seemed equally excited about discussing the details of the business as he was talking about the athletes and the gymnastics. Zmeskal-Burdette had told me that she thinks of the process of creating routines as an "art project." For Burdette, the "art project" seemed to be figuring out new systems and business strategies for the sprawling gym. They started Texas Dreams in 2001, ten years after Zmeskal-Burdette Indianapolis triumph, though they've been in the large facility I visited only since 2013.

The school, he explained, was a solution to the problem of having a business that essentially shut down from 10:00 a.m. to 4:00 p.m. every single weekday. Those would be the hours when the gymnasts were in class—either homeschool or public or private. He would even sometimes turn the lights off in the cavernous 36,000-square-foot warehouse space, which sits on a stretch of Wrangler Drive filled with other similarly boxy, gray lookalike buildings.

Hosting school on the premises allowed Burdette to stagger team workouts throughout the day. While one group is in school, the other can be out on the equipment, and vice versa. The gym wouldn't be sitting empty for hours on end.

This also would decrease the competition for time on the equipment. Though there is an impressive amount of equipment at Texas Dreams—three full-floor exercise areas, eighteen regulation-height beams (as well as a variety of lower ones for practicing new elements), eight full sets of uneven bars, and with many single-rail stations, trampolines, Tumble Traks, and a wealth of primary-colored, plush training aids—nearly every piece is in use. This is especially true during the after-school hours, when the teams share space with the recreational program. Froemming wished that they had room for more apparatuses, though she did acknowledge that this would probably do little to ameliorate the congestion. The gymnasts and coaches would come up with new ways to spread out and fill the space. It's the same problem faced by traffic engineers—no matter how many lanes they add to the 405, the traffic never seems to diminish. If you build it, they will fill it, whether it's a freeway lane or a balance beam.

By the time four o'clock rolled around, Froemming's prediction— that the gym would become a madhouse—was fulfilled. Hundreds of gymnasts and dozens of coaches started their afternoon workouts, complete with Christmas song singing. (I visited in early December.) Amid all this din, the Dreams Team, which is composed of the elite and pre-elite gymnasts, were trying to do yoga, which they did every Tuesday before their second workout of the day. They started the class on the vault runway, which annoyed Froemming, the ringmaster, since another group was scheduled to use it for its intended purpose—vaulting. They always do this, she said to me. Froemming had set aside half of a floor mat for them to run through their sun salutations. But I understood why the Dreams Team routinely ignored her assignment—the vault runway, while not exactly Zen, was probably the quietest spot in the gym. It was the farthest point from the entrance, where a steady stream of parents and little gymnasts were coming and going.

It was Zmeskal-Burdette who introduced yoga to their weekly mix of stretching and conditioning. She's an avid practitioner and takes private sessions every Wednesday night. She credited it for helping restore some strength and range of motion in her wrist, which had been chronically injured during her days as an elite gymnast. In addition to her personal affinity for the practice, adding yoga or additional stretching to training has become something of a necessity in the current era of women's gymnastics that emphasizes strength building, which can compromise flexibility.

It's hard, however, to imagine her coaches, Martha and Bela, bringing something like yoga into the gym, but as she said in the FloGymnastics documentary about Texas Dreams, "Chris and I are not Martha and Bela. We don't have their background, we don't have their history. So the environment is lighter than what it was for me growing up."

Zmeskal-Burdette boiled down the differences in her and Chris's coaching styles from her own longtime coaches to the type of behavior they allow around the chalk tray. In a gym, the chalk tray is like the office water cooler—a place where everyone gathers at some point during the workout to chat. In Texas Dreams, the girls spoke excitedly and freely as they adjusted their hand guards between turns as Burdette hovered nearby, spotting gymnasts through pirouettes and handstands. The amount of time a gymnast spent reapplying chalk and adjusting her hand guards seemed directly proportional to the amount of time they spent eating mat after a fall. The rougher your practice seemed to be going, the more time you needed at the chalk bowl to talk and collect yourself for your next attempt.

Things were a little different for Zmeskal-Burdette back at Karolyi's in Houston. "The expectation was to not be talking, so we would start talking without moving our lips. Bela, in recent years, was like, 'I know I always used to hear sounds coming from that bowl, but I would look at you and no one was moving their mouths.' He thought he was hearing things," she recalled in the documentary.

Zmeskal-Burdette laughed as she recounted this anecdote. In fact, she did not appear bitter or resentful when talking about her time as a gymnast at the Karolyis'. She and Burdette have remained close to the legendary coaching duo. They even got married at the Karolyi Ranch, which is where the couple had met back when Zmeskal was attempting a comeback for the 1996 Olympics and Burdette was just starting out in gymnastics as a coach. On the Tuesday afternoon

I arrived at the Coppell gym, Burdette was wearing a new hunting jacket, which he had purchased in preparation for his upcoming trip to Nicaragua with Bela and a couple of the other national team coaches. The camouflage detail seemed to clash with his hipster, Warby Parker–esque black-framed glasses and ear-length straight brown hair.

Burdette's background in gymnastics is very different from that of his better-known wife. Serendipity seemed to be one of the major factors behind Zmeskal's ascent up the ranks. She just happened to be enrolled in recreational classes at a Houston gym that just happened to be bought by the Karolyis in 1982. Bela spotted her at age six and fast-tracked her toward elite and U.S. gymnastics history books. It seemed almost as perfectly scripted as Comaneci's gymnastics fairy tale.

"I was the exact opposite of Kim," Burdette told me. "I was really interested in gymnastics from a young age, had the body type, and I had the build, had the shape, and didn't have a gym that was less than thirty-five minutes away. So I did North Texas traditional-type sports, soccer since I was little, played football and got beat up on that football field. I was one hundred pounds."

"It's amazing to see how passion can come from two entirely different sides of the spectrum," his wife said with notable admiration. "You know, someone who's been in it their whole life and almost didn't know any better versus someone who wanted it forever and ever and learned everything about it."

When Burdette got his driver's license at sixteen, he drove to the nearest gymnastics club and tried out for the team—at the age when his future wife was retiring from the sport for the first time. After a short-lived competitive career, Burdette turned to coaching, eventually landing a job at the Karolyis' during the run-up to the 1996 Summer Olympics when the Romanians were coaching Dominique Moceanu, transplanted Belarusian Svetlana Boginskaya, Kerri Strug, and of course, Zmeskal.

Unlike the Dreams Team at Burdette's gym, which has to fight for space among the recreational groups, the elites at Karolyi's trained in a separate facility from the rest of the team. The other coaches seldom entered. One day, Bela called him in to ask him to help with some spotting. "So I came in during floor, shut the door behind me. The blinds are pulled, and I mean, even as coaches, we weren't allowed to watch that workout. And I came in and stood next to Bela while he finished up his work."

Burdette had been expecting to experience something uniquely intense. He had heard all kinds of stories about Karolyi. This was the mid-'90s, during the heyday of the *Little Girls in Pretty Boxes* era. Instead, what he saw seemed like an average gymnastics workout. He spotted the gymnasts through some basics on bars. "And when bars was over, they went to beam, he said, 'Okay, thanks.'" That was it. Burdette left to return to the optional gym. He remembered feeling disappointed at that first encounter with the elite program. "I kept walking around him going, 'Really? That's it?'"

Burdette told me that MTV had been interested in shooting a reality series based on Texas Dreams at one point. They even sent a camera crew and producer down to Coppell to shoot a pilot. "That went up the chain of command, and then it got to the top where the executive producers finally looked at it and they said, 'It's just not dramatic enough for us. It's a little dull,'" he recalled. Just like that one practice he witnessed at Karolyi's.

After spending two days watching practice at Texas Dreams, I can understand MTV's perspective. They were not actually interested in showcasing gymnastics. Rather, the producers were hoping that these practices would be the backdrop for greater interpersonal drama. Nearly all pop culture iterations of the sport—from the ABC Family soap opera *Make It or Break It* or the Jessica Bendinger movie *Stick It* to the *Law & Order: Special Victims Unit* episode about gymnastics (because there's an *SVU* episode about *everything*)—is built around a certain set of assumptions about adolescent female friendship: that the girls are catty, highly competitive with one another, and boy crazy. (And in the *SVU* example—spoiler alert!—homicidal.) These narratives are less about gymnastics and more about the media's expectations about how young women behave. That Texas Dreams failed to live up to those expectations is a point of pride for the coaching duo.

Even the falls weren't particularly dramatic. In practice, the stakes are relatively low. Falling in this setting is not a big deal, so long as you don't get injured. And since it was early in the season, the gymnasts were practicing their skills onto soft landing surfaces to minimize the pounding on their joints. The elites were several months away from their next competition, so they were in the skill-building phase. Bailie Key, the 2013 Junior National Champion and one of Texas Dreams's Olympic prospects for Rio, repeatedly missed the high bar as she attempted to catch a new release move. As a precaution, she wore heel guards, which were really just volleyball kneepads slid down to her ankles. These would protect the bottoms of her feet should she fly too close to the rail. That, however, was not her problem on that particular day. She was often too far from the bar, reaching over her straight legs for the rail, but not getting her hands back on the apparatus. Key landed on the mats underneath, fully prone. Then she picked herself back up and headed over to the chalk bowl to regroup. And of course, talk.

Because Olympic gymnastics is the only form of gymnastics to which the majority of the mainstream audience is exposed, many would probably believe that training elites is the goal of any gymnastics coach—just as they think the Olympics are the dream of any gymnast who does a cartwheel across the balance beam. But most gyms don't have elite programs. Burdette went into great detail, explaining the difficulty of maintaining a high-level program—the hours, the expense, the time spent out of the gym traveling to training camps and international competitions. If your gymnast is chosen for the World Championships, you'll be away from home for a month. If they're selected for the Olympics, you'll be gone even longer. And while you're away, you have to have someone to coach the remaining athletes and run the business.

In fact, Key, their star athlete, was a transplant from a gym south of Dallas because it had decided to drop its elite program around the time Key and teammate Macy Toronjo were thinking of making the jump to that level. That's when they decided to switch to Texas Dreams.

Toronjo had been training at Woodland Gymnastics Academy alongside Key. "They had an enormous amount of talent there," Toronjo's father noted. Talent notwithstanding, the gym owner decided to cancel the nascent elite program at WGA, which was a huge blow to the two coaches there who very carefully developed a bevy of gifted youngsters. These gymnasts would be forced to leave if they wanted to go elite. From the gym's standpoint, this made financial sense. An elite program can be a huge financial and manpower commitment, especially if resources are scarce. "You have to have these coaches that can go to the ranch. If they [the gymnasts] get chosen for an international assignment, you have to have a coach who can go to Italy. Or Japan," Toronjo explained, echoing the same points Burdette had made about managing a high-level team.

This is when Macy started agitating to move north to train at Texas Dreams. She had seen Zmeskal-Burdette at Texas meets and was quite taken with the former World Champion. Though Zmeskal-Burdette, at those competitions, probably didn't say more than three words to the young athlete, "She just had this passion for Kim," her father said. He said he even has a video of Macy watching Zmeskal-Burdette, then pregnant, coach her athletes at a competition. "I think that's what she made her decision on. She liked the way she [Kim] was coaching girls," he said.

Zmeskal-Burdette and her husband bring very different styles and temperaments to the table that seem to complement each other. "Chris jokes around with them all the time," Toronjo said. "Kim is focused. You don't see her on her cell phone. You don't see her chit-chatting around a whole bunch. She's laser focused. She's a World Champion." Zmeskal-Burdette may allow the girls to gossip at the chalk tray, but she's still very much a product of her disciplined gymnastics upbringing at the Karolyis.

Toronjo explained his daughter's move away from home at age twelve very matter-of-factly, first A then B then C. In his telling, Macy's move seemed almost inevitable. "They slowly develop this passion and then you, as the parent, you're just fading into the background." Their progress through the levels creates its own momentum, and for parents the choice seems to boil down to either get on the train or get off the tracks.

I arrived at Texas Dreams for the Wednesday morning workout at roughly seven and walked into the cavernous gym with Burdette. The Dreams Team was already assembled. This, I learned, was something of an unwritten rule both at the gym and at the Karolyi

Ranch, where being on time was tantamount to being tardy. Martha Karolyi expected the gymnasts to be there early and ready to work out by the time she arrived. And Zmeskal-Burdette seemed to expect the same thing.

But she wasn't there that morning. She and Burdette alternate mornings at home and at the gym. It was her turn to get their three children off to school, so Burdette was starting the workout. He had chosen the Black Keys Pandora station to accompany the hour of conditioning, which probably suited only his tastes, not those of his female teenage gymnasts, whose ages and social media postings indicate a preference for Nick Jonas, Justin Bieber, and One Direction. For this reason alone, I was grateful that the gym was not a democracy.

Courtney McCool, a 2004 Olympic silver medalist, was there in Zmeskal-Burdette's stead. She helps run morning workouts at Texas Dreams twice a week. The rest of the time, she works with the team at Texas Women's University. This team, unlike the powerhouses at Florida or LSU or Georgia (which McCool competed for), is not at all notable. Texas, despite having some of the best clubs in the United States, doesn't have any of the top-ranked NCAA gymnastics programs.

That morning, Kurt Hettinger, an assistant coach at Auburn, a rising force in the powerful SEC conference, was also there observing possible recruits for his team. Per NCAA rules, he was not allowed to speak to the athletes, so he just stood on the sidelines, talking with McCool.

The gymnasts started their warm-ups by jumping rope, which was not an activity that any seemed particularly good at. The diminutive Ragan Smith, one of the top juniors in the country at the time—a double silver medalist on beam and floor exercise at the

2014 Junior National Championships—struggled mightily to get more than two consecutive revolutions around while crisscrossing the wires.

As the girls jumped and tripped, Hettinger and McCool chatted, not about gymnasts to recruit, but of their own desire to do the skills and exercises the young ones were performing. "I still think I can do it," Hettinger said to McCool, who just nodded. Their sincere longing for gymnastics explained, in part, why the Dreams Team gymnasts willingly submitted themselves to the grueling conditioning regimen I was watching.

I was reminded of the time, a few months earlier, when I sat at the World Championships next to Georgia Cervin, a former international elite-level gymnast from New Zealand. As we watched Simone Biles, the current top American gymnast, float into the rafters on her double layout and land it with a smile, Cervin leaned over to me and whispered, "I know why she's smiling. Those skills are really fun to do. It's the closest you get to flying."

If she had been there, I'm sure Zmeskal-Burdette would have chimed in with Hettinger and McCool. More than any other former elite gymnast I spoke to, Zmeskal-Burdette spoke with the greatest passion about how much she missed *doing* gymnastics.

Doing is also how Zmeskal-Burdette characterized her coaching style. "I coach by doing," she explained the night before after the Dreams Team had finished their Tuesday-evening workout. The former World Champion doesn't seem to have gotten much taller since the days that NBC and ABC listed her height at four feet seven. Zmeskal-Burdette, in person as an adult, seemed even more petite than she appeared on TV at the end of her competitive career in 2000; though still fit, her upper-body musculature had seemingly shrunk. She no longer needed swimmer-style shoulders to muscle through giant swings or to do pull-ups on the bars.

"You're the only one out of the 1992 and 1996 U.S. Olympians who is coaching at this level," I pointed out to her. "You're the only one who is—"

"Crazy," she interjected and laughed. "I like the game of it. It hasn't gotten old yet." She told me that she felt more fortunate than some of her former Karolyi teammates because she truly loved every day she spent in the gym. "Just because you're good at it doesn't mean that you like it," she pointed out. "I have a teammate of mine who said, 'I'm jealous of you.' I was like, 'No, don't say that. That's silly.' She was like, 'No, you really like this.' That makes me feel very sad. There are people who are good at something and feel like they need to see it through and that's responsible. In some ways, I feel lucky, and in others, it's torture. It doesn't go away. The level doesn't change. The intensity level. I'm a little different day to day in here, but it doesn't change. I don't remember a day of feeling like, 'Are we done?' "

Several times during our conversation, she clutched at her chest, right over her heart. "In my heart, if I was physically capable, I could still do these things," she said, echoing the same longing that I heard from McCool and Hettinger. She only retired because her legs gave out on her at the end of her career as she was trying to make a run for the 2000 Olympic team. Though this campaign was ultimately unsuccessful, she doesn't regret going for it. "Regret doesn't happen from the result. It happens from not knowing," she said. "But I still would do it again versus not knowing. Even with all of the extras. I stayed in gymnastics until I was almost twenty-four. I don't regret that at all because there is no 'I wonder what . . .' Everyone has to get to that place differently."

She views one of her responsibilities as a coach as protecting her athletes from that sort of regret. "A lot of this is us trying to be the guardian of their hindsight," she said. "There is no way for someone this age to have the same kind of perspective as someone who has lived through and watched others live through.

"There isn't a bad decision," she explained regarding staying with gymnastics or leaving the sport, "but I always tell them, 'I don't want you to have regrets.' "

Thoughts of the future and regrets are perhaps typically beyond most preteens, but Zmeskal-Burdette insisted that these gymnasts are not like typical tweens, at least in some ways. "I feel like I can have conversations with some of these girls who are not even twelve years old, ten-year-olds, about the ownership of what they're doing," she said. "Ultimately it's not a little-kid decision. It's in their heart, just as much as it would be an adult who put all of the pros and cons on paper. . . . This is not a little-kid sport."

Zmeskal-Burdette conceded that it can be difficult for others to see these young athletes as actors with agency, not only because of their chronological age but also because of their diminutive stature, which makes them appear even younger. She mentioned one of her especially small gymnasts, Ragan Smith, who was then a junior, fourteen at the time of our conversation but so short that she looked like she was closer to ten. It's hard to imagine someone who looks to be about ten making major decisions and dedicating themselves full time to a sport.

We also expect children to express happiness in very narrow ways, mainly laughing and smiling, and when young gymnasts don't do that, we're concerned. Zmeskal-Burdette argued otherwise. "You can watch people that are that little be happy without happy being defined as smiling and laughing. There's a difference in just being fulfilled by the challenge. That, I think, is hard for people to under-stand," she said.

Still, even though these youngsters are more mature and goal oriented than many of their same-aged peers, the former World Champion cautioned that as a coach, you still have to be careful. "At the end the day, remember when things get stressful, you are talking to teenagers, at best . . . When they are nervous about a test tomor-row, that's probably going to come out somewhere," she said. And that "somewhere" might be on the balance beam.

Zmeskal-Burdette used an example from the latter part of her career, when she was training in Cincinnati with Mary Lee Tracy and dating Chris, who coached other athletes in Tracy's gym. She approached Tracy and told her, "Before workout starts, I want to make sure you know Chris and I had it out." She needed her coach to know about the fight she had had with her boyfriend in case the subsequent practice went poorly. "If I'm not going to be able to let it go and have practice, she's not going to know the difference," she said. She needed her coach to understand that a bad practice on that particular day was not about gymnastics but about life outside the gym. And as a coach, she tries to keep that in mind when it comes to her own athletes.

But as supportive as the pair is, they do encourage competition among their top gymnasts. In the mini-doc about Texas Dreams, Burdette described how they use their gymnasts' innate competi-tiveness as a teaching tool. "The theory is if you have that fire, that competitive spirit, all I have to do is teach one Tkatchev [a com-plex release move on bars]," Burdette explained. "The other five will learn it that day. You gotta get the first kid to do it." In this setup, the coach shouldn't have to do much prodding. If a gymnast is motivated enough, simply seeing a teammate master a skill before she does should be all it takes to get her to let go of the bar and go for it.

Even at the lower levels, I saw coaches playfully stoking competitiveness between the young gymnasts. I watched a tatted-up coach with a beard that wouldn't have looked out of place in a Brooklyn bar, guide a group of eight-year-old girls through a drill on a grouping of single-rail bars low enough to the ground that each girl could jump up without assistance. He had them cast their lower bodies away from the bar and back while holding a block of foam between their knees to encourage them to squeeze their legs together. Some of the gymnasts were better at this than others, and when their feet came apart, they'd release the foam block, which flew back toward a teammate, who was on the bar behind her. "Cassie got mad at Allie," the coach said. "She threw a block in her face." He repeated this every time one of the gymnasts released her block. Though all of the girls giggled, I have no doubt that inwardly at least one über-competitive gymnast didn't find it funny and resolved never to let go of her foam block again. In five years, that girl will probably be training with the Dreams Team. She'd be the type of gymnast that Burdette wouldn't have to cajole into doing a new vault—she'd go for it simply because her teammate did. It's the gymnastics version of keeping up with the Joneses.

But of course, not everyone can win. It's a mathematical impossibility. There's only one first place. "Someone has to place fourteenth," Burdette said after the workout. "And the kid who placed fourteenth might not have placed first if you pushed her. You could have pushed her out of the sport." And you might have to coach that middle-of-the-pack kid differently than you do the high achievers.

Burdette used his own family as an example, pointing out that among his children, who are genetically related and are being raised in the same environment, there is diversity of personality. "My way or the highway doesn't work for your own kids," Burdette said. It stands to reason that there would be even greater difference in temperaments among genetically unconnected teens who are being raised in different homes.

The laid-back coaching attitude that I witnessed at Texas Dreams would probably come as a surprise to those who associate the sport with draconian taskmasters who like to yell. Some coaches, especially on the men's side of the sport, were repelled by women's gymnastics for the rep that it had, especially in the 1980s and 1990s. Kelly Manjak, a Canadian coach who started out working with men before switching to women, said, "I was turned off by women's gymnastics based on the coaching that I saw when I was coaching men."

"I don't like screaming," he went on. "I don't want to be more Catholic than the Pope. I don't want it more than them."

What Manjak described—yelling, pressure, kicking kids out of the gym—was the type of coaching technique (if it can even be called that) that Ryan described in great detail in her book. Many in the gymnastics community felt that the sport had been grossly misrepresented in *Little Girls*, since it mostly focused on a handful of gyms and extrapolated from those case studies to the sport at large. Dr. William Sands went so far as to call it a "work of fiction." Yet even he admitted that he used anger too much during his coaching days. "There's a place for anger, and I used it too much," he said. "There was a culture of coaching that was very different than now. The people who were productive at that time were slave drivers, and everyone went that way until we found out it didn't work that well. But it took awhile."

Ryan disputed the "fiction" accusation or any mischaracterization of her in-depth reporting. "Believe me, I've never done more research than I did for that book, knowing that it was going to be read and combed over with a fine-toothed comb, looking for an error so that they could dismiss the whole book and discredit me. So I was just so careful about everything."

Ryan admitted that she didn't follow women's gymnastics closely anymore, but from what she has seen and heard over the years, the sport has gotten much better. "It was a conversation that needed to happen. For the gymnastics community, it was like ripping off a Band-Aid—it hurt for a little while, but in the long run, wasn't it a good thing that we sort of stopped and looked at it and said, 'Is there a better way to do this?' We don't want to get rid of the sport. There's nothing wrong with the sport. What was wrong was how we practiced the sport, how we trained," she said.

Despite all of the time that has passed since *Little Girls* was published and all of the changes the sport in the United States has undergone, the specter of that book seemed to follow me throughout the research of my own. Prominent officials, including national team coordinator Martha Karolyi, turned down multiple requests for interviews. In the gyms where I did gain access, the book was invoked, explicitly or obliquely. "You're not writing anything scandalous?" Maggie Haney, head coach of MG Elite, asked several hours into my visit to her gym. "I probably should've asked you that sooner," she said, laughing. Haney had been a gymnast in the 1990s, around the time when Ryan was doing her research. She didn't share the experience that the subjects in Ryan's book had spoken about, but added, "I don't really know how it was for other people."

A few minutes later, however, she conceded, "It's just a different time now." She may have not been aware of other coaches' practices, but it seemed like she had heard some stories during her competitive days. If things are "different" in a good way, it stands to reason that they were once not great.

Haney was not the only one to obliquely reference the past scandals and negative media portrayals of the sport. Other coaches did, too, but, like Haney, opened their gyms to me anyway. Boorman, Biles's coach, told me, "I've got nothing to hide." Ditto for Burdette and Texas Dreams. He explained that given the size of the team, college recruiters and visitors are in and out of his gym all the time.

His team coordinator confirmed the frequency of recruiter visits. "The top schools are in here all the time," Froemming said. They even had crib sheets prepared for them that listed all of the top-shelf gymnasts, the last level they competed at, and whether or not they had committed to an NCAA program. If Burdette was indeed putting on a show for visitors, he'd really have to keep it up all day, every day.

Burdette told me that if I really wanted to get the scoop on what's going on inside gyms, I should talk to a college gymnastics recruiter. They spend most of the year on the road and can speak about the culture inside a wide range of gyms.

Tom Farden, now co–head coach of the University of Utah's gymnastics team, had been the team's chief recruiter when I interviewed him. On the day that we met, he was flying to the East Coast on a redeye right after the Utes' Friday night home meet. "I'm the only Delta Diamond in the department, which is one hundred twenty-five thousand air miles a year," he told me. The number of gyms he visits each year varies—it depends on how large a class he needs to recruit. Farden also travels to competitions and invitationals to see how potential recruits deal with competitive pressure.

Farden had visited Texas Dreams and knew Kim and Chris well. "Their system is very Eastern bloc," he said, "like the Karolyis would've done. They adapted that to fit the model that you need to be successful with today's kids." The Eastern-ness that Farden seemed to be talking about was about scale—the gym was a large, complex, almost self-contained system, similar to the schools the Karolyis established, first in the Carpathian Mountains and then in the backwoods of Texas.

"Chris," Farden added, "has a lot of humor with the kids. You can see the chemistry with Chris and Kim."

Farden then went on to talk about Liang Chow, who is 2-for-2—Shawn Johnson and Gabrielle Douglas—when it comes to coaching Olympic gold medalists. "His whole model blows everyone else out of the water. He only trains them four to five hours [a day]. He doesn't get obnoxious with the hours," Farden said. Chow and Farden boiled it down to efficiency. "That doesn't mean we did less work . . . I believe the intensity and the efficiency is the key. It's not about [how] many hours that you put in. It's about how efficiently you can get the work done," Chow told me.

Chow, like Zmeskal-Burdette, had been an international elite gymnast into his early twenties, retiring from competition due to an injury shortly before the 1992 Olympics. He then moved to the United States to study and coach at the University of Iowa. After seven years at the collegiate level, he and his wife struck out on their own and opened up a club. "We felt that we can do more if we start the athletes at a very young age," he told me, echoing the sentiment often expressed by Karolyi when he explained his own coaching philosophy back in the days of Comaneci.

Chow has achieved great success with his gymnasts, not by pushing them but by bringing them along slowly. His athletes often compete at lower levels of difficulty than they're capable of when they're younger, saving their more complex skills for their later years. He also emphasized technique. "I think that China has been known for the preciseness of the technique," he said. As a gymnast in the Chinese training behemoth, he was challenged to make even the most basic skills stand out. "You have to think in a way [about] how will you make your cartwheel better than others?"

At any other time in U.S. gymnastics history, Chow's repeated wins as a coach would have turned him into a legend. But in the crowded American club scene, his is just one gym out of many that have enjoyed significant international competitive success. Before Douglas won the all-around title under Chow's tutelage, World Olympic Gymnastics Academy (WOGA) in Plano, Texas, had back-to-back Olympic all-around titles in Nastia Liukin and Carly Patterson.

Farden's description of different modes of coaching illustrated that despite the homogenizing potential of the national team training camp system, coaches can still retain their individual ways of doing things. "The common thread with all of them," Farden said, "is that they're extremely hardworking and ask a lot of questions, which means they're still hungry. So if they can have those things going, if they can keep their kids happy, healthy, and hungry, they're going to be successful."

Compared to Texas, everything is smaller in the Northeast. That includes its gymnasiums. MG Elite is smaller than Texas Dreams by at least half. To put it into airplane hangar terms—because all gyms, big or small, somehow resemble hangars—TD can host a Jumbo Jet, and MG Elite is just large enough for a propeller plane.

The team at MG Elite in Monmouth County, New Jersey, is also much smaller than the one at Texas Dreams by several orders of magnitude. This, like TD's largeness, is by design, head coach Maggie Haney explained. Approximately twenty-five gymnasts try out, but they only accept three to five every year. There are only two team coaches—Haney and one of the gym's owners, Victoria (Vicki) Levine. Haney teaches the older, more advanced gymnasts, and Levine develops the next generation. There are four to five gymnasts in Haney's group and fewer than ten work with Levine. Combined, this group isn't as large as the training squad that works out regularly with the Burdettes every morning. And the Dreams Team is just a small part of the overall competitive program down in Dallas.

Yet it takes only one standout gymnast to put your gym on the map. More than half the battle is finding the talent. In 2012, MG Elite had a breakout year when Laurie Hernandez, then eleven, strutted her way onto the national gymnastics scene at the U.S. Classic. She didn't place high in the rankings—her difficulty level was too low to put up formidable scores—but she got everyone talking about the confidence and ferocity of her dance.

The following year, Hernandez, who had just turned thirteen, rocketed up the standings to second place at the Junior National Championships. She had also added tremendously to her difficulty on every piece of equipment. Another MG Elite athlete, Ariana Agripedes, then twelve, won the junior national title on the vault. And one year later, Jazmyn Foberg, the third in the gym's trio of elites, won the junior all around.

"Once you have that first elite, then it's easier to have the second and the third," she pointed out. "The program is in place and it's easier to develop those kids."

I first visited MG Elite right after Foberg, then fourteen, had been crowned as the top junior in the United States. Her win was something of a surprise—she hadn't even been a member of the national team when she won. To win the junior title before you were added to the national team and traveling squad is a little like putting the horse before the cart. Key, the 2013 winner, had been on the national team for over a year and had already competed internationally before she won her first title.

The morning I first visited, Haney showed her pupils pictures of her daughter's first day at kindergarten as the girls stretched and warmed up their joints with multicolored Thera-Bands, pulling them overhead to loosen their shoulders, wrapping them around their arches to tug on their ankles.

It was one of their first practices back after Junior National Championships and the team had been off for nearly two weeks, which is practically an eternity in gymnastics time. And the girls were rusty, Hernandez, most of all, since she was two months out of training after major knee surgery to repair a torn patellar tendon.

Hernandez is Haney's other baby—she's been coaching her since she was six years old. Sometimes Hernandez crashes at Haney's house to catch a ride to practice in the morning. As with Biles and Boorman, the two of them seemed to be learning the ins and out of elite gymnastics together.

"It's so funny—I can remember when she learned her round-off–back handspring–back handspring. I know there's a video of the first day she did two back handsprings in a row. Her sister came to pick her up and she was, 'Oh my god, I can't believe that's my sister.' " Haney recalled many of Hernandez's other firsts—her first glide kip on bars, her first competition. She's probably only missed Hernandez's first words, first steps, and first haircut.

Haney comes from a competitive gymnastics background, though she didn't compete as an elite as Zmeskal-Burdette did. She was born and raised in Texas and competed through the Junior Olympic program to completion. At fourteen, she left home to train at another gym in the hopes of going elite, but it was probably too late for her to make that push. She remained a Level 10 and ended up accepting a scholarship to North Carolina State.

Hernandez and Foberg, then just fourteen, both had their hearts set on going to the University of Florida, home of the defending NCAA champions. "Don't be close-minded," Haney advised her athletes about college. Haney thought that she would go to Auburn in Alabama until she went on her official recruiting trip during her senior year. Back then, she commented, they did the recruiting the "right way." No recruiting until five trips early in their senior year. But when she visited the campus, it didn't feel quite right.

"When you go somewhere," she tells her girls as they worked out on beam, "you'll know. You might have in your head one thing, but don't rule other things out." That's how Haney settled on North Carolina State, where she became one of their all-time greats. She even scored Perfect 10s, a first in the history of the school.

The girls didn't heed their coach's advice. By the time I visited the gym for a second time a couple of months later, Foberg and Hernandez had verbally committed to Florida. Verbal only because they were too young to sign the formal paperwork. Hernandez and Foberg had been adamant about competing in college together. "They're the best thing for each other," Haney said. Hernandez is fun loving and outgoing—her dark brown curly hair is as bouncy as her personality. Foberg is a bit more serious. They seem to balance each other out as training partners.

Their demand to remain together was not a hard one to satisfy. Not many NCAA gymnastics programs would be opposed to the idea of taking two of the top juniors as a package, just as one would adopt two sister kittens.

They may end up sharing a dorm in Gainesville, but it's unlikely they'll be sharing a room together at the Olympic Village in Rio. At best, Haney and MG Elite can hope to place just one of them on the five-person American team.

If there's a major downside to the new American system and the volume of talent rising from the grassroots, it's that many potential World and Olympic medalists won't even get the chance to compete internationally. There's just so much talent and not enough room on the major teams. If any of these girls—the ninth, tenth, and even eleventh seeds—were competing for less gymnastically power-ful countries, they'd be the stars of those teams. But in the United States, they're often alternates and second fiddles. At the 2015 Tro-feo Città di Jesolo, a friendly competition held every year in Italy, the Americans brought two Olympic teams' worth of gymnasts and ended up dominating, occupying nine out of the top ten spots in the all-around. The U.S. gymnasts in the lower half of the top ten hand-ily defeated athletes from Italy and Canada that will have no trouble making their countries' Olympic squads.

Tracy spoke about this seeming unfairness. "It's hard when you're in the middle of the pack," she said. "It becomes a lot of the coach's responsibility of how you keep your athlete motivated when all the time, you're sitting on the alternate or bubble spot." Because you never know. "Things happen," she added, "so you always have to be ready for when that window of opportunity opens, which we've seen happen a million times."

To get both of her athletes onto the Rio Olympic team, the win-dow of opportunity will have to open quite wide for Haney and the girls of MG Elite.

———

Hernandez seemed to rely more on Haney throughout the workouts I observed. This was perhaps due to the fact that she was still very early in recovery from knee surgery, which is a discouraging time for any gymnast. When a gymnast is injured, she's excluded from the group during the workout, forced to condition or do therapy exercises off to the side while her teammates get to do the fun stuff. At Texas Dreams, I watched as Peyton Ernst, one of their top elites who was on the mend from shoulder surgery, spent much of the four-hour workout on the sidelines, stretching and strengthening the joint while the rest of the team tumbled. Injury rehab requires a tremendous amount of self-directed practice and can be an extremely lonely time for an athlete. Zmeskal-Burdette told me that right after an injury or surgery, she'll give the gymnast the option of staying away from the gym because she understands how hard it can be to be in this environment and not be able to do anything. But that's only in the immediate aftermath. After a couple of weeks, the athlete has to come back because there are still things she can do while she rehabs the injured body part. "There's still a lot they can do," she said. At her gym, I saw a gymnast very heavily braced from upper thigh down to mid-calf working on bars, being carefully spotted on cast handstands by Burdette, who gently lowered her to the mats so she didn't risk an awkward landing on a surgically repaired ACL.

According to Sands, this tendency to work around an injury has made it difficult for epidemiologists to construct a database of gymnastics injuries, which is a project he is currently working on. The typical criteria for a sports injury, he told me, is to have missed a day of practice. "Unfortunately, that's not how most gymnastics injuries occur. Most gymnastics injuries are skill specific," he explained. "If you sprain an ankle, in almost any sport, you're out for awhile until the ankle heals. But in gymnastics you can just do bars and land on your butt in the pit," he pointed out. "The one that is pretty devastating for gymnastics is a wrist injury. If that's severe enough, you're usually done. But other than that, you can find something to do that doesn't aggravate the injury and prevent you from training." He'd like to tweak the definition for sports injury to better fit gymnastics. "Does it prevent you from training at full capacity? That's an injury. So that tries to take into account the sore ankle, but you can do bars. The sore back, but you do beam," he said.

Though she's very limited in the first workout I observed, Hernandez showed flashes of why she was one of the standout gymnasts in the country. It was all in the little things. In a handstand, her shoulders are flatter than those of her teammates. When she sits in splits, her arches are so flexible, she can touch the toes of her front leg to the mat. Her legs looked more extended than Foberg's, whose knees seemed to pucker a little bit even when completely locked out. To her, Haney said, "You will get straight knees, you will get straight knees, you will get straight knees," as though writing it punitively on a chalkboard on *The Simpsons*. Hernandez, brace and all, sat easily in a split with her hips squared and facing forward. Haney let her be but stood behind Foberg and stretched by pulling back on her shoulders and pressing her hips down. "I've been given a mission from Martha to get Jazzy more flexible," she told me. She pulls back on Foberg's shoulders a bit more as the gymnast grimaces a little. "As if I'm not already trying."

Haney seemed to be coddling Hernandez a bit—no stern words, jokes and encouragement only. When she jumped down from the bars after a failed attempt at a stalder to a pirouetting skill, her frustration, as measured by the number of flyaway hairs around her face, was obvious. "That's fine. Don't freak out. You haven't done gymnastics in a long time," Haney reminded her.

"I can remember feeling so scared up on that beam that I couldn't stand up after my mount," Haney told me. "And your coach can say something to you and make you [believe], 'That's okay, I can do this.' I think that it helps me to be a better coach just because I remember the mental aspects of the sport, and hopefully I can say the right things to my kids, or do something to ease their mind, or to give them the energy they need for that day."

At the end of the bar workout, Haney reassured Hernandez that she had come far in less than a week back in training. "The fact that you're doing stalders and the pak. And then tomorrow, [we'll add] releases. That's everything." Well, everything except a dismount, but it would be awhile before Hernandez would be able to absorb landings on her surgically repaired knee. But the gymnast took this encouragement to heart. Her eyes widened, and she smiled with genuine pleasure. She, like her coach, was raring to go.

When I visited again in December, Hernandez had been cleared to train all skills, on all events. That winter workout didn't take place in MG Elite. Twice a week, the team trained at Gymland. This facility was much bigger and had more training aids and equipment than their home base. And it was empty during the day—Gymland's team trained only once a day, and so the enormous gym sat idle until 4:00 p.m., when the kids trickled in from public school. Renting out the gym to MG Elite was Gymland's way of dealing with a business that is, in essence, shuttered between 10:00 a.m. and school dismissal, as Burdette had observed when he set his school plan into motion.

That day, they were working on floor routines. Haney, who choreographs all of the MG Elite exercises, was stressing out over the music for her star pupil's routine. "I just want everyone to love her," Haney said of the kind of pressure she's placing on herself to create

Hernandez's new floor routine. After almost a year out of competition due to injuries and a knee surgery, Hernandez isn't going to be the American gymnast with the most difficulty. "She's not going to do the hardest tumbling," Haney acknowledged. To get her to stand out, she's going to need the best choreography and performance value.

The gymnast spent the floor rotation practicing tumbling passes onto a soft landing surface. She consistently undertwisted, and Haney called out corrections from across the gym as she worked with Foberg. Finally, Hernandez fully rotated it—a front layout to a front two-and-a-half twisting somersault. She looked from side to side to see if anyone had noticed, but Haney had been solely focused on Foberg at that particular moment. Hernandez caught my eye and I nodded, assuring her I had seen it. She smiled and walked down the mat for another try.

I later mentioned to Haney that Hernandez seemed to need a lot of reassurance—after every turn on bars, she looked immediately to Maggie, her saucer eyes searching for a correction. I relayed the anecdote from earlier in the practice session. "She needs positive approval," Haney agreed.

In that way, Hernandez is similar to Zmeskal-Burdette. Burdette spoke about his wife as a gymnast as also wanting a lot of input from the coaches. "Kim wanted someone to watch every turn and give corrections. If you wanted to make her mad, don't give her corrections," he said. But with the large Dreams Team composed of so many gymnasts taking turns simultaneously, how would it be possible to give all of the girls that degree of attention? Burdette answered that you could have a team with one Kim but not with six Kims.

Though she was intense as a gymnast, Zmeskal-Burdette seems

to be much more lighthearted as a coach, striking a balance between seriousness of purpose and playfulness. Lauren Hopkins, founder and editor of the popular gymnastics site, The Gymter.net, recalled watching the Texas Dreams girls conditioning on the uneven bars before a competition. This particular set of bars was quite squeaky and as the girls moved through their strengthening exercises, "Kim was like, 'Who's farting?' " Hopkins said. For her, this was not an example of the atypical but the typical in American women's gymnastics. She has been covering the sport for more than five years and has seen very little screaming at competitions or in gyms. This generation of coaches and athletes seem quite adept at moving back and forth between seriousness and fun. As Walt Whitman wrote, they contain multitudes.

But if the emotional palette has expanded for both gymnast and coach, the selections of floor exercise music has not. Midway through our conversation in Texas, I heard the opening chords of a familiar selection of music. It was a big band piece called "Hooked on Swing."

"I recognize that," I said to Zmeskal-Burdette with a wry smile. It was her old floor music, the piece she clinched the 1991 World all-around title with.

"When I heard it, I said, 'Johnny, are you kidding me?' " she told me. "She almost got fired because she didn't know it was my floor music," the former World Champion joked. Zmeskal-Burdette has recycled the selection for her own gymnasts, too. "I put it in Bailie's," she said. Key no longer performed to that piece of music, but when she did, Kathy Kelly, the former vice president of USA Gymnastics, pointed it out to Zmeskal-Burdette just as I did. It's floor exercise music as gymnastics allusion, an inside joke for those who obsessively follow the sport, really no different than the pop culture savants in Nick Hornby's *High Fidelity* or the hip-hop head who can tell you all of the beats that are sampled in any given rap song.

Most of the Karolyis' U.S. athletes performed to music that was identifiably American, such as swing or rock and roll. Zmeskal-Burdette's 1992 Olympic floor routine was set to "Rock Around the Clock." In that routine, she briefly mimed the playing of the guitar as a teenager rocking out to records in his parents' garage would. In 1996, Moceanu performed to "The Devil Went Down to Georgia," which was a clever bit of pandering to the Atlanta audience, which ate it up as intended. Kerri Strug, also a Karolyi gymnast and the hero of those Games, performed to a rock medley. Karolyi chose catchy tunes for his athletes, the type that the crowd could easily get into, unlike the Soviets, who often presented more challenging fare to the audience. Could there be any music more challenging to audience engagement than Igor Stravinsky's "The Rite of Spring," which was performed to bizarre perfection in 1989 by Olga Strazheva? Perhaps these catchy selections represented Karolyi's actual musical affinities. Or maybe it was the savvy showman in him who knew how to play to the cameras and how to get the audience on his gymnasts' side. To paraphrase Haney, maybe he simply wanted the crowd and judges to love his gymnasts.

But in the end, no matter how many jokes your coach cracks, no matter how many training camp photos you post to Instagram, training as an elite gymnast in the United States is incredibly grueling work. At the end of the FloGymnastics series on Texas Dreams, Burdette acknowledged as much. "It breaks my heart what I see happen in this gym. And I don't mean in a negative way, of kids having to endure injuries and certain obstacles," he said. "I don't understand how they go in and endure the boot camp that they endure. It's just insane to me what they do. But I can't show that on the floor. I can't step on the floor and say, 'Yeah, you're thirteen years old and you need to be training this many hours a week and you need to make this many sacrifices and you need to move your family.' I say, 'That's what has to happen. This is what you do.' "

But after the the workout, Burdette and the team hug it out. "We're able to be human again. We're able to say, 'Jeez, it's incredible what you commit. We're proud of you.' "

THE WINNERS AND LOSERS
OF THE NEW SYSTEM

On the final day of competition at the 2014 World Gymnastics Championships in Nanning, the International Gymnastics Federation (FIG) held a press conference. About a hundred reporters and photographers decamped in the conference area, sitting in the kind of desks you'd find in a university classroom. I slid into a desk near a young female reporter who was working for the local organizing committee, putting out competition reports and grabbing quotes from the athletes in the mixed zone. She leaned over to me and whispered in my ear, "Everyone at that table is so old, male, and white."

I glanced up at the dais, and saw that she was right, at least about half of the table. The left side of the table seemed reasonable under the circumstances—a gymnastics competition held in China— a female Chinese translator and the president of the host nation's gymnastics federation. They were representative.

But to my right, it was a different story. That was where the two FIG representatives were seated—President Bruno Grandi and Secretary General Andre Gueisbuhler. As my colleague observed, they were old, white, and male. Though they were in Nanning representing the interests of the sport, they didn't really represent the sport demographically. At least not in the twenty-first century. The top two men's teams in Nanning were the Chinese and Japanese with the United States in third. (The British men had placed fourth. This was the closest that a Europe-based team got to the men's team medal stand that year.) The men's all-around champion was Japanese Kohei Uchimura. In 2014, the Japanese gymnast had won his fifth consecutive World all-around title. (And in 2015, he'd pick up his sixth.) Uchimura hasn't lost a major all-around championship since 2008, when he placed second as a teenager at the Olympic Games in Beijing to China's Yang Wei.

On the women's side, all of the gold medals were won by Asian and American gymnasts, with Simone Biles picking up three individual gold medals. The best that Russia and Romania, the traditional victors, could muster were a couple of silvers and bronzes. In the last decade, the power and growth in men's and women's gymnastics had shifted from Europe to Asia and the Americas.

If you want to get a sense of the whole range of international gymnastics, attend a World Championships in the middle of an Olympic cycle: 2006, 2010, 2014, and so on. Though you probably won't get the opportunity to watch the eventual Olympic champion during any of those years, since she's likely still too young to compete internationally, those midcycle World Championships offer a glimpse at the largest cross-section of elite gymnastics globally. Or what passes for elite gymnastics in some parts of the world.

The year after the Olympics, FIG doesn't host a team competition at the premier international event. Too many teams find their ranks decimated by post-Games retirements. Gymnasts (and their tendons) tend to hold on for the Olympics. After this culminating achievement, many athletes retire from the sport, which often leaves their countries' programs bereft of talent, at least until the promising junior gymnasts age into senior competition. Some countries opt not to send delegations during this year, saving their money and resources for a competition that allows them to bring a full squad of gymnasts along with them. Or if they do, they may send fewer gymnasts than they're allotted.

And the year before the Olympics is also not representative of the full spectrum of global gymnastics. That field has already been whittled down to the top twenty-four teams, from best to thoroughly mediocre. If you really want to see *everyone*, you need to attend a championships in the middle of the cycle when any country that is up to date on their FIG dues can send a full team of six gymnasts plus one alternate. It's basically an open-enrollment competition. For countries such as India, Israel, Qatar, Egypt, and Iceland, these World Championships are their Olympic Games. Since they are unlikely to qualify a full team for the following year's championships, they will have to wait another four years to compete as a team again at this level.

In 2014, the World Championships were inclusive. That year Nanning, the capital of Guanxgi province in southeastern China, hosted the competition. China didn't compete internationally in gymnastics until 1974 but started winning major titles almost right away. Gymnastically speaking, they are Athena, sprung fully formed from Zeus' skull. They didn't parade subpar beam routines in front of the judges and dominant Soviets. They were ready to win the minute they saluted the judges. Just a few years after China's appearance at the 1974 Asian Games, Ma Yanhong won the gold medal on the uneven bars at the 1979 World Championships, demonstrating ramrod-straight handstands, exceptional toe point and form that have since become the hallmarks of Chinese gymnastics on that event. This despite the fact that in those early years, as former U.S. international women's judge Delene Darst pointed out, they were at an enormous disadvantage because they didn't speak English, French, or German. "They had a lot of trouble conversing with the other officials, so they were kind of like out there on their own. They come into a meet and have absolutely fantastic athletes, but they don't have any alliances," she said.

By contrast, the Americans have participated in international competition since the inception of the modern era of the sport yet took much longer to start winning medals. Cathy Rigby won the first medal for the USA at the 1970 World Championships but couldn't follow it up with anything at the subsequent Olympic Games. It wouldn't be until 1978, when the U.S. women found themselves back on the podium, winning the bars title and picking up other medals. While it is certainly true that corrupt judging panels and Eastern bloc alliances held the Americans back, for the most part, they weren't nearly as good as their Soviet and Romanian counterparts.

The United States has certainly come a long way from those days in the early '70s when every medal was a milestone. In 2014, they entered the arena as the clear favorites. To lose the team gold to the top nations such as China and Russia, they'd have to record multiple falls across all of the apparatuses. But in the preliminary sessions, they weren't competing head-to-head with either of those countries. Rather, the U.S. women, the best squad in the world, would be competing alongside one of the worst—the Indian team.

Since training sessions mirror competitions—teams that draw the same subdivision work out together at the same time in the same training hall in the same rotation order that they will eventually compete in—the U.S. women trained alongside their Indian peers. I had come to watch the best team in the world work out but also got to see the thirty-eighth-ranked team on the planet. The difference between them was stark.

First of all, the Indian women seemed to be learning on the job, so to speak. They were training skills that clearly hadn't been mastered yet. The coaches were stepping in to offer significant spotting and assistance to the gymnasts. This is not something you're supposed to see mere days before a major competition.

The Americans, by contrast, moved with assembly-line speed and precision. On each apparatus, the seven gymnasts would quickly warm up skills before they started doing their full routines in competition order. After completing one to two routines on each apparatus, they would either work on segments that had given them trouble or sit and wait until the rotation switch was announced.

The activities of the American coaches seemed to be as carefully choreographed as those of their athletes. Each one knew exactly when to step in to pull a mat or move a board, or exactly how far from the vaulting table to place a gymnast's springboard. And like the gymnasts, who wore identical leotards, not only in the competitions but in all of the practice sessions, the coaches wore matching attire, too. One of the coaches confessed to me that she was happy to be home after over a month away from her family, in part, because she'd like to be able to choose what to wear every day. The coaches' attire, furnished by U.S. team sponsor Under Armour, was chosen by Martha Karolyi. Occasionally, the coaches would point out that the ensemble she selected didn't match. "Martha would say, 'Well, I think it looks good,' " the coach recalled, laughing a little. In Nanning, the coaches were rehearsing for the competition just as the gymnasts were.

But by the time the U.S. women arrived in Nanning, their training sessions were less practice than dress rehearsal. Their hair was neatly done, slicked back into buns or ponytails marked by Minnie Mouse ribbons. Their makeup was stage ready because even if they were not yet on the podium, it didn't mean that they weren't being watched. Media and coaches from other countries wandered in and out of the Americans' practice sessions to see what the gymnasts were up to. Kelly Manjak, who was in Nanning as the coach of the Canadian alternate gymnast, briefly sat down next to me during one of the workouts. "They're awesome," he said of the American girls. What impressed him as much as the difficulty level that Americans demonstrated was their consistency in training. They could go up and do their routines, error free, over and over if need be.

This consistency in practice was the reason that the U.S. gymnasts were usually done before the other teams were. They had completed full sets without any trouble. The Indian girls were still working hard as the Americans were packing up their gear and receiving physical therapy treatments from the team trainer. The U.S. women, unlike their competitors, had done all of the hard work at home. At the meet, they could practically coast.

The Indian women, despite their lowly ranking, were not exactly complete unknowns inside the gymnastics community. Earlier in 2014, Dipa Karmakar, one of their gymnasts, had won a medal at the Commonwealth Games. She did this on the vault where she performs—or I should say, attempts—a double front somersault. Called the Produnova, it is named for the only gymnast to ever successfully compete the skill—Russian Amazon warrior princess Yelena Produnova. The Rostov-on-Don native performed this skill back in 1999 at the World University Games on the old vaulting horse that was far less safe and aerodynamic, yet she still managed to land upright.

But Karmakar, despite her medal, had never once stood one up in competition. At best, she has pulled the skill, which entails two and a half flips from her hands, around just enough so that her feet touch before her butt grazes the mat, landing in a squat so deep that her knees are practically level with her shoulders. And that's on a good day. But the Produnova vault is so difficult and so highly rated that even a fall or a near fall or an out-of-control landing can't stop it. The available deductions simply aren't adequate. You can fall on that vault in qualifications and still make it to the event finals.

This is why gymnasts such as Karmakar or Fadwa Mahmoud of Egypt (which placed just two spots above the Indian team in thirty-sixth) or Yamilet Peña of the Dominican Republic do the double front vault—it rockets them into the medal round. Peña has even made the vault final at the World Championships and Olympic Games. And if you're from a gymnastically weak country, a finals berth is something you can take home to your sports federation and demand additional funding.

Vault is the safety school of apparatus finals, the back door to the medal rounds. Most female gymnasts, especially the all-arounders, do not have a second vault in their arsenal. They probably could learn one, but they don't want to take away training time from the other apparatuses or don't want to risk injury on an additional skill. And since they can get by in team and all-around meets with just one really good vault, most don't bother to learn another, which takes them out of the running to make the finals on it. In 2014, only twenty-eight women bothered doing a second vault in the preliminary round, which meant that nearly a third of those eligible made the finals. That's how weak the field is on this particular apparatus. Imagine if Harvard had an acceptance rate of 28 percent.

———

For a country with India's population size and economic growth, there's reason to believe that it could eventually do very well in gymnastics if they get funding and the right coaches. For India, there's nowhere to go but up.

But for several of the traditional gymnastics powers, their trajectory has run in the exact opposite direction—down. The year 2014 was an excellent one to observe the shifting fortunes in international gymnastics, with the United States and China topping the team stands, in first and second, respectively, while former perennial powers Russia and Romania scrambled for the bronze. And no team has seen its fortunes reversed as dramatically as the team of Nadia.

The Romanians' unraveling was on display in 2014 during the team qualifications. The rules were simple—six gymnasts per team, five compete on each apparatus, four scores count. The top twenty-four teams would qualify a full squad to the subsequent World Championships in Glasgow. The top eight teams after preliminaries would advance to the medal rounds. No one doubted that the Romanians would be in the latter group.

They entered the arena to dainty-sounding music, which was played at every single one of the women's sessions. Like all gymnasts, regardless of country, they marched with rigidly held upper bodies, and their straight arms swinging sharply at their sides. All that was missing was the goosestep. This mode of entry harkens back to the nineteenth-century militaristic roots of the sport, but it looks utterly incongruous on slight, teenage girls in iridescent spandex leotards and eye glitter. The solemn marching worked a little bit better for the judges, who walked in like a line of blue blazers to music befitting fighters entering the Thunderdome. The judges were the 181st Blue Blazer Brigade. The announcer politely asked the audience, "Would you please raise the roof?" A general rule of thumb: if you add "please" to that particular idiom, you clearly don't understand what it means.

In Nanning, the Romanians only had one competent gymnast—Larisa Iordache. The eighteen-year-old was the veteran of the team. The rest were rookies to major international competition. In 2012, she had been a rookie herself, an adorable sprite in a yellow leotard bearing a strong resemblance to Pikachu. She started off the year quite well, "unofficially" winning the all-around at the European Championships. (There was actually no all-around that year, just team.) But by the time Iordache showed up with the Romanian team in London, she was hobbled by a painful heel injury. In 2013, Iordache had been in the running for an all-around medal but fell. In 2014, however, the Romanian seemed to be coming into her own, accepting her role as team leader and performing difficult sets with confidence and style. This evolution did not come a moment too soon, because in Nanning, the entire Romanian squad collapsed around her. One gymnast did so poorly that her score was practically a 10—10.033. In the new *Code*, scoring this close to a 10 is not a good thing—it's a disaster.

Iordache singlehandedly dragged her team into the finals in Nanning. She pitched in with the highest score for the Romanians on every single event and was the third-highest qualifier to the all-around final. She also qualified to the medal rounds on the balance beam and floor exercise events. (Iordache would eventually win a pair of silvers for her work in the all around and on floor exercise.) As I watched her nail set after set, I was reminded of Winston

Churchill's quote about the Royal Air Force and its defense of the nation during the Battle of Britain: "Never in the field of human conflict was so much owed by so many to so few." At the end of preliminaries, the Romanians were in seventh. They had just made it into team finals.

But in 2015, they would not be so lucky. At those World Championships, which doubled as an Olympic qualifier for Rio—the top eight teams in preliminaries earned automatic berths to the Games— the team from Romania completely self-destructed. It started on the bars with all but one gymnast staying on the apparatus and not counting a grievous error. This casualty list included 2014's heroine, Iordache. And the Romanians didn't even do well on their pet events, beam and floor. They ended the competition without any qualifiers to the individual event finals. Most shocking of all, they didn't earn a spot to the Olympic Games. They placed thirteenth, miles from the medal podium and a team finals spot. They'd have to go to Rio in the spring of 2016 and qualify at the Olympic test event. Forty years after Nadia, her team was in shambles, their Olympic qualification in doubt. Comaneci, who had been in Glasgow to see the meltdown firsthand, commented that it made her sick to her stomach.

Perhaps more than any of the other top teams, the Romanians were most adversely affected by the elimination of the 10 that their countrywoman had made famous in 1976. The Romanians have been uniquely weak as a team on the uneven bars since the '90s. Under the old system, they always figured out a way to do just enough to reach 10.0 start values on their bar routines. "They planned to lose by two points on bars, hope like hell they can make it up on beam," Paul Ziert said. On the balance beam in particular, the Romanians competed very difficult skills with astonishing speed and surefootedness. They were *the* beam team.

On floor, they performed hard tumbling skills and were good on vault, too. The 1996 and 2004 Olympic champions on the event were Romanian. And the Amanar vault that the United States had used to dominate the team competition in London was named for one of their all-time greats, Simona Amanar. The Romanians were the three event gymnasts of teams.

But when the new rules were introduced in 2006 and the 10.0 scoring cap was removed, it blew the lid off the kind of math that allowed the Romanians to fall behind on bars and make it up on the other three. Now countries such as China, which has a long tradition of mastery and innovation on the uneven bars, and Russia, which has pioneered many unique skills over the years, were able to start racking up major points. The true distance between Romania and the other teams on the uneven bars became apparent. The new scoring system laid bare just how far behind they were. And while they could be impressive on the other three, they were not nearly far enough ahead on those events to come back from that kind of scoring deficit.

There are a lot of theories about the Romanians' lack of bars prowess. The most popular among them is that as youngsters, Romanian gymnasts don't practice with hand guards, which are better known as grips. Not only do grips protect your hands from rips and sores, the dowel, a slim foam roll under the leather guard, makes it easier to regrasp the bar after release moves and to hold on during giant swings. Training without them, in theory, means not being able to practice as long on the event because a gymnast's hands are more likely to be shredded.

Romanian gymnasts, for the most part, are culled from the lower socioeconomic strata from families who simply can't afford to buy them grips when they are young. By the time they start training at the higher levels where their costs are covered, many gymnasts have simply gotten used to swinging bars without this piece of equipment.

The problem with this theory is China and Russia. In both of those countries, the gymnasts are sometimes introduced to grips at a later age due to similar economic constraints. And both of those countries, especially China, are known for their prowess on the uneven bars. Russian legend Svetlana Khorkina didn't use grips through her long career yet managed to win five World titles and two Olympic gold medals on the event.

It seems that the trouble is less adequate equipment and more the Romanian style of coaching, which emphasizes the other three apparatuses to the detriment of bars. Mihai Brestyan, a Romanian ex-pat who now coaches in the United States, does not have a strong track record of instructing gymnasts to success on the uneven bars. Both of his best-known athletes, Olympic champion Aly Raisman and World champion Alicia Sacramone, excelled at vault, floor, and beam but were very weak on the uneven bars. Sacramone, who spoke about being actively afraid of the event, stopped training on bars altogether in 2006 to focus on the other three apparatuses. Raisman and Sacramone were essentially Romanian gymnasts who were trained in the United States. And both come from upper-middle-class families where cost was not an issue. They had been using grips from an early age. Their problem was one of ability and probably also instruction.

Or it could've been one of selection—if you are a coach known for technical teaching prowess on the power events but are unable to develop an athlete with a natural aptitude for the only upper-body apparatus in the women's repertoire, you're less likely to retain that type of gymnast. She might quit, or she might leave your gym for another where there is better bars instruction.

When I asked Cristian Moldovan, a Romanian national team coach since 2007, about the team's unique weakness on the bars, he disputed it. "It is a false reputation created by the lower performance compared to other apparatuses," he wrote to me in an email. He pointed out that Romania has had medalists on this event in recent years—Ana Porgras and Steliana Nistor. But these gymnasts won their bars medals in the weakest of years—the mid-quad World Championships—when several other, more favored gymnasts made mistakes. This is not to say that they didn't deserve these medals. They hit and others missed. That's how competition works. But no one gymnastically knowledgeable would look at these two athletes and say that they're actually *good* on bars.

Romania's problems, however, run much deeper than bars. Unlike the Americans and the Chinese, the Romanians didn't actually select a team for the Worlds. "Selection" implies an array of options. The Romanians had none. In 2014, Diana Bulimar, their number two gymnast behind Iordache, was injured and couldn't compete. This meant that they had to bring every single uninjured senior elite gymnast in the country with them to China. They had no benchwarmers. The reserves were on the team. In 2015, something similar happened yet again. Bulimar was back, albeit not fully prepared after returning from another injury. And on the eve of the competition, they lost their second-best all-arounder to an ankle injury. They didn't sub their alternate, who was struggling with her routines. That was it. They had no one else they could call up.

How did a team that brought the world the first Perfect 10 and presented a truly credible threat to Soviet gymnastics dominance become so depleted of talent and resources that it could barely field a complete team for a major international competition?

The simple answer: they don't have the numbers anymore.

Since the end of the Cold War, Romania's population has declined due to diminishing birth rates—they ranked number eleven on Bloomberg's list of the world's fastest shrinking countries—and emigration to other, more economically prosperous nations. And this decrease has been mirrored in their gymnast population.

The slide, which began after the fall of Nicolae Ceausescu in 1989, wasn't immediately apparent in the Romanian results. They still had a stable core of senior and junior athletes that learned their fundamentals during the Communist days. In fact, after the end of the Cold War, Romanian gymnastics went on something of a winning spree—capturing all of the team World Championship gold medals from 1994 until 2001, and winning back-to-back Olympic team titles in 2000 and 2004.

But this success does not mean that the Romanians were flush with talented gymnasts—they were just really good at managing their meager resources, of transitioning promising junior stars to senior Olympic gold medalists. For years, the Romanians were punching way above their weight.

But over time, their athlete pool shrank. Of the gymnasts who competed at the Junior European Championship in 2010 for Romania, only Iordache and Bulimar progressed to successful senior careers. The rest left the sport for education and other opportunities.

"Unfortunately, the decreasing number of gymnasts practicing in Romania was reflected in the results of recent years," Moldovan explained. "Because of this, internal competition decreased greatly and led to a complacency of our athletes, which is not enough to keep you in the world elite."

Many of the U.S. athletes have noted that their motivation to train and work hard in the gym is due to the competition they face to make international team rosters. In the crowded domestic field, simply earning a spot on a team is no small feat. U.S. coach Terry Walker noted, "It should have to be more stressful to make the team and the lineup than competing at the competition."

The decreasing numbers also applies to the coaching population. Like the rest of their countrymen, many coaches have left their native land for better jobs abroad. "Many Romanian coaches chose to leave the country because of the salary level of the Romanian education system," Moldovan said. Former Romanian champion Daniela Silivas, who now lives and coaches in the United States, observed in a recent online interview that in her day the Romanians were quite good on bars—she is the 1988 Olympic champion on the event. Their success was due to coaching. "We started being great on bars after Adrian Stan came to the national team," she recalled. "He is the best bars coach in the world." Stan is no longer in Romania; he's been coaching in Great Britain for years. That country has shown a special aptitude on the uneven bars as they've climbed the global rankings.

Moldovan rejected the idea that the new scoring system has at all harmed Romanian gymnastics results. In fact, he likes the new *Code* for the same reasons that those in favor of it praise it—it is easier to distinguish between gymnasts. As for Romania's downturn, he said, "It's all about preparation and organization."

"We need to increase the number of gymnasts practicing this sport for a solid foundation," he explained. To that end, Romania has spearheaded a new program to help return their gymnastics program to dominance for the Olympic Games in 2024. OMV Petrom, an oil company, has invested over two million euros to help create six gymnastics training centers for approximately two hundred six- to seven-year-old gymnasts. The campaign to recruit these young-sters is called "Country, Country, We Want Champions." This is a play on an old Romanian children's game called Country, Country, We Want Soldiers, making the connection between athletes as mili-tary proxies for the state even more concrete than their toy soldier marches on the podium do.

I first learned about this new recruitment strategy from Comaneci, who spoke about it quite excitedly back in her offices in Norman, Oklahoma. She had filmed spots for the campaign, as did several past Romanian gold medalists. Octavian Bellu and many other former gymnasts traveled to the tryouts. "Thousands of kids showed up," Comaneci told me. "It was really hard to make the cut." It was like *American Idol* for Olympic gymnastics.

In the twenty-first century, Romanian gymnastics recruitment has moved beyond a coach creeping around the playground, observ-ing little children.

The decline of Russian gymnastics since the fall of Communism shares many similarities to their Romanian counterparts—they, too, have seen state support shrink from total to virtually nothing. They have also lost coaching talent to the United States, Great Britain, Australia, and other Western nations. The science and coaching techniques behind the sport were the most advanced in the former Soviet Union, and when their coaches started leaving for better-paying gigs overseas, they took their knowledge with them. Rus-sia's loss was the West's gain. "Past secrets," gymnastics journalist John Crumlish wrote, "are now published agendas." The carefully guarded gymnastics playbooks were now widely available.

But it wasn't like the information was completely lost to the Russians. Many talented, highly knowledgeable coaches remained to train the next generation. And Russia, unlike Romania, has many top-notch academies. Russia's problems are more complicated than those of the Romanians', which seems to be a more straightforward case of lack of resources, both financial and human.

For the Russians, their recent troubles seem to be the management at the very top—specifically Andrei and Valentina Rodionenko. Since 2005, the Rodionenkos have been at the helm of gymnastics after longtime head coach Leonid Arkayev was fired after the 2004 Olympics. Since that time, the Rodionenkos have hired and fired five head coaches in as many years. Their last high-profile sacking took place after the London Olympics, when they relieved Alexander Alexandrov of his post.

Alexandrov is one of the most respected coaches in the sport. He is one of the few to have taught World and Olympic champions on both the men's and women's sides of sport. He first rose to prominence in the early '80s as the coach of Dmitri Bilozerchev, the 1983 World all-around champion. After the Soviet women's team was defeated by a surging Romanian squad at the 1987 World Championships, Alexandrov was appointed the head coach of the women's program to prepare them for the 1988 Games, replacing Andrei Rodionenko. The Soviets won easily in Seoul and again in Barcelona in 1992. After leading the Unified Team to its final team title, Alexandrov, like many other Soviet coaches, left to work in the United States and landed in Houston, where he coached American gymnasts, including 1996 Olympic gold medalist Dominique Moceanu, who credited him with teaching her almost all of her high level skills.

In 2008, Alexandrov was brought back to Russia by the Rodionenkos. The Russian women had just left the Beijing Olympics completely empty-handed—no medal in the team competition, none in the all-around, none in the event finals. Even North Korea managed to win a vault gold medal. The Russian program, now flush with cash from corporate sponsor, VTB Bank, was determined to reclaim its past glory.

In the early aughts, Round Lake, the famed training center outside of Moscow, had been regularly featured in NBC's coverage of the Olympics as a symbol of Russia's post-Communist decay. The doors were rusted. The paint on the walls was peeling. Unlike the full color wheel you see in U.S. gyms, Round Lake was all beiges and grays. The Russian gymnasts, who under the old regime allegedly feasted on caviar, were shown eating what looked like watery gruel as though they were wards of the state, not highly prized athletes.

With a refurbished training facility and a new head coach, Russian gymnastics seemed poised to reclaim the top spot in international competition. Just two years into the new cycle, the Russian women scored a major win—the team title at the World Championships. This was their first as a team since the breakup of the Soviet Union. While it was by no means a rout—they defeated the United States by just a few tenths—it seemed like a sign of good things to come. The year 2010 also marked the emergence of Aliya Mustafina, who won the all-around title and qualified to all four event finals, the first to do this since fellow Russian gymnast Svetlana Khorkina did it in 1997. Mustafina looked to be the most dominant gymnast of her generation. Alexandrov acted as the rising gymnast's personal coach in addition to carrying out his duties as team head coach.

And more talent was in the Russian pipeline. At the same time that Mustafina was slaying the senior field, Viktoria Komova was doing the same to the juniors, completely dominating the inaugural Youth

Olympic Games, competing with a surpassing level of difficulty and with the soft precision for which the Soviets had been known.

But in 2011, Mustafina tore her ACL and would be out of competition until the Olympic Games. And Komova, hobbled by a foot injury and a growth spurt, didn't transition as smoothly to the senior ranks as the Americans' very talented junior class did that year. Though the United States dominated in 2011, the Russians still won the silver and several other medals. They had been defeated, but they hadn't been trampled.

The Russians brought their A game to the Olympics in 2012. Mustafina was back in the lineup. Komova upgraded almost all of her routines and seemed to be gunning for the all-around title. Promising junior Anastasia Grishina was now a senior. The Americans were still heavily favored to win, but if the Russians performed up to their potential, the United States wouldn't be able to run away with it. And if the Americans had made any mistakes and the Russians went error-free, they could win.

That was not how it played out. The Russians, already working from a start value deficit, made enormous mistakes on the floor exercise and were trounced by the Americans, who were faultless, by five points. Still, they earned the team silver, adding a silver and bronze in the all-around, bronzes on the vault and floor exercise, and a gold for Mustafina on bars. Mustafina, just fourteen months after her devastating ACL injury, left London with more medals than any other female gymnast. This was quite a comeback for the gymnast and for the Russian program that four years earlier hadn't won any medals. You'd have thought that Alexandrov would be feted for these accomplishments.

And you would be wrong. After London, Alexandrov was told that when his contract with the Russian Gymnastics Federation (RGF) expired at the end of the year, it would not be renewed. The pretense was that Alexandrov was not allowed to train a personal athlete while acting as the team's head coach, but few bought that. He had taken over Mustafina's coaching when no one else wanted to work with the notoriously headstrong gymnast. Alexandrov seems to have a soft spot for gymnasts with strong personalities, having worked in the past with the likes of Svetlana Boginskaya (who admitted in a GymCastic podcast interview to biting her competitors when she was a very young gymnast) and Bilozerchev.

The RGF offered Alexandrov the opportunity to stay on as Mustafina's personal coach, but he viewed this as a demotion and decided to leave Russia for Brazil, the fifth ousted coach of the Rodionenkos' reign. "Five head coaches in the past five years have been dismissed, but the unsinkable Rodionenkos are still here," he said in an interview published on the website Rewriting Russian Gymnastics shortly after his departure.

Since Alexandrov was fired, the fortunes of Russian's women's gymnastics, which seemed to be on the upswing from 2010 to 2012, went south. The Russians were hit by the injury bug. Almost no one from the 2012 Olympic team, save Mustafina, was able to compete during the following years. While injuries are not uncommon in gymnastics and are typically not any one person's fault—they're often more the work of chance—when these injuries struck, it became evident that the Russians, like the Romanians, couldn't replace their fallen athletes. They didn't have the strength in numbers that the United States enjoys.

So Mustafina (literally) limped through 2013, picking up some medals at the World Championships, and then through 2014, doing the same yet again, because the Russians simply couldn't spare her.

She, like Iordache and a military recruitment slogan, was an army of one.

In Nanning, the Russians won the team bronze, a step down from their finishes in 2011 and 2012. And in 2015, without Mustafina, who was recovering from injury, they sank even further. Their final placement matched their number of falls—four.

The turmoil in Russian gymnastics management seems to have trickled down to the training hall. Before Nanning, I had been warned by many writers and fans not to expect much from the Russians' practice sessions. I had been told that little gymnastics actually happened there. There were tears, partial routines, stretching, tears, and occasional arguments with the coaches. The Russians did not train with the assembly-line efficiency of the Americans. One of the American coaches in Nanning commented to me that she had been shocked by the lack of discipline and respect that she witnessed in the Russian sessions.

Mary Lee Tracy spoke more generally about the breakdown of discipline and organization within the former Eastern bloc gymnastics programs. "As we gained more and more discipline and a broader base, it seemed like everybody else was doing the opposite." The way that Tracy described what ails the Russians, it sounded almost active, as though they were deciding to change their traditional mode of training rather than reacting to a breakdown of their long-standing systems. And as she noted about the Americans, their leadership is stable. "They're [Karolyi and Liukin] very secure in their positions," she noted. This is something that cannot be said about any Russian head coach.

———————

The changing fortunes in international women's gymnastics is not just the result of upheavals in the traditional powers and stability and resources in the United States. It's about the changing physical demands of the sport that for some, especially the Russians, seem to be an affront to their artistic worldview. For them, that means ballet and the accompanying body type—thin, flexible, strong but only deceptively so.

"It's hard for a Russian female gymnast to not do eighty percent of her floor routine in relevé because that's how they're brought up," Ziert observed. "They were the ones that started on the podium to stand in fourth or fifth position when they're getting up." If you look at photos from award ceremonies in the '80s, the Soviet didn't stand on the podium like little toy soldiers with their feet parallel and their backs ramrod straight. They stood in turnout with their shoulders relaxed as the medals were draped around their necks. Ballet is part of the Russian soul, even in the midst of an ostensibly athletic competition.

"Some countries want to compete but they can't give up their souls in the process. Some countries are willing to sell their souls to a *Code of Points*," he said.

This seemed to be a dig at the Americans, who have no such guiding aesthetic principles. The United States is, above all else, pragmatic. The American coaches and program directors aren't seeking an aesthetic ideal when they look for prospective talent. They're looking for gymnasts they can win with. And right now that means developing gymnasts with strength and speed in mind.

"The Russians, the Ukrainians, and Belarus lose to their rivals from other countries because they are weaker physically," Kim explained in a post-2014 Worlds interview. "Current gymnastics has become very dynamic and strength based." Kim, though she was something of a power gymnast herself, was not pleased with this development. She'd prefer to see gymnasts with body types as before—small yet deceptively strong—but she merely pointed out the reality. "Their performances lack elegance, finesse. But they perform like catapults, jump so high."

Even Svetlana Boginskaya had been reshaped by the American method when she moved to the United States after the 1992 Olympics. She noted a change in her physique when she started training in the United States for the 1996 Olympic with conditioning-obsessed Bela Karolyi. "I remember that even the Belarusian gymnasts told me at that time that I was no longer a 'ballerina' like I was before," Boginskaya said in an online interview. "I had such muscles as never before. But thanks to that endurance and physical reserve, I was participating in exhibition shows for the next three years after the Atlanta Olympics." With her increased muscle bulk, she was able to add difficulty to her program even though she was competing in an older, twentysomething body. So why should it matter if her shoulders were broader later in her career?

Because in movement art forms such as ballet your body type is significant. It's not just about your ability or musical interpretation. It's about how you look. Misty Copeland, the first African American principal for the American Ballet Theatre, has spoken about how she was repeatedly told that she didn't have the right type of body. The criticism she received wasn't a commentary on her ability but on her appearance. Copeland has stated that she was drawn to ABT because they seemed more accepting of a wide variety of body types, unlike other classical companies such as the Kirov in St. Petersburg, which is far less inclusive. The female dancers all pretty much look the same.

Back during the Cold War, you could say the same thing about

the Russians, of course, with a handful of notable exceptions. (Boginskaya was tall for a gymnast at nearly five feet five.) "The Russians
were all within probably two inches of each other," Ziert said.

The 1983 World all-around champion Natalia Yurchenko spoke
about Soviet selection procedures during her day. "To make any of
the competitive sports teams, you had to match a lot of criteria," she
said to Rewriting Russian Gymnastics. "For gymnastics, body type,
flexibility, toe point, feet, knee structure, level of natural strength
as well as the height and body type of the gymnast's parents were
all factors." This type of early selection likely had a homogenizing
effect on gymnasts' physical statures.

"Now you see the teams, and they all look totally scrambled.
I think they're all in chaos as to knowing who do we pick, why do we
pick them, what can they do, this is our heritage, but are we going to
forsake it because we've got to be competitive?" Ziert said.

The idea of picking and choosing certain athletes when they
are very young to the exclusion of others is alien to the American
gymnastics process. In the United States, we don't select—we moni-
tor. No one is excluded from training if the parents are willing to
pay tuition. A gymnast who may not have looked promising at first
might still become a gymnastics powerhouse. This is how a partici-
patory, rather than elite, model works. Everyone can play as long as
everyone pays. And sometimes you end up finding talent in the most
unexpected of bodies.

But this can't happen if you're not given the opportunity to continue in the sport. In the former Eastern bloc and in China, the
gymnasts are chosen at young ages mostly based on a few athletic
measurements such as speed, flexibility, and vertical jump height,
and, of course, body type.

China excels at bars but, in particular, seems to have struggled to put together lineups on half of the events: floor and vault. These are the power events where being short is still certainly an asset but being tiny is not. The best vaulters and tumblers in the world possess some muscular heft in their lower bodies. In Nanning, some of the Chinese gymnasts were so tiny that I wondered if they'd be able to compress the springs at all when hitting the springboard before a vault. Shang Chunsong, one of the best gymnasts on the team, was so short that she had to stand on an overturned bucket in the mixed zone to be eye level with Chinese reporters. Shang, who placed fourth in the all-around in 2015, could've easily medaled if she was only powerful enough to perform a higher-valued vault. (That year, it was revealed that Shang, who is uniquely small even on the Chinese team, had grown up very poor in a rural area of China where she had been undernourished as a child, which probably impacted her overall stature.)

When you mention how small the Chinese gymnasts are compared to the rest of gymnastics population, you run the risk of being accused of racism by gymnastics fans who suggest that you simply are biased in favor of Western bodies. But that takes a very narrow view of body diversity within China. After all, it spans a continent and has a population of over a billion. Before the start of every session of competition in Nanning, the local organizing committee treated the spectators to different dance-style performances. The dancers, unlike the gymnasts, were far from homogenous in terms of body composition, and nor were they all minuscule. Why, I wondered, were none of these athletic-seeming people selected for gymnastics in preschool? It seems to be more a problem of selection than of available human resources. In a country as vast and diverse as China, it shouldn't be too hard to find a few more vaulters.

Ziert acknowledged that many of the countries, especially China, may be choosing the wrong body type. "Who knew we were going to go to football players doing gymnastics, you know?" he said.

Football players might be a little bit too big for gymnastics, their centers of gravity a little too high. But as in dating, the gymnastics world is learning that it's not the best idea to cling too rigidly to your so-called type.

———

"If you get a runaway train with any one or two countries, then it almost ruins the rest of the competition for everybody else," Steve Butcher, the president of the Men's Technical Committee, told me. There's little suspense. The results are foregone conclusions.

That's exactly what has happened on the women's side of the sport. The United States is so dominant that the only question is exactly how much they're going to win by this time. As in professional wrestling, the outcome in the women's competition seems practically predetermined.

In 2014 and 2015, the Americans won the team title virtually uncontested. This is, in part, due to the fact that when the United States walks into the arena, they already have a multipoint advantage. When two basketball teams face off on the court, they all start from zero. Though there are clearly better teams and worse teams, great players and mediocre ones, when the clock starts, everyone has the same number of points. But under open-ended scoring, the playing field isn't even level at the start.

"Before the new *Code of Points* was implemented in artistic gymnastics, there were quite a few gymnasts who could have a pretty even fight per se for the medals/top spots," Alexander Alexandrov commented. "Many gymnasts were equally strong and pretty even with each other skill-wise largely because of 10.0 scoring system."

He acknowledged that something needed to be done to better separate the very best from the rest, but one of the unintended consequences of this change is that one team has charged so far ahead of all the others that they're virtually out of sight. "Before there were many more girls who could fight for the all-around title, and it was definitely much more interesting to watch, in my opinion, because there was some unpredictability and someone unexpected had a fighting chance," he said.

While that might not have been fair to the very best competitors to be ranked so closely to their less-talented peers, it did allow for exciting competitions where you felt that anyone could win. If the dominant Soviets fell, the Romanians could sneak in for the title. In the good ol' days, the results were not foregone conclusions.

The Americans are clearly the "runaway train" to which Butcher had referred. Except that phrasing suggests that something is out of control, and that's the exact opposite of what is happening. The United States is dominating through discipline and control (and an abundance of resources). Perhaps it would be more apt to describe the Americans as an airplane following its flight plan to the letter; the other countries are having trouble getting off the ground.

"I think an adjustment to the rules might be necessary over time not only for the women but also for the men to keep it competitive between all of the countries," Butcher acknowledged.

In the past, adjustments to the rules have been made to make the sport more inclusive. In 1974, after five of the six Soviets occupied five of the top seven all-around spots at the World Championships in Bulgaria, the rules were adjusted to allow only three per country to advance to the all-around final and two per nation to event finals. (That number was later reduced to two for the all-around.) The East Germans, the other gymnastics power at the time, won six of the remaining spots in the top fourteen. The World Championships in Varna was basically a dual meet between two countries.

The purpose of the rule change was to create opportunities for gymnasts from less gymnastically powerful countries to win medals, or at the very least, make the finals, which could encourage investment and growth in the sport in less-dominant countries.

But one of the other consequences of the rule change meant that potential medalists were kept out of the medal rounds because they had the misfortune to compete for the best team instead of one of the lower-ranked ones. It also meant that the true extent of Soviet dominance was not apparent simply by looking at the final standings after any given competition. "If you go back to the eighties and watch the Russians—any Russian—their difficulty was markedly better than any American," Walker recalled. The first gymnast in the Soviet lineup—and the first gymnast up was usually the sacrificial lamb of the team, since scores tended to start low and then increase throughout the rotation—might've been better than the last one up for the United States, but she wasn't going to make the finals and win a medal.

But changing the rules expanded opportunities, at least somewhat, for other gymnasts to win medals or earn finals berths, results they could bring home to their sports federations to demand greater support and investment in gymnastics.

That Butcher, who asserted that his main job is ensuring proper application of the rules and correct rankings, is also concerned with the overall competitiveness of the field and the entertainment value of the competitions, underscores just how little anyone involved in the sport, even at the highest levels of FIG, takes its continued popularity for granted.

"If only the top three are your clear medalists, it's just not as exciting," Butcher said. Indeed, it's like a game of musical chairs where, when the music stops, everyone has a seat.

———

It's hard to be a fan of gymnastics and to not be dismayed about the downturn in the Romanian and Russian programs even if you're also happy that your team—the Americans—is winning. Most of my favorite performances are not from the Americans. They're from the Soviets in the 1980s. This era and this team, for many, was the golden age of the sport. The difficulty level took off quickly after Olga and Nadia, and by the 1980s, Soviet gymnasts were competing skills that were so far ahead of their time, they would remain competitive for more than thirty years. In addition to difficulty, they brought artistry to the table. Choreography in a Russian floor routine wasn't just filler between the tumbling passes; it expressed the music. A Soviet exercise had a beginning, middle, and end. It conveyed an idea. A Russian floor exercise truly was greater than the sum of its parts.

And it is unlikely that in today's more athletically driven sport that we'll see another team like the Soviets of the '80s. But that doesn't mean it's all been doom and gloom in the world of women's gymnastics, even if you're not from the United States. Over the past decade, new players have emerged. The British men went from not fielding a full team for Beijing to winning the team bronze on their home turf in 2012. That year, the British women placed a historic sixth in the team finals in London. Beth Tweddle, the veteran of their team and a past World Champion on the uneven bars, won the bronze on her specialty. This was a first for the British women's gymnastics.

The hits kept on coming for both programs. In 2015, again on home turf, the men topped the *Chinese* men for the silver medal, the night after the women overcame Russia in a Romania-less field for the bronze, their first-ever team medal in World or Olympic competition.

The British have enacted a program similar to that of the Americans: they invest in gymnastics at the club level, with an emphasis on athlete *and* coach development. British gymnastics has instituted a system of training camps and coaching clinics. Instead of centralizing the talent and knowledge, they spread it around. They may not have a ranch in Texas with a Romanian doyenne in charge, but for a country that's roughly the size of Oregon, they are punching way above their weight.

The perennial top four—United States, Russia, China, and Romania—is no more. A new women's gymnastics world order has finally arrived. It is no longer just four against the world.

10

THE PERFECT 10:
THE COLLEGE YEARS

On October 1, 1975, Greg Marsden posted a short recruitment ad in the *Utah Daily Chronicle*. "Women's gymnastics team tryouts," it tersely began. "Wednesday-Friday; 4-6 p.m." Underneath this text, there was a similar posting for women's field hockey tryouts and notices for a ski club meeting and water polo competition. Seven girls answered Marsden's ad, and they all made the team. That year, Marsden and his hastily recruited squad went to nationals and placed tenth.

This was near the beginning of the Title IX era in women's college sports and Marsden, then twenty-four and a graduate student in sports psychology at the University of Utah, had been tapped to create a women's gymnastics team despite having no experience with the sport. For this, he received a part-time coaching salary of $1,500 a year.

Around the time that Marsden was getting the Utah women's gymnastics program off the ground, a thirteen-year-old Nadia Comaneci was starting her ascent up the global gymnastics ranks. Less than a year after Marsden posted his ad and assembled his ragtag group of gymnasts, Comaneci would go on to earn the sport's first Perfect 10s and earn worldwide fame.

Fast-forward forty years. Elite gymnastics has gotten rid of its iconic score. But that doesn't mean that the 10 has completely disappeared from the sport. It's simply matriculated. The Perfect 10 has graduated high school and headed to college.

———

On the night of the University of Utah's gymnastics' team January 2015 showdown with Pac-12 rival UCLA, I had arrived at the Huntsman Athletic Center with more than forty-five minutes to spare before the official 6:00 p.m. meet start time. This, I discovered, was barely enough time to find a parking spot. All of the adjacent lots were already filled, and I had to park in a distant one. Earlier in the day as I sat in co-head coach Marsden's office, he announced the presale numbers for the competition later that night—twelve thousand. It certainly seemed like I had passed at least half as many cars as I trekked to the arena.

In 2014, Utah gymnastics led the country in attendance for women's sports, averaging more than fourteen thousand per home meet. Alabama gymnastics came in second with more than thirteen thousand in attendance at their home competitions. Women's basketball entered the crowd rankings only in third place, behind these two gymnastics powerhouses.

On that night in Salt Lake City, more than fourteen thousand showed up to watch the two best teams in the Pac-12 conference vault it out. But before the actual competition started, the gymnasts were introduced to the audience. After the visiting UCLA gymnasts were warmly if somewhat tepidly received, it was time to bring out the home team. These introductions were done with all the razzle-dazzle production values of an NBA all-star game. In front of the near sellout crowd, the Utah gymnasts, clad in black lamé warm-up suits, their long hair tugged back into ponytails with varying configurations of braids and ribbons and team decals on their cheeks, were announced, one by one, to the mat where they were greeted by loud cheers. Once on the mat, each gymnast danced with the school mascot, Swoop, a red-tailed hawklike bird indigenous to Utah. Each girl seemed to have her own shtick with the mascot. One even butt bumped with him before taking her place in line next to her teammates.

This is a far cry from the reserved introduction ritual you see at elite competitions. And that's largely been Marsden's doing.

Shortly into his tenure as head coach, he recalled, Utah started winning National Championships, yet media attention seemed to lag. Marsden started bugging the local press to cover his competitions. "Finally someone had enough of me and said, 'Coach, it's not our job to promote the program. It's our job to report on what people are interested in hearing about. When you get four to five thousand people in the seats up there, you won't have to call us anymore. We'll be there,' " Marsden recalled.

"I really took that as a challenge," he said. "I became as passionate about getting people here to watch us as I did about the success of the team on the floor." Now the team has its own beat writers from the *Salt Lake Tribune, Deseret News*, and other local publications.

To get to that point, Marsden started studying other popular spectator sports, such as basketball and football, to try to find a shared thread that ran through them. The commonality, he concluded, was spectacle. The audience was always being entertained. "I felt we had to create an event that was fast moving, that people could understand, so it was important to have a good announcer to educate people," he said. In particular, he used NBA basketball games as his template. At basketball games, he noted, "Every time there is a time-out, they've got something going on. Girls dancing, marketing stuff, giving away freebies. They're entertaining people all the time. People are never just sitting there with nothing to watch.

"I think at that time gymnastics had the image of, it was like going to a dance recital," he recalled. "That you sat very quietly and politely applauded at the end of the routine. We wanted to change it to more of an athletic experience—yell and scream and boo and clap."

That Friday night, I was seated next to a couple of retirees who have been season ticket holders for Utah gymnastics for twenty years. The husband explained that he and his wife had been longtime supporters of Utah's men's football and basketball. His wife wanted to add a women's sport to the mix, so they decided to give gymnastics a try. They were hooked by the spectacle of it, they said, just as Marsden hoped they would be. Their son, who was a young teen when they first started attending home competitions, has remained steadfast in his loyalty to the gymnastics team to this day. He was there that night with them.

I heard something similar from an elderly woman I met on my way out of the Huntsman Center. She had been coming to the gymnastics competitions for thirty-nine years, long before the Utes started competing in the main arena, back when Marsden had to drag bleachers into the practice facility for spectators. Like my seatmates, she came to women's college gymnastics from a passion for Utah college sports in general, not from any particular interest in or connection to gymnastics. She was also an avid supporter of football and basketball at Utah. That night, she told me she was there with four generations of her family.

These two examples indicated that Marsden figured out how to do something I didn't think was possible—he managed to embed gymnastics within the greater college sporting culture of the university. In the Huntsman Center, banners of the gymnasts hung alongside those of the basketball players. And it's safe to say that the gymnasts, the shortest athletes on campus, were at least as popular as the tallest.

(Not that there weren't young gymnasts in the audience. I saw many little gymnasts identifiable through their warm-up suits or their elaborate ponytails and glitter eye makeup or crutches. I don't have any official numbers, but I'd venture that gymnastics meets probably have the highest percentage of audience members in casts or orthopedic boots.)

Marsden is something of a gymnastics populist—he's concerned with keeping the sport as accessible to as many people as possible. Like a coach of any Olympic sport at the college level, he knows that gymnastics is vulnerable. The number of programs—for women but especially for men—has decreased markedly from the time he took the reins at Utah. There's only one surefire method to protect an athletic program at the collegiate level: "You want to save a sport? Make it popular," Marsden told me emphatically. Sports that sell out arenas don't find themselves on the chopping block when administrations need to cut budgets.

"When I started in seventy-six, there were two hundred twenty-eight programs or something like that. We competed against USC and Oregon and Northern Colorado and University of Colorado. All those programs are gone. And they've been gone for years now, but back when I started, almost everybody had a team," he said. "And I know a lot of people think, well, you know, Title IX made that possible . . . Well, that's really not true. I mean, maybe that helped us get going, but it hasn't saved us."

Not that Marsden was worried about his program at Utah getting the ax. "Now, it would be really tough for my athletic director to make a decision to eliminate women's gymnastics," he said. "Why? Not because we won, you know, ten National Championships twenty years ago, or that we do relatively well now. I mean, there are plenty of examples of teams that were doing well that got cut. But the reason it would be tough for him is because of our popularity, because we put fourteen and fifteen thousand people in the stands, because all three newspapers have beat writers that cover us, because the sport sells."

And for Marsden, one of the key selling points of NCAA gymnastics is the Perfect 10. According to the legendary coach, eliminating it was one of the biggest mistakes elite gymnastics has ever made.

"Gymnastics became known for the 10," he pointed out. "You could not go out and get a marketing firm and pay them one hundred million dollars to brand gymnastics the way we were branded with the 10. The 10 was everything—in our culture, it became the movie *10*. You don't walk away from that brand." While acknowledging the problems that had arisen while trying to maintain the 10 in international gymnastics, Marsden was still emphatically opposed to the scoring change. "That was the stupidest thing we ever did," he said.

Jill Hicks, the former head coach at Cal State Fullerton, echoed a similar sentiment. "They [the audience] don't understand what the girl is doing in the air. They don't get the skills. They get the sticking [the dismount], and they get the 10," she told me. The 10, she pointed out, is hitting a home run at a baseball game. "You have to have that thing that keeps people in their seats and grows your program." But despite the promise of the 10, Hicks's program at Fullerton was canceled in 2011.

That college gymnastics has maintained the 10 and elite gymnastics has rid itself of it is not simply due to the fact that savvier marketing heads prevailed within the NCAA. It is because elite and collegiate gymnastics don't have the same goals. Their scoring systems reflect different priorities. Elite gymnastics is, well, elite. It's about pushing the envelope on innovation and difficulty. You're always trying to add a half twist to a vault and extra flip to a beam sequence. The rules found it difficult to accommodate this kind of progression under the 10.0 without major changes every four years and occasionally during the intervening ones.

In college, gymnasts compete according to modified Level 10 rules, which are far less demanding and far more stable than those used by the elites. They perform fewer skills in any given exercise and those skills are much less complex. The emphasis instead is on execution and team performance. In the elite world, the most vaunted title is the women's Olympic all-around. But at the NCAA Championships, the best all-around gymnast is determined, not by a separate round of competition, but in the team preliminaries when the twelve schools that have qualified to nationals are trying to make the Super Six. The all-around competition is practically an afterthought; the team is what is sacrosanct. And since they are still using the Perfect 10, there isn't a lot of scoring breathing room between the teams. Every tenth counts, the way it once did at the elite level in the early 1990s, a time that Zmeskal-Burdette jokingly referred to as the "battle of the 9.9s." Now the NCAA is the battle of the 9.9s.

The former World Champion understands the appeal of the NCAA arrangement, especially to elites competing under the open-ended scoring regime. "There's a part of me that would like to go back to just trying to do a perfect routine," she said. "I think that that change has made it an enticing reason for these elite athletes to do the sport they know but play a different game."

The reason the game is different at the NCAA level has to do with the stage. Most gymnasts are winding down their gymnastics careers in college. It is not preparatory for higher levels of competition the way that college track or diving or soccer or basketball or really any other NCAA sport is. Many NCAA track and field stars go on to win medals at the Olympic Games. A small percentage of college basketball players are offered contracts to compete for the NBA. Some college football players move on to the NFL. But there is no professional league for gymnasts. Further, female gymnasts peak younger than athletes in other sports do, typically before they get to university. For all but a handful of gymnasts, NCAA gymnastics is the end of the road, and the rules reflect that.

(Men's NCAA gymnastics, unlike the women's side, is preparatory because male gymnasts don't approach their peak until college, if not after. This is why the men have adopted a slightly modified version of the international rules for NCAA competition. Men's college gymnastics does not use the Perfect 10.)

But Marsden's point about the magic of 10 and marketing, regardless of the difference between college and elite, is a valid one. In 2014, it was LSU's Lloimincia Hall's Perfect 10 on floor exercise that got the mainstream media to pay attention briefly to college gymnastics. At the beginning of the season, Hall, who was then a junior star, performed with her typical crowd-pleasing braggadocio to a medley of funk and gospel in front of a packed house on home turf. She launched her tumbling passes into the stratosphere and landed each one easily. After she finished her performance, her teammates ran onto the mat to hug and congratulate her, even before her score was flashed.

That routine, as great as it was, could have received a 9.9 or a 9.95 or a 9.975. All three of these scores would have been as fair as the 10 she ended up getting that day in January. Her 10, like some of the earliest perfect marks in elite gymnastics, was an appreciative score—it was greater than the sum of each individual element. It wasn't about scrutinizing every skill for flaws but about the overall impression of the routine, the explosivity of her tumbling, the swagger of her choreography, and the crowd's excitement. It was also the culmination of a successful floor rotation for the Tigers, who put up five very strong routines before Hall saluted the judges. The scores had been steadily escalating from 9.800 to 9.85 to 9.875 to 9.9 to 9.925. Hall's teammates had created momentum for her to get that 10, as had been the plan when the coaches drafted that rotation order and put Hall in the anchor position.

The initial wave of excitement over this score lasted just a few minutes until the crowd's cheers died down. But then, a few months later, a website called Total Sorority Move found the video of Hall on YouTube and posted it. It is unlikely that they would've come across the clip had it not had the label "Perfect 10" somewhere in the header. If she had scored a 9.975, also a justified mark, it is likely that the routine would have gone unnoticed by anyone other than hardcore LSU and gymnastics fans.

Hall's "perfect" routine was viewed millions of times and posted all over social media. The gymnast went from being a gymternet favorite to a viral phenomenon. She was even interviewed on *Good Morning America*, where the host cluelessly asked, "Will Hall ever go for the gold at the Olympics?"

The short answer: No. Hall was not on track to make the Olympics nor had she ever been. As a club gymnast at Texas Dreams, she hadn't even competed as an elite, much less made the national team and represented the United States abroad. But the fact that the *GMA* anchor even asked this question underscored the fact that most people are incapable of thinking of gymnastics outside the context of the Olympics. They assume that every gymnast dreams of making the Olympic team from the moment they first prance across the balance beam. In a sense that's true, but only in the way that little kids dream of growing up to be a cowboy or an astronaut or a police officer. It's mostly fantasy stuff.

Earning a spot on the U.S. Olympic team is akin to winning the lottery—not only do you have to be *that* good but you also have to be healthy and ready at the exact moment of selection. Luck plays an enormous part in this. Getting an NCAA scholarship, on the other hand, is the attainable dream. It is not determined by chance in the same way making the Olympic team is. Colleges are recruiting athletes to compete for four years, not just one week for a single event every four years. A gymnast might get recruited while they're injured. And it's not unusual for an athlete to arrive on campus for the start of their college career nursing an injury. When Christine "Peng Peng" Lee, one of the best Canadian gymnasts of the last quadrennium, showed up at UCLA at the start of her freshman year, she was on the mend for ACL surgery—she had torn it right before the Canadian Olympic Trials. She didn't compete her freshman season, and she had to redshirt her sophomore year, too, since the original reconstruction didn't take and she had to undergo the procedure all over again. She was out of competition for more than two years. Lee clearly had no luck when it came to timing and injuries, yet she still managed to hold on to her scholarship and spot on the UCLA team.

The first time I met K. J. Kindler, the head coach of the 2014 NCAA co-champion Oklahoma Sooners, was at the junior session of the 2014 Secret Classic, which served as a qualifier for the U.S. National Championships held six weeks later. She and Jay Clark, the assistant head coach at LSU, sat down next to me in the lower level of the stands adjacent to the uneven bars. *Of course, they're at the junior session*, I thought as they took their seats. *These kids—the twelve-, thirteen-, and fourteen-year-olds—are the only top-shelf gymnasts who haven't already been recruited.*

It's a curious thing—over the last forty years since Nadia and Olga, a lot has been made about the youth of elite gymnasts, how they're too young to commence high-level training and face that sort of competitive pressure. But since 1970, the age minimums in international competition have inched upward, first to fourteen, then to fifteen, and finally to sixteen, where it sits at present. At the same time, the age of college recruitment for these same athletes has trended downward. Now, the top echelon of gymnast in the United States is deciding at thirteen or fourteen years old where they will be going to college at eighteen.

This is a departure from how things used to be done. MG Elite head coach Maggie Haney, who had been a star at North Carolina State, didn't get recruited until her senior year of high school. "I took five recruiting trips my senior year. They were all official recruiting trips, and the schools paid for all of them. I visited all five schools, I picked the school I wanted to go to," she told me. "That's what the rules are set up for. Now they're recruiting so young there are not even rules actually in place for it.

"What I mean by that is," she added, "up until ninth grade, there really are no rules. You're allowed to talk to kids in seventh and eighth grade." Her gymnasts verbally committed to the University of Florida as high school freshmen, which meant that they were probably talking to coaches before NCAA rules even applied to them.

"The NCAA rules are insane," said David Toronjo, whose daughter Macy was recruited to UCLA. "Before they turn a freshman in high school, they [the coaches] can actually talk to you all they want to. But once they become a freshman, they can't initiate a conversation." The parents and athletes can, however, reach out to the coaches as much or as little as they want. But they don't leave messages because, per NCAA rules, the coaches can't return the calls anyway. "You got to have your phone on 24/7. . . . You're taking calls any time," Marsden said.

But most bets are off if the gymnast sets foot on campus. In that event, she and her parents can talk to the coaches as much as they wish. Of course, those early trips are self-financed unlike the "official" senior-year recruiting trips. "The parents take the kids on the recruiting trips. You have to pay for everything," Toronjo said. Haney pointed out a gymnast like Laurie Hernandez can't afford to go on several under her own steam. Early recruiting presents a challenge to gymnasts whose families don't have a lot of extra money.

None of the coaches I spoke to—at both the elite and the college levels—were particularly pleased by the early recruitment phenomenon, but none felt empowered to do anything to change it. "You know, we're all frustrated by it, but we all continue to do it," Marsden said. "And each year, it just gets earlier and earlier."

"Now you're just recruiting till you fill a class, and then you're recruiting the next class," Marsden continued. "You're out all the time. You never feel like you can be out enough. And we get pressure from clubs and regions to show up."

And it's not just the club coaches who are calling the college recruiters about their athletes; the parents are also highly involved in this process. "I've gotten calls from, this summer, from parents of sixth graders, seventh graders, wanting to know if we have any interest, where they are on our list," he added.

When I was at Utah, I asked Tom Farden what he looked for in athletes, especially ones that were so young and several years away from competing in college. He admitted that the recruiting is, at best, an educated guess. "But what I look for is, obviously, if they are doing the skills that we'll need them to be doing when they're eighteen, nineteen, and twenty, and we're recruiting when they're fourteen and fifteen and they're close to mastery of those skills now, that's a big bonus because they're going to spend the next four to five years of doing those skills that we need them to compete, which is muscle memory. The more muscle memory they have, the more confidence they have with those skills, the probability is a little bit better that they'll compete them in the decisive moment when the pressure is on rather than somebody who just learned them or learned them a little bit later."

This is somewhat different from the answer I heard from Kurt Hettinger, the Auburn assistant coach and recruiter I met while I was visiting Texas Dreams. He told me he was more interested in physical traits and athletic abilities. He said he was less concerned with skills because the skill demand in college is markedly lower than it is in elite gymnastics. Perhaps Hettinger was focused less on skills and more on athletic ability because gymnasts often lose skills when they go through their growth spurts and puberty, and only some successfully regain those elements. Both Farden and Hettinger were using different ways of trying to predict the athletic future of their potential recruits.

But Farden's focus on skill attainment at a young age makes sense, since the lengthy competitive season, which runs from January to April, makes it hard for gymnasts to add skills to their repertoire once they get to college. "The window [in which] we can teach skills is smaller," Hettinger pointed out. Shortly after the school year starts, they are already putting routines together. During the competitive season, the emphasis is on physical conditioning, not skill learning. The coaches and trainers are merely trying to keep their gymnasts reasonably healthy so they can compete every weekend for over three months. NCAA gymnasts compete a lot more than their club and elite peers. And more competitions mean less-forgiving landing surfaces, though certain allowances are made for the fragility of college gymnasts' bodies. Often, extra mats will be inserted into the corners of the floor exercise mat where they land their passes. A white line will be taped over the extra mat to denote in bounds and out. A coach or team manager will remove it when the gymnast lands the pass safely. The uneven bar rotation, in particular, has the feel of a NASCAR race, with assistant coaches and managers acting like a pit crew, pulling mats in and out throughout the routine, and then quickly adjusting the rail setting between gymnasts.

The day after the Utah versus UCLA showdown, I attended a Saturday-morning workout at the Utes' training facility. The girls were already on the spinning bikes when I arrived. Co–head coach Megan Marsden, who had been a standout Ute in the mid-'80s, explained that during the competition season, they maintain their cardiovascular fitness this way—on the bikes instead of hitting the pavement for a run or something similarly impactful—because the coaching staff is trying to preserve the gymnasts' bodies. After the girls were done with their cycling assignment, they headed into the main gym for a conditioning circuit. Greg explained that they like to bring them into the gym after a competition for a short workout in order to set eyes on them and see if anything physically is amiss, an injury or imbalance that might have been masked during the meet by adrenaline.

The training facility, though not as large as Texas Dreams down in Dallas, was more than adequate for the relatively small team of twelve to sixteen gymnasts that made up the squad. There were several sets of bars and beams of differing heights. All of the apparatuses adjoined foam pits to give the gymnasts the option of practicing their dismounts and tumbling passes onto soft surfaces. This gleaming, sunlit gym with adjoining cardiovascular and weight rooms, the trainers and the masseuse, they all highlight a paradox of which Marsden himself spoke. Though there are fewer teams than there once had been, the ones that remain are better funded and staffed than ever before. And as K. J. Kindler pointed out to me, there are now more scholarships available to the gymnasts. "In the early nineties was the time when our scholarship numbers went up dramatically. I would say that in 1990 most teams went from six scholarships to twelve, which basically doubled your opportunity to get a scholarship," she noted. "That's huge to walk out of school and have no debt."

This put the NCAA on the map for the parents of high-level gymnasts. And perhaps this is part of the reason that from the mid-'90s onward, more international elites seemed to pursue the NCAA, at least anecdotally. The year 2000 was the first when more than half of the Olympic team ended up in the collegiate ranks—Tasha Schwikert, Kristen Maloney, Elise Ray, and Jamie Dantzscher. (Also,

Alyssa Beckerman, the alternate, ended up in the NCAA.) The only two who didn't go that route were Dominique Dawes and Amy Chow, and they were returning 1996 Olympic gold medalists who had long since forfeited their eligibility in order to partake of the financial windfall from being a member of the Magnificent Seven.

Wendy Bruce, the 1992 Olympic team bronze medalist, recalled a different era when college gymnastics wasn't such a popular option for international elites. "It was the Level 10s that tried to get the scholarships, not elites," she said of the gymnasts in her day. Zmeskal-Burdette, Bruce's Olympic teammate, admitted that she hadn't even been aware of college gymnastics during her time as an elite, much less considered that route. "I didn't even know it existed," she said. "And we [Karolyi's] had several going off to college," including 1988 Olympic alternate Rhonda Faehn, who ended up competing for UCLA. Zmeskal-Burdette said she first became aware of NCAA gymnastics when she was invited to do an exhibition at a competition. Like Bruce, it was too late for her, since she had accepted money.

That Saturday morning in Salt Lake, the trainer explained the stations to the team. Former Red Rock Megan joined in, doing most of the stops on the conditioning circuit nearly thirty years after she retired from gymnastics. Her husband sat on the sidelines tossing a Frisbee back and forth with the family dog, Rocky, a three-year-old yellow Labrador possessed of enough energy to make it through a four-hour training session. Throughout the conditioning workout, Rocky would tear across the mat, jumping up in the air, practically turning 180 degrees to make the Frisbee catch. Megan told me that last year Rocky had to have surgery to repair a torn ACL. Because in gymnastics, even the coaches' dogs tear their ACLs.

A recruit from New Jersey was there that morning, too, sitting on the sidelines with her mother. They had been in town to watch the Pac-12 showdown. She had committed to enroll at Utah in the fall of the 2015. As we both watched the conditioning session, she commented to me that it seemed more lighthearted than her club workouts back home.

It's not just the workouts that look like fun—the competition does, too. After each vault, stuck or otherwise, 10 or 9.8, the whole team rushes down the runway to congratulate and high-five the gymnast. This happens after every single vault. Six vaults. Six trips down the runway for the entire team. These girls should wear Fitbits so we can know just how much extra cardio they get from this congratulatory ritual.

This vault celebration is by no means unique. This is how college gymnasts revel in every performance on every event. The routine (get it?) celebrations are part of the fun of watching the sport. These gymnasts are not demure or quiet or cowed in any way. They jump up and down and scream after each hit routine. To put it into *How I Met Your Mother* parlance, these are definitely girls who "Woo!"

"Fun" is perhaps one of the most important motivations for club gymnasts to continue the sport at the college level. "Ninety-nine percent of my clients when I ask them the question why college gymnastics, why do you want to do college gymnastics, the number one answer every single time is it looks like they're having fun. Every single time," Hicks, who now works as college recruiting consultant, told me.

Hicks doesn't consult with the country's top prospects—the elites like Bailie Key or Kyla Ross or the top Level 10s. She primarily works with what she described as "diamonds in the rough," the kind of gymnast who's healthy, has a passion for the sport, and may have been overlooked because she was not quite precocious enough. Hicks instructs gymnasts and their parents not to panic, that some of the scholarships promised to gymnasts at twelve or thirteen years of age might become available. It's inevitable that in the four years before college, some gymnasts who verbally committed will get injured and retire. Others will not weather puberty very well and might quit. And still others might simply want to move on from the sport they started as toddlers. "It's like a crap shoot because there's just too many years between then and their senior [year] in high school," Hicks said.

Though I met Kindler scouting the young prospects at the junior session of the U.S. Classic, she, too, had misgivings about early recruiting and has done a better job than most of the top coaches at bucking the trend, at least somewhat. "I believe I'm [the only] one of the top ten schools that hasn't offered a scholarship for 2018 yet," she told me late in 2014. "I really want to make sure that we're making good decisions, and I really am concerned about throwing those offers out so early." Kindler, in a small way, is like Martha Karolyi, who doesn't want to name her World Championship or Olympic team until the last possible moment. Of course, Kindler doesn't want to wait until one month before matriculation; rather, she'd like to be able to wait until a gymnast is just a couple of years away from starting her collegiate career before offering her a scholarship, if that's not too much to ask.

It's not just the coaches like Marsden and Kindler that Hicks would like to see exercise caution—it's the elites, especially the ones who have legitimate shots at the World or Olympic team. These elites are toying with the idea of going professional and signing endorsement contracts in the run-up to the Games. For an elite gymnast, this will probably be the only opportunity she has to make a significant sum of money. And because female gymnasts tend to peak before they reach university age, those in the running to make the Olympics rarely get to do both—earn money and receive a college scholarship. It's usually an either/or proposition.

Hicks acted as the chaperone for the women's team members on the 2012 post-Olympic tour, since most of the gold-medal-winning squad, with the exception of Aly Raisman, were not yet of legal age. Four of the five members had turned pro before being selected to the Olympic team: Raisman, Wieber, Douglas, and Maroney. Only Ross skipped the money (and most of the tour dates) to maintain her NCAA eligibility.

Not that Hicks blamed the other gymnasts for not thinking beyond the Olympics. "They can't even imagine past trying to make that team. There is so much pressure. There are so many hours. There is so much going on," she said. The gymnasts are teenagers who, at best, have a tenuous grasp on the future. Add to that the fact that these young women are fairly cloistered in their world of sport. Many are homeschooled and have less exposure to non-gymnast peers who are planning, not for the Olympics but for college.

And then of course, there's the money. If making the U.S. Olympic team is like winning the plain ol' lottery, then someone like Douglas won the Powerball. But her level of earning is specific only to her. You have to win the all-around to make the real money. For Douglas, the decision to turn pro in March of the Olympic year was a gamble that has more than paid off.

"The other kids, if you really look at what, with taxes, because it's thirty percent of their money is going to go to taxes, you know, so now we're looking at five hundred grand. Well, that's an education," she pointed out, with a little extra change in the bank. "A lot of times kids have absolutely no idea what an education costs. They have no idea what a scholarship is worth."

And this math does not take into account the intangibles—of being part of a team, of performing in front of sold-out crowds, of being local celebrities on campus. Farden said that Utah's record-breaking attendance numbers are a draw for many of the gymnasts he has recruited. "I can't think of a better platform to showcase your craft that you love so much than in front of fifteen thousand fans every weekend," he said.

"There's a sisterhood that goes [on] in college gymnastics that doesn't go on in elite gymnastics," Farden continued. The gymnasts live together in the dorms, train together in the gym. "For these kids, they're all going through the struggles with classes, first-time boyfriends, breakups, being away from Mom and Dad—at the same time and growing together."

Gymnastics, as a team sport, has always seemed a bit contrived to me. The team competition is basically a game of addition—each gymnast goes up, does her routine, and her score is added to the total. It's not a team sport in the way that basketball or soccer is, with the players on the field at the same time, interacting in footwork, passing balls, playing off one another. But even if the team format in gymnastics feels contrived, what is unmistakable is just how much these gymnasts seem to *need* to feel like part of the something bigger than themselves. So much so that a gymnast who has won an Olympic gold medal will do almost anything to be a part of a college team.

That January in Salt Lake City, I watched arguably the best gymnast in the Huntsman Center drag mats across the floor, check springboard settings, fill water bottles, and cheer loudly from the sidelines while her Bruin teammates swung on the bars and flipped on the beam. This sidelined gymnast was Jordyn Wieber, the 2011 World all-around champion and the 2012 Olympic team gold medalist. Now a student at UCLA, Wieber is the gymnastics team manager, a job that typically goes to an athlete who wasn't quite good enough to walk on to the team or a former team member who already competed for four seasons but is still at school finishing up her degree.

But Wieber ended up as the team manager for a different reason—she had forfeited her NCAA eligibility after she won the 2011 World title and became the presumptive favorite to win Olympic gold. Wieber extended her victory streak into 2012, winning the American Cup, the Pacific Rim Championships, and defending her U.S. national title. Her forward march was halted at the Olympic Trials, where she was defeated by the upstart Douglas. And at the Olympic Games, she didn't make the all-around final, placing outside the top two among the Americans.

Though Wieber toyed with the idea of returning to elite competition after the Games, she decided instead to matriculate at UCLA, where coach Val Kondos Field had promised to find a way to bring her on to the team in some capacity. Which is why she was pulling mats and filling water bottles. That's how badly this Olympic gold medalist and World champion wanted to be on a college team.

Despite the risk that some top prospects will turn pro before matriculation, it makes sense to recruit elites like Wieber out of the ninth or tenth grade. After all, they have the greatest gymnastics abilities. "It's always good to have someone, you know, an elite or two or three on your team," Marsden told me, "because they usually do bring execution and skill level. You know, most of them can back off dramatically. And so what they're doing is very easy for them, and so they're very consistent and execute very well." Some of the best NCAA gymnasts had once been former elites, such as 2008 Olympic silver medalists Samantha Peszek and Bridget Sloan, of UCLA and Florida respectively. In 2015, Peszek and Florida's Kytra Hunter, both former senior international elites, tied for the NCAA all-around title and each won one event apiece in the apparatus finals. And one of best college gymnasts of all time was Courtney Kupets. As an elite, she had been 2002 World Champion on the uneven bars, a member of the 2003 gold-medal-winning World Championship team, and double medalist at the 2004 Olympics. As a gymnast at Georgia, she led the Gym Dogs to four consecutive NCAA titles and won the all-around three times.

Despite the success that international elites often enjoy at the college level, they are by no means unbeatable. As Farden pointed out, "Level 10 is the great equalizer." It doesn't matter that an elite like Kupets or Ashley Postell has many more skills up her leotard sleeve—since scores in college are capped at 10, they don't get extra credit for going above and beyond. And if they're slightly off, they can be beaten by a Level 10 with an easier routine who performs it flawlessly. Tricia Woo, a former Nebraska star, spoke proudly of bettering elites during her college career. "I was just a Level 10, and I was kicking butt," she said in a podcast interview.

Kindler and OU, in particular, have been singled out for achieving more than expected without many big names in their lineups. They have relied on a bevy of rising elites and Level 10s who seem to get better in college. When I asked Kindler how she has managed to find these gymnasts, she said, "We keep teaching. I think they're really still hungry to keep learning so that's important."

"I would say with recruiting the way it is now, I'm super disappointed in it because it has made what we've been very successful at very difficult. I'm looking at 2018 graduates," she told me in the fall of 2014. "Well, they're freshmen and they really haven't reached the level," meaning Level 10, which is where the gymnasts need to be to get recruited. "I'm worried that gymnasts will actually quit the sport because they haven't received a scholarship yet and they're a freshman," Kindler said.

Kindler has another reason not to doggedly pursue elites. "They do have to survive another, well, in this case eight years. That's a long time to stay healthy when you're in the elite program and you're pushing those numbers and working the difficulty that you have to work," she pointed out. "There's four years between now and then, and then four years when they get here. There are so many unanswered questions. You'd know a lot more if they were juniors or seniors."

In addition to the physical wear and tear, many elite stars arrive at college with emotional baggage that other gymnasts don't bear—that of thwarted dreams. Regardless of training or selection tactics, at the end of the day, it's a winner-take-all system. There are only so many spots on any given team. "When you have the dream of the World Championship team or the Olympics, and only five or six young women get to be on that team, that's a gigantic dream and not very many people get to experience that. If you fall short of it, you are wounded," Kindler said.

And even those who make the national team, the World Championship team, and even the Big O—the Olympic team—look forward to their collegiate experience. For some elite gymnasts, NCAA gymnastics is nothing short of redemptive.

This is how it was for Hollie Vise. In 2003, Vise was fifteen and a rising star on the national team after a superstar junior career. That year, she placed second in the all-around at the National Championships and was named to the World Championship team. In Anaheim, she helped the United States win the team gold. As an individual, she won a gold medal on the uneven bars, tying teammate Chellsie Memmel. But less than a year later, hampered by injuries, Vise failed to make the Olympic team.

After this blow, she couldn't bring herself to go back into training. Though she dutifully returned to the gym, she didn't really do much on the equipment. And then she stopped conditioning. Six months after the missed Games, she wasn't doing anything aside from coaching some youngsters. By her own admission, she was woefully out of shape.

This would have been fine had Vise officially retired from gymnastics, but she hadn't. She had accepted a college scholarship offer from Steve Nunno, Shannon Miller's former coach, who was then in charge of the women's team in Norman. At that point, OU was not a top-ranked school in women's gymnastics. It did well in its own conference but never threatened to win the National Championships or even make the Super Six, which is the NCAA team final. Vise, as a World gold medalist, had been one of the biggest names that OU had ever recruited. She was going to be expected to contribute scores to the team total.

At least on the balance beam. In an interview with *Inside Gymnastics* at the end of her collegiate career, she recalled the conversation she had had with Nunno. "He had said, 'As long as you can do beam for me, that's great.' I thought, 'Okay, that sounds easy enough,'" she told the magazine.

But shortly before Vise began her freshman year, Nunno was replaced by Kindler, who had led Iowa State to its first appearance in the Super Six. Vise later admitted that she was very nervous about meeting the new coach. She knew that she was in trouble.

Kindler recalled the beginning of Vise's freshman year. "She was very out of shape and very emotionally broken," she told me. "She shared with me that Coach Nunno really wanted her to do beam when she got here [to OU] and that he would be okay with that, just beam." But Kindler was not okay with that arrangement. "I said, 'Well I'm actually not. I really want you to do everything.' I think that really caught her off guard."

Kindler had a lot of work to do. Not only did she have to get Vise back into competitive shape, she had to renew her love for the sport. This isn't something Kindler had to do for just Vise. She had to do this for many of the elites she has recruited over the years. "I've had a lot of elites that have had very interesting stories," she said, "elites that maybe [were] incredibly talented women, amazing athletes, who, for one reason or another, had one sort of massive obstacle that prevented them from doing what they wanted to do at that level."

Kindler viewed it as her job to help these gymnasts recover from these types of disappointments and move forward. "I have to create this new experience and remind them why they do this sport, why they love it, why they started it, and why when they were five years old they wanted to keep going and do cartwheels in their parents' living room."

This is precisely what Kindler did with Vise. "I'll be honest, I was kind of intimidated. I walked in going, 'I'm going to coach the World champion? What am I going to teach her?' Well, it turns out I kind of had a lot to offer because she needed me in a different way." At first, Kindler was spotting Vise on the kip, which is a crucial yet elementary element on the uneven bars, an event on which Vise had once dazzled the world with intricate pirouettes and high-flying release moves. "I was spotting the World bar champion on kips and our goal was to make three kips before she left the gym in a row," she recalled. "And she couldn't. She could maybe do two sometimes. This is what we were struggling for."

Eventually Vise made it all the way back—first, on beam and then bars. By her senior year, she occasionally made the team lineups on every single apparatus. At the 2010 NCAA Championships, the Sooners placed second in the team competition, their best ever finish at that point. And Vise, who had only started performing on floor exercise during her senior year, placed second on the event in what would be her last competitive routine ever. Redemption complete.

When Vise reflected on the end of her collegiate career in 2010, she didn't seem to regret any of what she had to do in order to get through her four years at Oklahoma. In fact, she confessed to missing gymnastics. "I find myself thinking, *When I go in the gym the next time, I'll try this*, and then it's like, *Oh, there is no next time*. That's scary," Vise said. "As soon as it started getting really good, it's over."

"I feel like a lot of these girls graduate, and they're doing their best gymnastics. I really do," Kindler said, subverting the conventional wisdom for female gymnasts—that it's all downhill after you turn sixteen. This is probably why she and her staff have worked so hard to help gymnasts like Vise recover their skills and passion for the sport. "There was something we saw in them in the first place that we went after them. If we can just get them back to that place," she added, trailing off a bit.

Kindler was not just talking about the disheartened elites. She was talking about injured athletes, too. When she took over from Nunno, she said there were five athletes on medical scholarship, meaning that they had been given permission to leave the team due to injuries. "Something that speaks to our program is we've only had one athlete in nine years that was on a medical scholarship at all," she said. That's not to say that there haven't been injuries. It's gymnastics, which, according to some studies, is only second to football when it comes to injuries. Further, by the time these gymnasts arrive on campus, they've been pounding their bodies as club gymnasts for upward of eight years. If they don't show up at college injured, it is inevitable that their bodies will break down, at least somewhat, at some point, during their four years on the team. And when that happens, coaches, trainers, and gymnasts have to decide what they're going to do—do they want to rehabilitate the gymnast or will they let her quit? "We want to give them the chance to come back," Kindler said. "We want to motivate them to come back if they have an injury and not give up on them."

Marsden echoed Kindler's sentiments about the trajectory of the elites he has recruited over the years. As freshmen, the adjustment can be difficult, moving from elite to NCAA, from very difficult routines to simpler exercises masterfully executed. Samantha Peszek, a 2008 Olympian who graduated from UCLA in 2015, spoke candidly about how hard that transition had been when she first started competing in college. Though she was enjoying school, campus life, and being part of a team, "the only thing I wasn't loving was my gymnastics," she said in an interview with UCLA Athletics during her fifth and final year. "You come from an elite program where the skill level is a lot higher and you train a lot more, so kind of figuring out the whole college gymnastics adjustment was really difficult for me. I don't think I loved that part at the beginning."

During that first year or two in the NCAA, many elites will do okay but perhaps not great. "It usually takes a year or two for them to kind of recover from that and kind of rediscover the sport in a different way, and fall back in love with it," Marsden said. "And then in their last year or two, they are just on fire and unbelievable, and as good or better than ever."

Some collegiate stars have such a great time in the NCAA that they don't stop doing gymnastics after they graduate. In 2012, former UCLA star Anna Li was named as one of the alternates to the U.S. Olympic team. In 2004, UCLA had two representatives at the Olympics—Mohini Bhardwaj, who had already graduated, competed for the silver-medal-winning American squad, and Kate Richardson, still in college, made the Canadian team. Both gymnasts made the floor exercise finals that year with Richardson using her NCAA choreography (albeit with upgraded tumbling) on the Olympic stage. Utah star Daria Bijak competed for her country, Germany, in 2008 between college seasons. And Jessica Lopez, who had competed for Denver as a college gymnast, now represents Venezuela. At twenty-eight, she finished in the top ten in the all-around at the 2014 World Championships in Nanning.

Other former NCAA athletes sign contracts with Cirque du Soleil or move to Hollywood and get into stunt work. One of the top stuntwomen in the business, Heidi Moneymaker, is a former Bruin and member of the 1997 squad that won UCLA's first NCAA title. And of course, there's always coaching, a career path that many former gymnasts follow. Most of the newly appointed NCAA head coaches had once been gymnasts themselves. In addition to Kindler and Faehn, there is Tabitha Yim, former World team member and Stanford star, who is the head coach of the Arizona Wildcats. The 2000 Olympians Ray and Maloney are both assistant coaches at the University of Washington and Iowa State, respectively. And Jenny Rowland, the 1989 World team alternate, succeeded Faehn at the University of Florida.

Still, none of this—coaching, stunting, circus performing—is the same as doing gymnastics, four events in competition. These are all simply offshoots of the sport, ways to use the skills you developed for over twenty years to earn some income. It's a little bit like getting a law degree and using it in some other capacity—to help draft and parse contracts for your business. It's useful but not truly what your JD was designed for. But there is no such thing as professional gymnastics. For those gymnasts who wish to keep going past their college years, this is the best they can do.

———

While it may be tempting to consider collegiate gymnastics apart from its elite sister—after all, they use different scoring systems, they have separate requirements, and distinct priorities—the overall success of the U.S. national team in the past decade owes a lot to the NCAA's appeal to elite gymnasts as well as the Level 10s in this country. If the only thing a gymnast could possibly shoot for is the national team, then many would end up dropping out once they came to the conclusion that this was an impossibility. But the domestic scene in the United States is robust and competitive. This has more to do with the lure of college than of the Olympics. Hicks remembered speaking with USA Gymnastics president Steve Penny when she was still coaching at Cal State Fullerton and trying to fund-raise to save the program there. "We had a lot of conversations about how everybody needs each other," she said. "There's so many parents that think, *Maybe my daughter will go elite*, and it doesn't happen, but then they have this other track.

"I wonder, statistically, what it would look like if we didn't have that," Hicks added. It's hard to know—the college program has existed alongside the elite track for most of the modern era of the sport. In the United States, it's hard to imagine one without the other. But it is probable that the talent pool would be much shallower, not just for the Americans but for countries such as Canada or

Great Britain. Many of their Olympic-level elites end up competing in the U.S. collegiate system as well.

And what would the NCAA look like without the 10? This is not something that fans need to worry about. "We will never change it," Kindler said emphatically of the Perfect 10 in college gymnastics. Kindler is the chair of the Women's Collegiate Program Committee, which controls the rules of the NCAA game, so it's safe to say she has a lot of input on this subject. "A 10 means something in more than just gymnastics. You can ask anybody on the street what a '10' is and they know," Kindler pointed out. "Why would you take that away?"

Perhaps for the same reasons it was eliminated at the elite level—to better distinguish between good and great, to make sure that the winners are "correct." This, according to Marsden, is the wrong way to look at it. "My thing is—it doesn't matter who wins. It matters that a lot of people have a chance to win and that it's a kickass event," he said, banging on the table, "that everybody who comes walks out and goes, 'Wow, that was fun. That was exciting.' "

And forty years after Nadia, there's still nothing more exciting than watching a gymnast score a Perfect 10.

CONCLUSION:
THE 10 IS NOT A TIME MACHINE

At the 2015 World Championships in Glasgow, Scotland, Nadia Comaneci was on hand to watch the shifting fortunes in women's gymnastics—her team, the Romanians, failed to qualify to the Olympic Games while the Netherlands (literally) danced its way toward its first full-team berth at the Olympics in forty years. When asked what she would bring back to the sport from its gloried past, the most recognizable gymnast of all time answered, "It's hard for me to say bring the 10.0 back, but somehow somebody needs to figure out a way to bring it back. Somebody smart should find a way to bring the 10.0 back?"

This answer is hardly unexpected coming from the 10's most famous recipient. And in the decade since the iconic mark was stripped from the sport, Comaneci has not been the only person who has lamented its demise and argued for its resurrection. Many coaches and past champions have echoed the same idea. The 10—or the lack thereof—has been scapegoated for nearly everything that's wrong with the sport from escalation in difficulty to the demise of artistry to alleged declining popularity to lack of audience comprehensibility. (I'll stipulate only to that last one.)

But how would bringing back the 10 do all of the things that its most ardent supporters wish it would? It won't make the once-great nations—Romania and Russia—great again, because the material conditions and infrastructure that helped those countries excel have eroded since the fall of Communism across Eastern Europe. It won't bring the coaches who left for better paychecks back to the countries of their births. It won't make the sport more artistic. It won't bring back the world in which Korbut, Comaneci, and Kim won gold medals and global popularity, a world with just three television channels and no X Games.

Because the 10 is not a time machine.

———

"Development will never stop," Nellie Kim, the 10's second recipient, told me after the women's competition at the 2015 World Championships concluded. "If you see girls already performing double layout with a turn, so a little bit later, it will probably be a double layout with three turns," she added. The move toward greater complexity and difficulty is what imperiled and ultimately ended the 10. This forward march will continue until we reach the limits of what the human body can do, a line that keeps moving. After all, back in Comaneci's and Kim's day, everyone thought we were at the edge of human ability. And forty years later, we're still moving forward, albeit at a much slower pace than at the beginning of the Perfect 10 era.

In 2015, 1988 Olympic multiple gold medalist—and recipient of countless perfect marks herself—Daniela Silivas pointed out that not much has changed, difficulty-wise, since her retirement from the sport in 1989, more than two decades ago. "It really amazes me that they still do a lot of skills that we did twenty-five to twenty-seven years ago," she said. Silivas had been a key player in that staggering escalation in difficulty, becoming the first woman to perform a double twisting double somersault on floor exercise in competition all the way back in 1988. The skill now bears her name in the *Code of Points*. For all but the most elite of tumblers, the Silivas is still one of the most difficult skills that they can do.

The decrease in the rate of increase in difficulty has helped reverse one of the trends that Comaneci and her cohorts encouraged—that of the youthful gymnast. There are tweaks to the rules every four years, but in the absolute sense, the difficulty in women's gymnastics hasn't skyrocketed dramatically over the past twenty years, with the exception of on the uneven bars, an event that has been revolutionized since the introduction of open-ended scoring. What this means is that once a gymnast has mastered most of her skill set as a teen, she won't have to update it constantly in order to remain competitive with the up-and-coming youngsters. The real challenge for older gymnasts is not being outstripped by the rules but staying fit and healthy.

Despite gymnastics' reputation as being a sport for young teens, many elite gymnasts have been competing well into their twenties with great success. As Shannon Miller recently noted in a podcast interview, "There are so many athletes that are hanging around for two, even three Olympics." Gymnasts such as Russia's Ksenia Afanasyeva, who will compete in her third Games if she makes it to Rio, and teammates Viktoria Komova, Aliya Mustafina, and Maria Paseka, who will each be vying for their second Olympics. Romania has Catalina Ponor, who will going after her third berth after winning three gold medals all the way back in 2004. Italy's Vanessa Ferrari, the first World all-around champion under the new scoring system, is in her mid-twenties and still competing. Rio will be her third Olympics. "Gymnastics has more longevity than it ever has, I think it's good for the sport," Miller observed.

These older athletes are hardly an aberration. Nearly every country boasts a standout gymnast competing successfully into her twenties. Ponor won a medal on floor in 2012. Afanasyeva just picked a World Championships medal in Glasgow where Paseka won her first World title on the vault. These older gymnasts are not merely participating; they're still winning medals.

And in some nations, such as Poland and Uzbekistan, these older gymnasts are the only athletes they have. Which brings us to another reason for the seeming increase in gymnast age in the last decade: lack of competition coming up the ranks. In countries with underdeveloped programs, older gymnasts can maintain their positions on major teams without constantly being threatened by the younger cohort. In 2016, age in gymnastics really should be viewed through the lens of team depth; the greater the number of high-level gymnasts a country has, the younger the average age on the national team seems to be. This is another reason why Ponor can come out of retirement the year before the Olympics to make the Romanian squad: the former gymnastics superpower doesn't really have anyone better to take her place.

The only two countries that still seem to have deep reserves of young talent are the United States and China. They also have some of the youngest teams out on the floor. In London, the oldest gymnast on the American team was eighteen. And in Glasgow, half of the Chinese squad had just turned sixteen. Age may be nothing but a number, as Aaliyah sang, but team depth is significant.

Yet even on the incredibly deep American team, which has a seemingly endless supply of fresh-faced stars, older gymnasts can still find great success. At the 2015 World Championships, every single one of the gymnasts, including the alternate, was eighteen or older. Two were returning Olympic champions. This was the first

time in decades that the United States sent a team to a major competition without at least one member who was not yet old enough
to drive in all fifty states. This might be the first time that the years
are spread across the whole team, but with the exception of the Bela
Karolyi era—1991 to 1996—U.S. Olympic teams have always featured a range of ages, from the very young to women who can rent
cars. In 2004, the team featured two women in their mid-twenties
in addition to teenagers. In 2000, with the exception of one fifteen-
year-old, the entire team was eighteen or older. In 1988, Kelly
Garrison-Steves was married and in her early twenties.

This doesn't mean that youthfulness isn't still an important factor
in women's gymnastics. It's just that talent and ability have always
meant more. A thirty-year-old Simone Biles, if she's still training
at that age, will probably be able to defeat any teen gymnasts that
come her way.

And it's not just increased diversity in age that we've seen in the
post-10 era. President Grandi, in his closing remarks at the 2015
World Championships, noted the accomplishments of gymnasts
of color. He seemed pleased with the success of athletes like Biles,
Gabby Douglas, and Manrique Larduet, a black male gymnast from
Cuba who won his country's first World all-around medal. "Black
people have the possibility to win in gymnastics in fantastic mode,"
he said in his thick Italian accent.

Much was made of Douglas's Olympic all-around win in 2012, a
first for an African American gymnast. The lack of black gymnasts at
the top of the Olympic medal heap up until recently could be partly
ascribed to the shifting fortunes in global gymnastics. Up until 2000,
the dominant forces in international gymnastics were Russia and
Romania, two countries without significant—or any—black populations. The medal podiums reflected those countries' demographics.

But as the United States started to become the strongest force in women's gymnastics, black gymnasts started earning more international accolades. America has won every single Olympic all-around title since 2004. Douglas's win in 2012 accounts for one-third of those three Olympic victories. To get a sense of how diverse the ranks of U.S. gymnastics are, watch a college competition. Gymnasts of color are hardly the exception in the NCAA. And with the rise in the global rankings of other countries with minority populations like Great Britain, women's gymnastics promises to become even more diverse in the coming years.

Eliminating the 10 didn't bring about these changes. The world had changed and gymnastics along with it. And the 10, which had been at once beautiful and fraught, no longer seemed to work quite as well in a postmodern, data-driven sports world with the internet and instant replay. We might have always known that perfection is impossible, but I think we're less willing to lie to ourselves about it anymore.

The calls to bring back the 10 are less vehement than they were when the new *Code* was first introduced. "Everything new, it takes time for people to learn," Kim said. It's been nearly ten years, and it seems that the coaches, athletes, and even the public have adjusted to the points-based system introduced in 2006. In 2015, the BBC's ratings for the World Championships were high, outperforming perennials like athletics. Ticket sales were also strong with some sessions being completely sold out. The crowd in the SSE Hydro Arena was fully engaged the whole time. Loud cheers went up after nearly every exercise. Scores in the high 15s and low 16s were applauded as loudly as though they were 10s. And the audience for the sport is young. This bodes well for the future popularity of gymnastics, especially in places like Asia and the United States. The sport is doing just fine despite the 10's absence.

"Would you have wanted to compete under this *Code*?" I asked Kim. "Yes," she answered without any hesitation. "For me, it would be an absolutely perfect system." After all, she had performed a higher degree of difficulty than most gymnasts of her era, but with the 10 she was never more than a hair's breadth ahead of her competitors.

Kim's willingness to accept this *Code* underscored the differences that the 10 played in her life compared to Comaneci's. The Romanian had come to symbolize the score and the sport, but for Kim, the 10 was just a mark, a ranking, a gold medal. Kim became a politician and bureaucrat within the Federation, climbing the ranks to her present position. She was—and still is—only known within the gymnastics community. Kim wears the ill-fitting blue blazer of the judge; Comaneci wears designer clothing, goes to movie premieres, and is a Special Olympics ambassador.

Kim mused about whether her 10s would withstand her judge's scrutiny. "I have this temptation sometimes to evaluate my own exercises from the past," she said. "Actually on vault, I don't see many possibilities for deductions," she noted of the first of her two perfect scores in Montreal. "When I look at the vault, there is no deduction if you follow the rule in 1976." But not only are the rules different today, so is the mind-set of the judge. They are more motivated than ever before to find a deduction. The judges have grown savvier along with their audiences. "You can always find something," Kim added. They will never give the gymnast the 10, the pat on the back she's been craving, the "That'll do, pig" from the farmer in *Babe*.

"I still should not complain because I think it was good [in] 1976," she said with a laugh.

But it wasn't the rules that made Kim, Comaneci, or Biles great. "The best gymnasts will adjust to any *Code of Points*. The good gymnasts are always good. If you take myself or also Nadia, we would end up with the same results with this *Code of Points*, too."

The gymnasts and the sport have been and always will be greater than the scores affixed to them. That part will never change.

AFTERWORD FOR THE PAPERBACK EDITION

On August 9, 2016, the five-member squad for Team USA—Simone Biles, Madison Kocian, Laurie Hernandez, Aly Raisman, and Gabby Douglas—won the team title at the 2016 Games in Rio. It was the result that everyone had predicted long before the team was formally chosen at the beginning of July. They competed in a dominating fashion, hitting every single routine start to finish, besting Russia by more than eight points. As they celebrated their win on the podium, they announced their team name to the audience and cameras. They were, as they said, "the Final Five." For the next Olympic Games in 2020, team size will be reduced to just four gymnasts. "The Final Five" is also the last team of Martha Karolyi's tenure as national team coordinator for USA Gymnastics. Forty years after Nadia Comaneci, her most famous pupil, scored the first Perfect 10s in Montreal, Karolyi had declared that Rio would be her final Olympic Games. Moments after winning, the Final Five huddled around Karolyi to reveal their team name and the seventy-two-year-old coach burst into tears, covering her face with her hands.

If only the story of American gymnastics in 2016 had ended here. A month after the team's win and the U.S. women's record medal haul—nine—a member of the 2000 Olympic team filed a lawsuit against USA Gymnastics, alleging that the former team doctor,

Larry Nassar, had sexually abused her from the time she was a junior level athlete until she retired from elite gymnastics at eighteen to attend college. The suit claimed that the former Olympic medalist and NCAA champion hadn't come to terms with the abuse she'd endured during the course of medical treatments administered by Nassar until July 2016. The gymnast, identified as "Jane Doe" (who, since filing her suit, has come forward and revealed her identity. She's 2000 Olympic bronze medalist Jamie Dantzscher who was interviewed in Chapter 6) in the suit, claimed that he fondled her breasts and spoke frankly about sex with the then-underage athlete. She also alleged that he penetrated her vagina with his finger without gloves or lubrication (and without written consent of a guardian), under the guise of medical treatment.

Jane Doe's accusations were mirrored in almost every detail in the account given by Rachael Denhollander, a former club gymnast who had been treated in the early aughts by Nassar in his home state of Michigan. Nassar was on the faculty of Michigan State University and saw patients at the clinic. He also worked with their NCAA gymnastics team. Soon, more women came forward, telling very similar stories. They all claimed that Nassar had digitally penetrated them during the course of treatment, usually for hip or back pain. Nassar, through his attorney, maintained that any procedures he had done were legitimate parts of osteopathic medical practice.

The accusations against Nassar came on the heels of an investigation by the *Indianapolis Star* looking into how USA Gymnastics handled allegations of sex abuse against coaches. According to depositions obtained by the paper, the leadership of USA Gymnastics kept files on coaches who had come under suspicion of sex abuse but did not immediately report them. USA Gymnastics required that either the victim or the victim's parent make the complaint before they acted. As many pointed out, this standard gives insufficient support to victims, many of whom are too scared or ashamed to come forward to the authorities or even to their parents. The *Star*'s investigation prompted Denhollander to file a criminal complaint and tell her story to the newspaper. Her complaint and the first Jane Doe's lawsuit opened the floodgates of allegations against Nassar.

About a month after the first suit was filed, a second former national team member, also referred to as "Jane LM Doe," filed suit against Nassar; USA Gymnastics; president of USA Gymnastics, Steve Penny; and past president Bob Colarossi. This second lawsuit, however, also implicated both Bela and Martha Karolyi, as well as the Jane LM Doe's personal coaches, Galina Marinova and Artur Akopyan. The suit claimed that the national team staff and coaches created an environment of secrecy and fear, which enabled a sexual abuser like Nassar to thrive.

As of this writing, more than eighty women have come forward, most from Michigan. Several women have joined ranks to file suit against Nassar's former employer, Michigan State University, USA Gymnastics, and other individuals for failing to protect them from the doctor.

In mid-December 2016, Nassar was arrested by the FBI on child pornography charges. In the trove of 37,000 images found on Nassar's hard drives, the FBI discovered GoPro footage of Nassar molesting victims in a pool. Before this arrest, he had been out on bail after having been formally charged with first degree criminal sexual conduct with a person under thirteen. The abuse allegedly took place between 1998 and 2005 in the doctor's home. This girl, unlike most of the victims who have come forward, was not a gymnast.

I first heard of Larry Nassar in 2013 when I listened to an interview with him on the GymCastic podcast, quoted in Chapters 6 and 7 of this book. Though my knowledge of the sport was deep and comprehensive, it had never occurred to me to think about the doctors who treat the athletes. I hadn't considered who provides the medical treatment at the national team training camps and competitions. Up until that episode, I never realized that one man had been at the helm for so long.

In the interview, Nassar came off as caring and passionate about athlete well-being. He singled out the 2000 team for sympathy and praise. The squad had placed fourth at the 2000 Olympics in Sydney. Coming after the Magnificent Seven's triumph in 1996, their placement was seen as a failure and the team was largely forgotten by the media, which was quick to move on to the next generation of gymnasts who won several medals in the 2001–2004 quadrennium.

I was heartened to hear Nassar acknowledge this particular group and all they had gone through in 2000. I, too, had felt they had gotten a raw deal—both from USA Gymnastics, which had upended their preparation schedules less than a year before the Games with grueling training camp and the media, who made their fourth place finish seem like a loss. (As mentioned in Chapter 6, their finish was upgraded to third in 2010.) And I was even more pleased when Nassar spoke about the improvements to training and injury care at the Ranch. He told Jessica O'Beirne, the host of the podcast, that Martha Karolyi had him check in with coaches to make sure they weren't pushing their athletes while they recovered from injuries. This was what all those who loved the sport wanted to hear—that the training, while still tough, was less extreme than it had once been and that the athletes were better looked after than they had been before. Nassar spoke of it as an evolution—from bad to better.

It was unusual to hear someone involved in USA Gymnastics in any official capacity to even acknowledge the negatives publicly. This was why I had sought him out for an interview.

At the time, there wasn't cause to question his assertions. He seemed like a credible source, one who didn't stand to gain much from the success of any individual athlete. It didn't matter to his career which athletes were named to the squad and which ones were left behind. He was charged with keeping the *whole* team healthy through the long competition season.

Now, with the knowledge of what Nassar is alleged to have done, what to make of his assertions of improvement in the national team training system and the treatment of athletes at the Ranch?

As of this writing, it is unclear whether USA Gymnastics knew the extent of his activities with national team members. In a statement, the organization revealed that, upon being notified of "athlete concerns" in the spring of 2015, they removed Dr. Nassar from his position with the national team and reported him to the FBI.

"It's a perfect storm," Wendy Bruce Martin, a 1992 Olympic bronze medalist, told me. "He had his pick of kids. Then you also have the trust, the wanting to be in that inner circle," she explained. "What would you sacrifice to be on the team? If they did feel like something was wrong, would they have ever said anything to jeopardize their position?" Athlete health can be a factor in team selection, which meant that someone like a doctor could be influential, even if he didn't have a seat on the selection committee. Perhaps an abused athlete might worry about whether or not she'd be allowed to compete if she came forward to the coaches about the invasive "treatment" she had been subjected to.

If she even realized that something abusive had taken place. In the first Jane Doe suit, the former gymnast acknowledged that she hadn't told anyone about what had happened to her as an elite gymnast until more than a decade after the abuse had ended. She had been young, just thirteen or fourteen, when the abuse had started and didn't realize at the time that the way the doctor treated her crossed any legal or moral lines.

"Gymnasts aren't taught to speak up," Bruce Martin told me. This is why gymnasts like Jane Doe didn't come forward sooner.

Still, it was surprising to most in the gymnastics community when the allegations first surfaced against Nassar. I spoke to several insiders shocked by the absence of rumors swirling around the doctor. When 1984 Olympic coach Don Peters was banned from the sport in 2011 for sexually abusing his athletes, it came after decades of whispers about inappropriate behavior.

After the first allegations about Nassar were made in September 2016, stories—some dating back more than a decade—started to surface. One Michigan State University softball player alleged that she had complained to staff in 1999 about the treatments she had received for a back injury; her complaints were brushed aside. A young woman filed a police report in 2004 regarding treatment received in Nassar's office. The matter seemed to end with the complaint. The police never sent the charges to the county prosecutor. In 2014, MSU investigated a complaint from a female graduate student who alleged sexual abuse during an examination, which resulted in a Title IX investigation. Nassar was cleared by MSU staff and doctors who had longstanding relationships with him. Yet again, Nassar's prestige protected him, and word of his misconduct never seemed to move beyond the people immediately involved in each incident.

Nassar had also constructed a good guy persona as someone who was always available to help. "He was my go-to guy," Bruce Martin said. She told me that she reached out to him, via Facebook messenger, to get his professional opinion on her daughter's cheerleading injury just over a month before the lawsuits and allegations were made public.

In a thread on GymCastic's Facebook page, Aimee Boorman, Simone Biles's coach, spoke to the kind of trust that Nassar had garnered over the years. "I can honestly say that, knowing Dr. Nassar for five years, there was no sign of him being a predator. I had heard nothing from other gymnasts or other coaches. I trusted this man. I confided in this man. I would have considered him my friend," she began. But Boorman wasn't rushing to Nassar's defense. "It is sickening," she continued, "what he has done to these poor children for so many years."

Below Boorman's comment, Christy Sharp, a renowned gymnastics photographer and a former gymnast at Michigan State University, also admitted to being clueless despite close proximity to Nassar. "I have known him for seventeen years, he was my team doc at MSU . . . and the same was true for me. I had no idea."

Bruce Martin, who remembers him working with the national team when she was an athlete in the early and mid '90s, also can't recall anything suspicious at the time. "There weren't a lot of signs as far as I was concerned. I didn't see him go into anybody's room or do anything weird. I didn't see any of that. If I did, I don't even think I would've thought it was strange," she said. Part of it was the culture then. No one was talking about sex abuse.

"You're thinking, he's alone in a room taping an ankle. Or he's alone in a room and he dropped off an ice bag and some Bengay. You're not thinking, he's alone in the room with somebody, crossing boundaries," she said.

This behavior—of treating unchaperoned athletes, of being alone in rooms with the gymnasts—points to a problem not in the memories and perceptions of these former athletes who were young and under a lot of pressure but with the practices of USA Gymnastics. It may have figured out how to better train athletes and win medals, but it clearly has not fully worked out how to protect athletes.

While USA Gymnastics has announced it has hired a former prosecutor to review its protocols and guidelines regarding sexual abuse and athlete safety, change is most likely to come from the outside. In early 2017, the USOC officially opened SafeSport, which will assume responsibility for handling sexual abuse complaints coming from athletes in America's forty-seven Olympic sports organizations.

———

In writing a book about women's gymnastics, I wanted to concentrate on the history and development of the sport from the postwar era to the present without exclusively focusing on its pathology. While sex abuse in youth sports, including gymnastics, is not uncommon, I, like many others in the gymnastics world, had been unaware that the trusted doctor, a man who *everyone* went to, was one of the worst offenders.

I still believe that women's gymnastics is bigger than just what ails it, but the sex abuse and failure to protect athletes cannot be ignored. Nassar, who has pled not guilty to all of the charges, is unlikely to beat the charges against him and will probably remain locked up (he is currently being held without bail on the federal child pornography charges), but this is not where the story ends. Nassar's arrest highlights the need for expanded protocols and greater oversight, and steps taken by USA Gymnastics and individual coaches will hopefully create institutional change. Keeping gymnasts safe has to go beyond mats and foam pits, beyond protecting them from broken bones and torn ligaments. It has to be creating an environment where they feel as empowered to speak up as they do to flip on the beam and where the adults who are tasked with training them care as much about their overall well-being as they do for their athletic success.

ACKNOWLEDGMENTS

There are so many people who have supported me as I wrote this book. First, there are my neighbors. Michael, Michelle, Jason, and especially the denizens of 6A (Cynthia, Phoenix, and Orion) for helping take care of my dog while I was out of town researching the book. And for walking her when I was in town but way too stressed to leave my desk.

Members of the gymnastics writing and media community—Jess, Elizabeth, Cordelia, Georgia, Blythe, Lauren—for reading over parts of the book and making sure my logic and command of facts were sound. And to Bea, for not only reading chunks of the book but helping with translation of texts and interviews from Romanian to English. To my gymnastics coach Lisi for introducing me to the sport and getting me to do the skills I was afraid of. And, of course, for putting up with a very sarcastic ten-year-old.

Lindsey—thanks for first planting the idea of writing this book in my head. Andrew, for helping me get through the year of writing and research. Avi, who spent so much time reading chapters and reassuring me that the book wasn't going to be terrible. To my agent, Allison, for putting up with a very neurotic writer and taking me out for drinks when I was falling apart. And to my editor, Michelle, for having to deal with my obsessiveness and tendency to overwrite.

ACKNOWLEDGMENTS

To all the coaches, judges, and gymnasts who spoke to me and allowed me into their gyms to watch practices and get in the way.

To coffee for animating me: mind, body, and spirit!

And of course, to my mother who drove me to gymnastics practice every Sunday morning even though, as she told me often, she really wanted to stay in bed and sleep. She understood how important the sport was to me.

CHAPTER SOURCES

INTRODUCTION

The description of McKayla Maroney's vault from the 2012 Olympic Games is derived from the NBC broadcast of the competition. The discussion of Yelena Shushunova's and Daniela Silivas's routines in 1988 are also based on review of Olympics broadcast footage, this time from ABC.

Quotes from Nadia Comaneci's writing can be found in the gymnast's memoir *Letters to a Young Gymnast* (New York: Basic Books, 2009).

The status quoted came from Larry Nassar's Facebook wall, which he made public, https://www.facebook.com/larry.nassar/posts/534205519998527.

CHAPTER 1. SINEW AND SPANDEX: THE FIRST–AND LAST–PERFECT 10S

Description of Nadia Comaneci's first Perfect 10 on the uneven bars is derived from ABC Olympics footage.

Quotes from Comaneci from the "Sporting Greats," episode of the Sky Sports documentary series, https://www.youtube.com/watch?v=WMVxnUqnmuM.

The rest of the Comaneci quotes are from interviews conducted with the Olympic champion in Norman, Oklahoma, on December 17, 2014.

Nellie Kim's quotes were recorded on November 1, 2015, in an interview in Glasgow, Scotland.

Quotes from Abie Grossfeld were recorded at the 2015 U.S. National Championships in Indianapolis, Indiana.

Olga Korbut's account of her thwarted 10s was taken from her memoir *My Story: The Autobiography of Olga Korbut*, with Ellen Emerson-White (London: Century, 1992). Korbut's 2012 assertions that she deserved a 10 for her performances in Munich were taken from an interview with Gigi Khazback, WOGymnastikA, http://www.wogymnast.com/2012/11/olga-korbut-i-am-first-perfect-ten.html.

Description of Ludmilla Tourischeva's routine on the collapsing asymmetric bars is derived from footage of the competition, https://www.youtube.com/watch?v=3TuQSnVShdw.

CHAPTER SOURCES

Roslyn Kerr talks about the renegade style of Olga Korbut's coach, Renald Knysh, in "The Evolution of Women's Artistic Gymnastics Since 1952," her master's thesis, University of Sydney.

Larisa Latynina's quotes about Nadia Comaneci at the 1976 Olympics have been recorded in several articles and publications, both from that time and later. One quote can be found in the New York *Daily News*, 2000, http://www.nydailynews.com /archives/sports/olympic-moment-nadia-comaneci-article-1.877128. The other appears in the *New York Times*, 2012, http://www.nytimes.com/2012/08/01/sports /olympics/gymnast-larisa-latynina-is-elegant-reminder-of-olympics-history.html. Rigby's quotes can be found in the same article and in Charles Michener, *Newsweek*, August 1976, http://amanaradmirer.tripod.com/articlenadia76.html.

The letter to the editor, *International Gymnast*, October 1976. Frank Deford's account of the Games and Comaneci's performance, "Nadia Awed Ya," *Sports Illustrated*, http:// www.si.com/vault/1976/08/02/615419/nadia-awed-ya. And Rod Hill's description of the Romanians' tour of the United States in early 1976 also appeared in *International Gymnast*, October 1976.

Comaneci's account of the extreme conditioning regimen can be found in her memoir *Letters to a Young Gymnast*.

Paul Ziert's comments come from interviews conducted in his office on December 15 and 16, 2014.

Ioan Chirila's 1977 book *Nadia* is liberally excerpted in this chapter (and chapter 2). The translation was provided by Beatrice Gheorghisor.

Observations about Romanian technical prowess are drawn from Bill Sands and Mike Conklin's *Everybody's Gymnastics Book*.

The description of the Radio Shack ad that Mary Lou Retton appears in can be found at https://www.youtube.com/watch?v=8RlKvPPGvkI.

The descriptions of the floor exercise final at the 1992 Olympics were based on the broadcast, https://www.youtube.com/watch?v=LDbqzoDUtq0.

CHAPTER 2. I DON'T CARE ABOUT YOUR ART: HOW GYMNASTICS BECAME LESS ARTISTIC AND MORE ATHLETIC AFTER NADIA

In Bob Ottum's "The Search for Nadia," *Sports Illustrated*, he describes the minimonsters and a postpubescent Comaneci, http://www.si.com/vault/1979/11/19/824185/the -search-for-nadia-the-author-plunges-into-the-mists-of-transylvania-in-quest -of-the-worlds-favorite-gymnast-nadia-comaneci-she-had-been-perfect-then -she-had-faded-from-view-now-it-develops-there-is-a-new-nadia.

Paul Ziert's comments about gymnastics' "primitive" years was found "With her all time record set to fall, little known Latynina looks back" in *Sports Illustrated* in 2012, http://www.si.com/olympics/2012/07/10/larisa-latynina-michael-phelps -olympic-medals-record.

The description of Chelle Stack at the mall is derived from ABC's 1988 profile of the gymnast, https://www.youtube.com/watch?v=D5EExWlGwuI.

Laddie Bakanic describes her gymnastics career from the 1940s in an article on the website *Jezebel*: "Female Gymnasts Used to Compete on the Rings, but the Game

CHAPTER SOURCES

Changed," http://jezebel.com/5932478/female-gymnasts-used-to-compete-on-the-rings-but-the-game-changed.

The description of female gymnastics comportment in the 1930s was derived from footage uploaded to YouTube, https://www.youtube.com/watch?v=IW4VTuAdsjA.

Mary Lou Retton's words about looking up to gymnasts eight years her senior were found in her autobiography *Mary Lou Retton: Creating an Olympic Champion*, with Bela Karolyi and John Powers (New York: McGraw Hill, 1985).

Quotes from Vera Caslavska about the youth revolution in gymnastics were culled from Minot Simons II, *Women's Gymnastics: A History*, vol. 1, *1966 to 1974* (Carmel, CA: Welwyn, 1996).

The video of Johanna Quaas performing on the parallel bars at age eighty-eight can be found at https://www.youtube.com/watch?v=CTWo9EfQ4Hc.

Grossfeld's grandfatherly quotes about the olden days of gymnastics come from an interview I conducted with the respected former gymnast, judge, and official.

Bela Karolyi's words on the fearlessness of young gymnasts can be found in Anita Verschoth, "A Great Leap Backward," *Sports Illustrated*, April 1976, http://www.si.com/vault/1976/04/12/616332/a-great-leap-backward.

Roslyn Kerr explains the evolution of difficulty for pre-Nadia gymnasts such as Ludmilla Tourischeva in "The Evolution of Women's Artistic Gymnastics Since 1952," master's thesis, University of Sydney. She also describes how the body changes we witnessed in gymnastics during the 1970s and 1980s might have been informed by trends in the wider culture outside of the sport.

The description of the documentary *You Are in Gymnastics* was derived from https://www.youtube.com/watch?v=TkdsKhGwde8. The content was verified by Vladimir Zaglada, who then worked at the Soviet gymnastics club Dynamo. Quotes from Zaglada and Gary Goodson come from interviews with the author recorded in 2015. This article about Yelena and Mikhail Klimenko demonstrates their athlete-coach relationship, http://www.gymn-forum.net/Articles/SS_Mukhina78.html.

Information about Yelena Mukhina, the 1978 world champion, was derived mostly from the death notice posted in *International Gymnast*, http://www.intlgymnast.com/index.php?option=com_content&view=article&id=38:yelena-mukhina-dies&catid=2:news&Itemid=53. The gymnast's later remarks were broadcast in *More than a Game*, the documentary series about women's gymnastics, https://www.youtube.com/watch?v=j3QzwAruIMU.

Much of the information about Bela Karolyi's life in Romania (and later in the United States) comes from his autobiography *Feel No Fear: The Power, Passion, and Politics of a Life in Gymnastics*, with Nancy Ann Richardson (New York: Hyperion, 1994).

The discussion of body specialization starts with David Epstein's *The Sports Gene: Inside the Science of Extraordinary Athletic Performance* (New York: Penguin, 2013). It continues with Joan Ryan's *Little Girls in Pretty Boxes: The Making and Breaking of Elite Gymnasts and Figure Skaters* (New York: Grand Central Publishing, 2000). The latter book is referenced repeatedly throughout the chapters. "The Role of Intensive Training in the Growth and Maturation of Artistic Gymnasts" by Robert M. Malina, Adam D. G. Baxter-Jones, Nell Armstrong, et al. [*Sports Medicine* 43 (2013): 783–802], is the study that suggests that claims that high-level training stunts growth are not well founded, http://link.springer.com/article/10.1007%2Fs40279-013-0058-5#/page-1.

CHAPTER 3. PEAK 10: HOW GYMNASTICS' MOST POPULAR SCORE REACHED ITS BREAKING POINT

The discussion of the poor judging in 1988 starts with E. M. Swift, "How Perfect Can You Be?" *Sports Illustrated*, http://www.si.com/vault/1988/10/03/118559/gymnastics-how-perfect-can-you-be-despite-some-soaring-performances-by-the-soviets-poor-judging-stole-the-show. It continues with discussion of judging and quotes taken from ABC's Olympics broadcast of the competition.

The profile of Hardy Fink and his mission to eliminate the Perfect 10 was the result of several interviews, mostly conducted in China during the fall of 2014. Interviews with Jim Holt and Jeff Thomson were conducted during the same period in Nanning, China. The author also spoke with Esther Hyde and Karen Bevins, the two New Zealand judges, during this time in 2014.

Jeff Thomson's discussion of the judge-gymnast feedback loop was quoted from an essay, "Balancing Art and Sport," in *Gymnastics in Perspective*, a photo anthology by Eileen Langsley (Crémines, Switzerland: Imprimerie Roos SA, 2000).

Dwight Normile's remarks can be found in an op-ed, "Take Our Breath Away," *International Gymnast*, January 2005. Delene Darst's interview, "You Be the Judge," appeared in the November 1998 issue of that magazine.

CHAPTER 4. BLAME IT ON THE MEN: THE 2004 OLYMPICS AND THE END OF THE 10

Discussion of the scoring fiascos at the 2004 Olympics in Athens is derived, in part, from NBC's coverage. The high bar final can be seen at https://www.youtube.com/watch?v=MEBnMqOj-xI.

Nellie Kim's comment about Comaneci comes from "Sporting Greats," an episode of the Sky Sports documentary series, https://www.youtube.com/watch?v=WMVxnUqnmuM.

"The Task Complexity of Judging Gymnastics," Hardy Fink's study about the difficulty of gymnastics judging, was quoted from the December 1985 bulletin (no. 147) published by the Fédération Internationale de Gymnastique.

Discussions about judging with Jeff Thomson, Karen Bevins, Esther Hyde, and Chris Grabowecky were all recorded in October 2014 in Nanning, China.

Dwight Normile's comments on the 2004 men's high-bar final come from *International Gymnast*, October 2004.

5. NEW *CODE*, NEW GYMNAST: THE RISE OF SIMONE BILES

The account of Vanessa Ferrari's victory in 2006 was drawn from John Crumlish, "Formula Won," *International Gymnast*, December 2006.

Author's conversation with Enrico Casella was recorded in Nanning, China, in October 2014. The quotes from Nellie Kim and Nadia Comaneci were recorded in October 2015 and December 2014, respectively.

CHAPTER SOURCES

Bart Conner's comments about the all-around competition in 2006 is drawn from the Universal Sports coverage of the event.

The section of the chapter that discusses the racist comments from the Italian camp is excerpted from the author's article that was published by *Deadspin* called, "Simone Biles vs. the Racists: Are Black Gymnasts the New QBs?" http://deadspin.com /simone-biles-vs-the-racists-are-black-gymnasts-the-ne-1443998882.

Andre Agassi's comments about the pitfalls of perfectionism are found in his memoir *Open: An Autobiography* (New York: Alfred A. Knopf: 2009).

Elizabeth Booth's description of Biles as the "true protagonist" of open-ended scoring was taken from her site, Rewriting Russian Gymnastics, http://rewritingrussian gymnastics.blogspot.co.uk/2014/11/women-artistic-gymnastics-at-turning .html.

In this interview with ESPN, Simone Biles talks about her 2014 and says the word *fun*. A lot. http://espn.go.com/espnw/news-commentary/article/12003448/simone-biles -power-personality-endless-potential.

The standing double back that Biles attempted as a junior gymnast can be found at http://wogymnastika.blogspot.com/2014/03/simone-biles-attempting-standing -double.html.

David Foster Wallace's quote was taken from his *Esquire* essay, "The String Theory," which was published on September 17, 2008.

CHAPTER 6. THE GUINEA PIG GENERATION: THE 2000 OLYMPIC TEAM AND THE BLUEPRINT FOR AMERICAN GYMNASTICS SUCCESS

The account of the 2010 bronze medal award ceremony for the 2000 Olympic team was taken from the FloGymnastics record of the event, which is available on their site. Also, quotes from Kelli Hill and Donna Strauss were taken from the site's coverage, http://www.flogymnastics.com/event/237471-2000-us-olympic-team -receive-bronze-medals/videos.

In this additional video, Hill goes into detail about changes in the role of the national team coordinator that had taken place since 2000, http://www.flogymnastics.com /video/353002-2000-womens-olympic-team-head-coach-kelli-hill.

USA Gymnastics' own coverage of the fraught origins of the training camp system is detailed in its online series *Behind the Team*, episodes 2 and 3, https://www.you tube.com/watch?v=4PltieSKM6k.

Svetlana Boginskaya's interview with Russian journalist Elena Vaitsekhovskaya, which appeared translated on Rewriting Russian Gymnastics, was published in 2013, http://rewritingrussiangymnastics.blogspot.com/2013/10/conversation-with -svetlana-boginskaya.html?view=mosaic.

Discussion of the "Kim Kelly" episode from the 1992 Olympics was drawn from Diane Pucin, "Dreams Turned Upside Down: Kim Kelly Had the Women's Gymnastics Team Made. Then a Special Meet Was Held. She Postponed College for a Chance to Compete in the Olympics," *Philadelphia Inquirer*, http://articles.philly .com/1992-07-11/sports/26028292_1_championships-and-trials-okino-and -campi-steve-nunno.

CHAPTER SOURCES

Vanessa Atler's comments after Trials were taken from this account in the *Philadelphia Inquirer*, http://articles.philly.com/2000-08-21/sports/25593919_1_vanessa-atler -gymnastics-trials-alyssa-beckerman.

The account of the team, Bela Karolyi's unhappiness in Sydney, and the postcompetition recriminations can be found in Josh Eisenberg, "Finger Pointing Is the Next Event After U.S. Gymnasts Fail to Medal," *Baltimore Sun*, http://articles.baltimore sun.com/2000-09-20/sports/0009200232_1_karolyi-gymnasts-team-competition.

Much of what team physician Larry Nassar is quoted as saying in this chapter came from his interview with GymCastic, episode 63, http://gymcastic.com/63-doctor-larry -nassar/#.VqP1pVMrJp8.

Several quotes from Kristen Maloney and Elise Ray were drawn from their interviews with the GymCastic podcast, episodes 28 and 31, respectively, http://gymcastic .com/episode-28-kristen-maloney/ and http://gymcastic.com/episode-31-elise -ray/.

Dominique Dawes quote about Dong being the "forgotten victim" came from the *Hartford Courant* coverage of the medal ceremony: Jeff Jacobs, "Tears from 2000 Olympics Turns to Tears of Joy for the U.S. Gymnastics Team," http://articles.courant .com/2010-08-12/sports/hc-jacobs-gymnastics-2000-0812-20100811-7_1_elise -ray-chinese-gymnasts-kristen-maloney.

In addition to the GymCastic episodes, several of the quotes came from interviews the author conducted with Kristen Maloney, Elise Ray, Vanessa Atler, and Jamie Dantzscher.

Matt Damon's idea about awarding Oscars ten years after the fact can be found in *Parade* (via *Today*), http://www.today.com/id/29682021#.Vv1OIJMrL_Q.

CHAPTER 7. CAMP KAROLYI: INSIDE THE NATIONAL TEAM TRAINING CAMP SYSTEM

Several of the quotes that appear in the chapter are culled from interviews the author conducted with Terry Walker, Mary Lee Tracy, Liang Chow, Kelly Manjak, Dominique Moceanu, and Wendy Bruce.

The author also interviewed Dr. David Toronjo, father to elite gymnast Macy, in his office in Huntsville in December 2014.

Frank Litsky's report on the "game of musical coaches" in the early-'80s U.S. gymnastics scene, "Gymnasts Move On to Seek Coaching," *New York Times*, http://www .nytimes.com/1984/03/16/sports/gymnasts-on-move-to-seek-coaching.html.

The allegations of sex abuse made against Don Peters were covered largely by the *Orange County Register*, http://www.ocregister.com/articles/peters-318708-yama shiro-gymnastics.html.

Richard O'Brien's account of U.S. coaches' discontent with Karolyi in the late '80s and early '90s, as well as Mary Lou Retton's comment about Karolyi's training, came from "Lord Gym," *Sports Illustrated*, July 1992. Here, too, Paul Ziert discusses Karolyi waiting until the last moment to protest the Bulgarians' springboard setting, http://www.si.com/vault/1992/07/27/126879/gymnastics-lord-gym-it-has -been-11-years-since-bela-karolyi-defected-to-become-the-undisputed-king-of -the-us-women.

CHAPTER SOURCES

Ecaterina Szabo's account of being hungry under the Karolyis in Romania was printed
originally in Romanian, http://www.gsp.ro/gsp-special/superreportaje/povestea
-de-chin-lupta-si-glorie-a-papusii-blonde-a-gimnasticii-mondiale-cati-szabo
-viata-pe-morfina-210961.html. Rick McCharles's corroboration of how slim the
Romanians looked in 1979 was posted on his site in 2010, http://gymnasticscoach
ing.com/new/2010/11/romania-starved-gymnast-szabo/.

In her *My Child, My Hero*, Claudia Miller writes of her daughter Shannon: "She placed
a distress call to us. She was hungry . . . Martha stayed with the gymnasts and was
closely monitoring the diets of her girls" (Norman: University of Oklahoma Press,
1999, p. 96).

"Same Karolyi, Different Tune," *New York Times*, a story about Bela Karolyi's emergence
from retirement in 1994, reiterates Kristie Phillips's allegations against her former coach, http://www.nytimes.com/1994/10/13/sports/gymnastics-same-karolyi
-different-tune.html.

Bela Karolyi talks about stalling the entry of the Romanian team in 1976 in his autobiography (with Nancy Ann Richardson) *Feel No Fear: The Power, Passion, and Politics
of a Life in Gymnastics.*

Juliet Macur, "Sacramone Still Waiting for That Call," *New York Times*, July 18, 2008,
chronicles the 2008 Olympic selection camp at the Karolyi Ranch.

"Last Leotard Standing," *Slate*, discusses the overtraining of the U.S. team in 2011, http://
www.slate.com/articles/sports/sports_nut/2011/10/usa_gymnastics_injuries
_the_united_states_women_keep_winning_gol.html.

Dwight Normile's criticism of the long selection process was published in *International
Gymnast*, July 22, 2008, "Just What I Think," http://www.intlgymnast.com/index
.php?option=com_content&view=article&id=461:just-what-i-think&catid=8
:stretching-out&Itemid=130.

John Geddert's blog post from the World Championships in which he argues for more
rest days, http://thegymnasticscoach.com/blog/2011/10/06/2011-world-cham
pionships-pre-competition/.

Martha Karolyi's quotes about consistency are found in Dwight Normile's interview
with the legendary coach in the September 2006 issue of *International Gymnast*.

McKayla Maroney's comments about the training camp and her experiences in 2012
were taken from her February 2016 interview with GymCastic, https://www.you
tube.com/watch?v=oOx1jLcM1XM.

Hollie Vise's comments about the public nature of the 2004 team selection were published in the profile, "Graceful Exist," *Inside Gymnastics*, May 2010.

Elizabeth Price's quotes were taken from an interview with the author in July 2014.

CHAPTER 8. A TALE OF TWO GYMS: THE NEW WAVE OF AMERICAN COACHES

The descriptions of Texas Dreams were culled from the author's visit in December 2014.
The descriptions of MG Elite were derived from two visits—the first in September 2014 and the second in December 2014.

Quotes from Chris Burdette, Kim Zmeskal-Burdette, Maggie Haney, and Mary Lee
Tracy were taken from interviews conducted by the author.

CHAPTER SOURCES

Leonid Arkayev's discussion of coaching was quoted from his essay "My Coaching Philosophy," in Langsley, *Gymnastics in Perspective*.

The four-part series about Texas Dreams was published on FloGymnastics, 2014, http://www.flogymnastics.com/article/27357-watch-now-full-texas-dreams-beyond-the-routine-series.

CHAPTER 9. THE WINNERS AND LOSERS OF THE NEW SYSTEM

The disadvantages faced by the Chinese during their early years competing in international gymnastics were discussed by Delene Darst in an interview, "You Be the Judge," *International Gymnast*, November 1998.

Observations of training and competition at the 2014 World Championships in Nanning, China, are from the author's firsthand reporting and notes.

Nadia Comaneci's comments about the Romanian performance in Glasgow were recorded on October 23, 2015, and published in several places, including on NBCOlympics.com, http://olympics.nbcsports.com/2015/10/23/nadia-comaneci-gymnastics-world-championships-romania-larisa-iordache/.

Interview with Cristian Moldovan was done through email. Answers were translated by Beatrice Gheorghisor.

Statistics on Romania's population decrease since the fall of Communism come from Bloomberg Business, August 2010, http://www.bloomberg.com/bw/lifestyle/content/aug2010/bw20100812_825983.htm.

Daniela Silivas's statements about the former uneven-bars prowess of the Romanians and the coaching of Adrian Stan on the event were taken from an interview with Gigi Khazback of WOGymnastikA, posted on October 4, 2015, http://www.wogymnast.com/2015/10/daniela-silivas-my-friend-told-me-i.html.

John Crumlish's remarks about the dissemination of gymnastics knowledge were originally published in "Art, Mind, and Muscle," in Langsley, *Gymnastics in Perspective*.

Dominique Moceanu discusses her time under Alexander Alexandrov's tutelage in her memoir *Off Balance*, with Paul and Teri Williams (New York: Simon & Schuster, 2012).

In addition to the author's exchange with Alexandrov through his daughter, many of his quotes come from an in-depth interview he gave to Rewriting Russian Gymnastics, August 2013, http://rewritingrussiangymnastics.blogspot.com/2013/08/alexander-alexandrov-in-his-own-words-1.html.

From the website Rewriting Russian Gymnastics: Nellie Kim's comments about Russian gymnastics after the 2014 World Championships appeared in, http://rewritingrussiangymnastics.blogspot.com.au/2013/10/nelli-kim-russian-gymnastics-has-closed.html. Svetlana Boginskaya's comments about how American-style gymnastics reshaped her body later in her career, http://rewritingrussiangymnastics.blogspot.com/2013/10/conversation-with-svetlana-boginskaya.html?view=mosaic. And Natalia Yurchenko's comments about athlete selection, January 2016, http://rewritingrussiangymnastics.blogspot.com/2016/01/natalia-yurchenko-exclusive-interview.html.

In Minot Simons II, *Women's Gymnastics: A History*, vol.1: *1966 to 1974*, is a discussion of how the dominance of the Soviet Union and East Germany in 1974 led to rule changes.

CHAPTER SOURCES

CHAPTER 10. THE PERFECT 10: THE COLLEGE YEARS

In addition to original reporting and interviews with Greg Marsden, much of the biographical information about him was furnished by John Walters, "Directing a Dynasty, Greg Marsden Has Coached the Women of Utah to 10 National Championships," *Sports Illustrated*, April 1, 1996, http://www.si.com/vault/1996/04/01/211561/directing-a-dynasty-greg-marsden-has-coached-the-women-of-utah-to-10-national-championships.

Records of women's gymnastics attendance numbers for 2014 that showed Utah and Alabama out front were published in several publications, including AL.com, http://www.al.com/sports/index.ssf/2014/03/alabama_gymnastics_attendance.html.

Jill Hicks's remarks on college recruiting were from an interview the author conducted with the former head coach of Cal-State Fullerton.

Hollie Vise's comments were taken from "Graceful Exit," *Inside Gymnastics*, May 2010.

Interviews with Tom Farden and Greg Marsden were conducted in person in their offices in January 2015. Interview with K. J. Kindler took place in December 2014.

Jordyn Wieber's bid to be included on an NCAA team despite forfeiting her eligibility was reported in "Point After: The NCAA's Golden Rule," *Sports Illustrated*, April 6, 2015.

Samantha Peszek's comments about adjusting to college gymnastics after her elite career were taken from a video interview published by UCLA Athletics, January 2015, https://www.youtube.com/watch?v=7oXJ9E3hHkY.

Tricia Woo's comments about competing against elites in college comes from GymCastic, episode 27, http://gymcastic.com/episode-27-tricia-woo-an-artistic-gymnast-finds-her-home-in-the-circus/#.VqRABFMrI0o.

CONCLUSION: THE 10 IS NOT A TIME MACHINE

Nadia Comaneci's comments about bringing back the 10 were published on the official site for the 2015 World Gymnastics Championships in Glasgow, October 23, 2015, http://www.2015worldgymnastics.com/news/2015/october/interview-with-nadia-comaneci-rou-winner-of-all-around-gold-at-the-1976-olympic-games-where-she-earned-seven-perfect-scores-of-100.aspx.

Daniela Silivas's statements about how difficulty hadn't increased staggeringly since her day were taken from an interview with Gigi Khazback of WOGymnastikA posted on October 4, 2015, http://www.wogymnast.com/2015/10/daniela-silivas-my-friend-told-me-i.html.

Shannon Miller's comments about gymnast longevity were uttered during her appearance on GymCastic, episode 168, http://gymcastic.com/168-shannon-miller-belarusgate-ned-vs-gb/.

The ratings for the 2015 World Gymnastics Championships were noted in Simon Briggs, "Perfect 10 for BBC as Gymnasts Help to Beat Cuts," *Telegraph*, http://www.telegraph.co.uk/sport/olympics/gymnastics/11967013/Perfect-10-for-BBC-as-gymnasts-help-to-beat-cuts.html.

CHAPTER SOURCES

AFTERWORD

The *Indianapolis Star* investigation into USA Gymnastics' coverup of coaches' sex abuse: Marisa Kwiatkowski, Mark Alesia, and Tim Evans, "A Blind Eye to Sex Abuse: How USA Gymnastics Failed to Report Cases," *IndyStar*, n.d., http://www .indystar.com/story/news/investigations/2016/08/04/usa-gymnastics-sex-abuse -protected-coaches/85829732/.

The Nassar victim count so far: Diana Moskovitz, "Police: 81 Have Accused Doctor to Olympic Gymnasts of Sexual Assault," *Deadspin*, February 22, 2017, http://deadspin .com/police-81-have-accused-doctor-to-olympic-gymnasts-of-s-1792652315.

This is the first news account of the lawsuit and investigation against Larry Nassar: Mark Alesia, Marisa Kwiatkowski, and Tim Evans, "Former USA Gymnastics Doctor Accused of Abuse," *IndyStar*, September 12, 2016, http://www.indystar.com/story /news/2016/09/12/former-usa-gymnastics-doctor-accused-abuse/89995734/.

The revelation that the original "Jane Doe" is Jamie Dantzscher: Associated Press, "Olympian Jamie Dantzscher Claims Sex Abuse by ex-USA Gymnastics Doctor," nbcsports.com, February 19, 2017, http://olympics.nbcsports.com/2017/02/19 /jamie-dantzscher-larry-nassar-gymnastics-sexual-abuse/.

The second lawsuit from Jane LM Doe, which named the Karolyis and the gymnasts' personal coaches in addition to Nassar, USA Gymnastics, and past presidents: https://assets.documentcloud.org/documents/3189553/Jane-LM-Doe-Complaint -FILED-10-27-16.txt.

The federal charges against Nassar: Tracy Connor, "FBI Says Gymnastics Doctor Larry Nassar Recorded Abuse on Go Pro," nbcnews.com, December 21, 2016, http:// www.nbcnews.com/news/us-news/gymnastics-doctor-larry-nassar-hit-new-sex -abuse-claim-n698741.

The GymCastic podcast that Nassar appeared on: "63: USA Team Doctor Larry Nas- sar," http://www.stitcher.com/podcast/gymcastic/e/63-usa-team-doctor-larry-nassar -30851164.

The quotes from Wendy Bruce came from in interview conducted in late 2016.

Tiffany Thomas Lopez, the MSU softball player's account of what happened to her in 1999: Scott M. Reid, "Suit by Former U.S. Softball Standout Outlines Alleged Sexual Assault by Former Team Doctor," *The Orange County Register*, December 21, 2016, http://www.ocregister.com/2016/12/21/suit-by-former-us-softball-standout -outlines-alleged-sexual-assault-by-former-team-doctor/.

These articles list additional accusations against Nassar, including the 2004 case: Marisa Kwiatkowski, Tim Evans, and Mark Alesia, "16 more women Accuse Former USA Gymnastics Doctor of Sexual Abuse," *IndyStar*, September 25, 2016, http://www .indystar.com/story/news/investigations/2016/09/25/16-more-women-accuse -doctor-sexual-abuse/90410436/; Matt Mencarini, "18 More Alleged Victims Sue MSU, Nassar," *Lansing State Journal*, January 10, 2017, http://www.lansingstatejournal .com/story/news/local/2017/01/10/larry-nassar-michigan-state-lawsuit/96246098/.

An account of the 2014 Title IX charges and investigation: Matt Mencarini, "Schuette: Nassar Is 'a Monster' and More Charges Coming," *Lansing State Journal*, February 22, 2017, http://www.lansingstatejournal.com/story/news

CHAPTER SOURCES

/local/2017/02/22/former-msu-doctor-larry-nassar-faces-23-new-sexual
-assault-charges/98220438/.

The opening of Safe Sport: Tim Evans, Marisa Kwiatkowski, and Mark Alesia, "Safe-Sport Center: Is It the Answer to Athlete Sex Abuse?" *IndyStar*, March 8, 2017, http://www.indystar.com/story/news/2017/03/08/safesport-center-answer-athlete-sex-abuse/98775554/.

INDEX

INDEX

Burdette, Chris (*cont.*)
on program management, 201, 207, 217, 226
and Texas Dreams, 200–201, 203, 205, 208–9, 217
Butcher, Steve, 68, 93, 95, 96, 256, 257–59

Cal State Fullerton, 266, 289
Campi, Michelle, 169
Carlos, John, 3
Carter, Jimmy, 165
Casella, Enrico, 104–6, 108, 109, 126
Caslavska, Vera, 10–11, 14, 38
Cazeneuve, Brian, 94
Cervin, Georgia, 210
Chetkovich, Liz, 77
China, gymnastics in, 254–56
Chirila, Ioan, 19, 38, 39, 40
Chow, Amy, 132, 134, 136, 140, 154, 276
Chow, Liang, 175, 178, 218–19
Chusovitina, Oksana, xvii, 28
Ciaralli, David, 119, 120
Cirque du Soleil, 288
Clark, Jay, 271
coaching, 105, 158, 168, 179, 186, 197–99, 210–15, 235, 288
Code of Points:
(1972), 11
(1992), "new life" rule in, 27
(1993–1996), 64
(2006), 103–9
(2009–2012), xiii
open-ended scoring in, *see* open-ended scoring
revisions to, 57–68, 72–74, 96–97, 178, 241, 245, 257–58, 293, 296, 298
Cohen, Sasha, 92
Colarossi, Bob, 141, 151
college gymnastics, 209, 217–18, 222, 261–90
competitions in, 274, 277
different priorities in, 267–68, 273–74
former elites in, 282, 287
having fun in, 277
modified Level 10 rules in, 267–68, 276, 282, 289–90
postgraduate continuation of, 288–89
recruitment for, 270–74, 278, 280, 282–83
redemptive nature of, 283–86
sisterhood in, 280

Super Six, 267, 284
as team sport, 280–82, 287
Comaneci, Nadia:
and aging, 9, 23, 24, 31–32, 51–53, 293
on Biles's talent, 126–27
and body types, 32, 37–38
and changing sports world, 49, 56, 93, 103, 199, 271
and Conner, 7–8, 9, 20
consistency of, 18–19, 23
defection to U.S., 7, 8
development of, 42, 261–62
endorsements by, 9
and European Championships, 41, 42
and fame, 9–10, 17–18, 39, 40, 44–45, 58, 77, 262, 297–98, 299
family of, 24–25
first perfect 10, xiv–xv, 6, 10–11, 13–17, 59, 81, 127, 262
influence of, xv, xviii, 9–10, 32–33, 34, 41, 42, 45, 103, 127, 138, 259, 290
and Karolyi, 4, 19–22, 39, 122, 172, 218
and Kim, 6–7, 8–10, 60, 63, 77
Letters to a Young Gymnast, xv, 16, 21
and Olympics (1980), 51–52
performance of (1976), 4–6, 11, 13, 23, 27, 32, 34, 37, 38, 42, 56, 59, 60, 62, 292
and recruitment, 246
and scoring systems, 29, 56, 57, 59, 63, 68, 81, 87, 93
as spectator, 126, 240, 291
talent/skill of, 19–20, 42, 47, 62–63, 68, 122, 298
Conklin, Mike, 23, 45
Conner, Bart, 6, 7–8, 9, 20, 56, 106
Conner, Dylan, 24–25
Copeland, Misty, 253
Crumlish, John, 107, 108, 246

Daggett, Tim, 146, 147
Damon, Matt, 160
Dantzscher, Jamie:
and Atler, 139, 149, 150–51
and Karolyi, 143, 153, 156
at Nationals, 132, 150
and NCAA competition, 132, 134, 157, 275
on Olympic team (2000), 132, 134, 137, 140, 151, 154, 160
on selection, 146, 151

324

INDEX

INDEX

INDEX

Phelps, Michael, 14
Phillips, Kristie, 174
Podkopayeva, Lilia, 64, 103
Ponor, Catalina, xvii, 293–94
Porgras, Ana, 243
Postell, Ashley, 282
Pozsar, Geza, 169
Price, Elizabeth, 185, 186, 187, 190
Produnova, Yelena, 236

Quaas, Johanna, 35–36, 37

Raisman, Alexandra (Aly), xiii, 111, 176,
    194, 195, 242, 279, 299
Rastorotsky, Vladislav, 45
Ray, Elise, 156–58
    as coach, 288
    injury to, 154
    and Karolyis, 156, 158
    and NCAA competition, 132, 134,
        156–57, 275
    on Olympic team (2000), 132, 134,
        145, 147–48, 154, 157
    and selection, 147–48
    style of, 140
    and training camps, 160
Retton, Mary Lou:
    and aging, 23–24
    autobiography of, 48
    and body types, 48
    consistency of, 166–67
    influence of, 34
    and Karolyis, 48, 163, 164, 168, 172
    and Olympics (1984), 75, 79, 135, 163,
        165, 168
Richardson, Kate, 288
Rigby, Cathy, 15, 38, 234
Rodionenko, Andrei and Valentina, 247,
    250
Romanian gymnastics, 238–46, 259
Ross, Kyla, 111, 118, 182, 193, 195, 277,
    279
Rowland, Jenny, 288
Russian gymnastics, 246–51, 254, 258, 259
Ruyak, Beth, 148
Ryan, Joan, *Little Girls in Pretty Boxes*, 51,
    170, 205, 215–16
Rybacki, Beth, 138–39, 149–50
Rybacki, Steve, 138–39, 145, 149–50, 160

Sacramone, Alicia, 176, 191, 192, 194, 242
Sakalova, Emilia, 46–47

Sandberg, Sheryl, 177
Sands, William:
    and coaching, 45, 46, 215
    on conditioning, 181
    Everybody's Gymnastics Book (with Mike
        Conklin), 23
    on injuries, 224
    on Karolyis, 143, 154
    on training camps, 144–45
Schlegel, Elfi, 84, 146
Schwikert, Tasha, 132, 134, 151, 152–54,
    156, 275
Secret Classic (2014), 271
Shade, Sheryl, 137, 150
Shang Chunsong, 255
Shaniyazov, Aman, 44
Shushunova, Yelena, xiv, 55, 56
Silacci, Philippe, 70, 88
Silivas, Daniela, xiv, 55, 56, 245, 292–93
Sloan, Bridget, 282
Smith, Ragan, 209–10, 212
Smith, Tommie, 3
Soviet National Championships, (1964),
    38
Soviet Union:
    breakup of, 132, 164, 176, 246, 248,
        292
    and competition, 41–43
    and scoring inflation, 60
    training techniques in, 46–47
sports, data driven, 94
Stack, Chelle, 47, 169
Stan, Adrian, 245
start value (SV), 71–72, 79, 82, 95, 192,
    240
Stoyanova, Boriana, 171–72
Strauss, Donna, 148, 158
Strazheva, Olga, 56, 229
Strug, Kerri, 131, 135, 136, 169, 205, 229
Swift, E. M., 55
Szabo, Ecaterina, 167, 171

Talavera, Tracee, 146, 165
Talent Opportunity Programs (TOPs),
    188, 195
Texas Dreams, 199–215, 217, 219,
    227–29
Texas Women's University, 209
Thomson, Jeff, 66, 67
Title IX, 261, 266
Toronjo, David, 183–84, 208, 272
Toronjo, Macy, 183–84, 207–8, 272

329

INDEX

ABOUT THE AUTHOR

Dvora Meyers is a New York–based writer and journalist. In 2012, she provided all the Olympic gymnastics coverage for *Deadspin* and *Jezebel*, chronicling the results of the competition as well as adding her own commentary. Her work on the sport has also appeared in ESPN, *Slate*, VICE, and *The Atlantic*. Her other non-gymnastics-related writing has been published in the *New York Times*, *Elle*, *Tablet*, *New York* magazine, and several other publications.